D0597048

*Eros, Imitation, and
the Epic Tradition*

· BARBARA PAVLOCK

Eros, Imitation, and the Epic Tradition

· Cornell University Press

Ithaca and London

First published 1990 by Cornell University Press.

International Standard Book Number 0-8014-2321-x
Library of Congress Catalog Card Number 89-36639
Printed in the United States of America
Librarians: Library of Congress cataloging information
appears on the last page of the book.

∞ The paper used in this publication meets the minimum requirements of the American National Standard for Permanence of Paper for Printed Library Materials Z39.48–1984.

In Memory of
Gilbert Sink
and
Walter Lee Horton

Contents

Preface

ALTHOUGH CLASSICISTS' source studies have demonstrated longstanding interest in literary imitation, the subject has in recent years become more methodologically oriented and theoretically grounded. In criticism of the genre of epic poetry, there has been a steady flow of valuable work over the past forty or so years on Vergil's use of Homer, from scholars such as Viktor Pöschl, W. F. Jackson Knight, Brooks Otis, and W. R. Johnson, who are sensitive to the Augustan poet's interest in shaping his great model to the needs of contemporary Rome. More recently, in *The Rhetoric of Imitation,* Gian Biagio Conte has posited an interrelation between the epic code, the conventions of the genre, and epic norms, the cultural and ideological concerns of a poet's own society. His approach to the *Aeneid* emphasizes the dovetailing of Homeric allusions with the surface meaning of Vergil's own text. He also indicates that Vergil diffuses the "bias" of the Roman norms, which often refer to the superiority of the state, by incorporating multiple points of view against the more focused vision of the hero Aeneas.

My own book assumes that Homeric allusions are an inherent source for the rhetorical power of the *Aeneid* and the poet's means of reflecting upon his own world. As a broadly comparative work, however, it follows the transformation of Homeric material through a wide historical range: Hellenistic Greece, late republican and Augustan Rome, and the Renaissance in Italy and later in England. The increased prominence of the erotic in heroic poetry, from the Alexandrian period to the Renaissance, has not been fully accounted for. I examine the history of that movement, at least partially, by considering the sources of eroticized material in Homer's two epics. By elucidating a process of literary imitation, I aim to provide one form of access to the problem of literature and the social, of poetic continuity and change in the epic. The importance of both Vergil and Ovid in the history of this process will also become apparent, as evidenced by the Renaissance writers who took up the challenge to produce epic for their own societies. Finally, each of the chapters is to some extent a discrete study, but their intersections will, I believe, contribute in a small way to a fuller appreciation of the relevance of generic norms.

The roots of this work go back a long way. At its earliest stage its purpose was quite different; it was concerned with the rhetorical adaptations of traditional material from Vergil onward which undermine the romantic surface of key episodes in heroic poetry. For their considerate advice and criticism of my work at that stage, I am most grateful to William J. Kennedy, W. R. Johnson, and Giuseppe Mazzotta, all of whom were then at Cornell University. M. H. Abrams, Frederick Ahl, and Pietro Pucci, also at Cornell, broadened my understanding of narrative poetry and literary influence. Without the inspiring instruction of my undergraduate teachers Lydia Lenaghan, Helen Bacon, and especially the late Steele Commager, I would not have pursued the study of classical literature.

I owe many debts from years of working on this book. I thank the following friends and scholars who read chapters of the manuscript at various stages: William S. Anderson, Albert Ascoli, James Degnan, J. Martin Evans, Frank Romer, Edward Spofford, and Giuseppe Mazzotta, who read a later draft in its entirety. James Zetzel, then the editor of *Transactions of the American Philological Association*, and two anonymous referees gave me very useful advice for improving the first draft of my article "Epic and Tragedy in Vergil's Nisus and Euryalus Episode," *TAPA* 115 (1985), © The American Philological Association 1985, which in revised form constitutes part of my chapter on Vergil. I am grateful to the editor of *TAPA* for permission to reprint. In more and less direct ways *en route* to this book, I have benefited from the conversation and advice of Matthew Santirocco, Jesse Gellrich, and Olivia von Ziegesar. The following individuals gave me crucial help in learning and using word processing for the manuscript: Fred White, Joanna Watt, John Balling, Harry Hopcroft, and Steve Bradley.

The Mary Isabel Sibley Fellowship in Greek, awarded by Phi Beta Kappa, enabled me to spend two quarters of leave time working on the first draft of the chapter on Apollonius's *Argonautica*. The staff of the library of the American Academy in Rome generously provided assistance during my fellowship period in 1981–82 and in several summers since then. Two other grants should also be recognized: one from Santa Clara University helped me to complete some research on Ariosto in Italy, and another from Bowdoin College enabled me to fill in some final areas of scholarship. The thoughtful criticism of two anonymous readers for Cornell University Press provided valuable direction for improving the quality and the clarity of the manuscript. Finally, I am grateful to Bernhard Kendler for his advice and expertise as an editor; to my copyeditor, Martha Rappaport; and to Roger Haydon for guiding the manuscript through publication.

A word or two on the quotation of foreign language texts is in order. I have used English translations for convenience unless discussion of aspects of the original language follows; in that case, I quote the original and supply a translation. All Greek has been transliterated.

BARBARA PAVLOCK

Bethlehem, Pennsylvania

*Eros, Imitation, and
the Epic Tradition*

Introduction

IN LITERARY epic from ancient Greece and Rome through the European Renaissance, eros often deters the hero's progress toward his social and political goals. A. Bartlett Giamatti eloquently traces one important facet of this dynamic: the hero's encounter with a female temptress in the *locus amoenus*, or beautiful landscape, and the difficult process of extricating himself.[1] Taking account of the classical antecedents, Giamatti emphasizes thematic variations in the conflict between love and duty, illusion and reality, in the seductive garden in Renaissance epic through Milton, who returns to the garden as a true ideal. The erotic takes many forms in epic, in general as an irrational force that acts against the prevailing values of the world in which the hero operates. Yet eros also has a more complex function, not only acting against societal demands but also, from the perspective of the poet as an observer and sometimes critic of his world, engaging in a confrontation and dialectic with the prevailing values.

Individual poets, of course, develop their own means of measuring erotic against heroic values, but there is a remarkable continuity of theme and of rhetoric in the major western literary epics. Specific forms remain constant even though epic is a very inclusive genre, containing lyric, comic, tragic, and other genres within its bounds,

[1] A. Bartlett Giamatti, *The Earthly Paradise and the Renaissance Epic* (Princeton: Princeton University Press, 1966).

and is subject to numerous kinds of adaptations. In the Hellenistic and Roman periods, for instance, epic was already considered anachronistic; poets continued to produce the genre in part by incorporating the aetiological narrative and elements of tragedy. In the Renaissance, epic tended to be assimilated with another narrative form, the popular romance.

This book relies on the basic assumption that both continuity and change are intrinsic to the vitality and the very existence of a genre. In a theoretical preface to his discussion of the fantastic as a genre, Tzvetan Todorov emphasizes the importance of perceiving the properties that a work has in common with other examples of its kind and of understanding that a work receives a place in the history of literature only by altering its genre in some way.[2] My approach assumes many of the views elaborated by Rosalie Colie about the relation of generic form to meaning.[3] Although not dealing specifically with epic, she discusses the close connection of genre to social and cultural concerns in numerous literary kinds in the Renaissance. Rather than a rigid structure, genre implies a link between a topic and the way it is treated in literature. Furthermore, value systems and modes of perceiving the world are rooted in the literary kinds so that in a compressed form a genre might serve as a type of metaphor when used in another work, as Shakespeare uses the sonnet in *As You Like It*. Colie also shows that generic assumptions enable one to comprehend the prolific adaptations of traditional types in literature in the Renaissance: *genera mixta*, which play off the meanings associated with different genres, and *nova reperta*, new kinds altogether for expressing new experiences and interests.

Recent work on the imitation of classical models in the Renaissance has illuminated the concerns and the methods employed by major writers. In a seminal book, Thomas Greene has defined the modes of imitation by which Renaissance writers not only acknowledge the primacy of the source texts but also clarify their own viewpoints: in the "dialectical" mode, the new poet cannot accept

---

[2]Tzvetan Todorov, *The Fantastic: A Structural Approach to a Literary Genre*, tr. Richard Howard (Cleveland: Case Western Reserve University Press, 1973), esp. pp. 5–8.

[3]Rosalie R. Colie, *The Resources of Kind: Genre-Theory in the Renaissance* (Berkeley: University of California Press, 1973).

the positions supported by the primary model but instead arrives at a new solution.[4] As Greene's model suggests, the discrepancy with a source text occurs through adjustments of form, deviations from the predecessor's poetic and rhetorical structures. His exemplary imitative poet, Petrarch, reflects a profound concern with the problem of temporality, in part by numerous allusions to Vergil that destabilize the Roman poet's rhetoric. In another study concerned with imitation, David Quint traces the transformations of the theme of the "source," which ultimately goes back to Plato, through a variety of Renaissance literary texts.[5] In relating this topos to poetics, Quint shows that for Renaissance writers, Vergil's version of the source myth in *Georgics* 4, which contrasts Orpheus and Proteus, served as a reflection on both poetic origins and forms of poetry. Beginning with Sannazaro's efforts at both pastoral and epic poetry, which offer two different ways of interpreting Vergil, Quint reveals the important opposition between historicist and allegorical modes of reading in the Renaissance.

Although their work stresses the importance of continuity and tension that informed the Renaissance approach to the classics, neither Greene nor Quint is concerned with imitation within a particular genre. Another Renaissance scholar has more closely approached the intrinsic concerns of Vergil's poem as epic and its influence on later literature, especially Shakespearian drama. Barbara Bono discusses the story of Dido and Aeneas as a dialectic between the hero's hard-won detachment after traumatic experiences of suffering and the queen's intense involvement with the past.[6] Dido's frustrated passion and the unresolved tensions in the *Aeneid* become fertile ground for transcendent reinterpretations in the autobiographical narratives of Saint Augustine and Dante, in Spenser's epic and, finally, in Shakespeare's integration of eros and civilization in *Antony and Cleopatra*.

The five chapters of this book illustrate in two paradigmatic types

[4]Thomas M. Greene, *The Light in Troy: Imitation and Discovery in Renaissance Poetry* (New Haven: Yale University Press, 1982).

[5]David Quint, *Origin and Originality in Renaissance Literature: Versions of the Source* (New Haven: Yale University Press, 1983).

[6]Barbara J. Bono, *Literary Transvaluation: From Vergilian Epic to Shakespearian Tragicomedy* (Berkeley: University of California Press, 1984).

of episodes the interplay between the erotic and core epic values. These episodes, which became highly eroticized in later epic, are derived from Homer: the abandoned female ultimately modeled on Nausikaa in the *Odyssey*, and the night raid of a pair of warriors based on the expedition of Odysseus and Diomedes in the *Iliad*. I focus on the imitation of thematic and rhetorical material from these paradigms in Apollonius of Rhodes, Vergil, Catullus, Ovid, Ariosto, and Milton. As an inherently social genre that is rooted in aristocratic values, epic conservatively keeps many of those concerns constant throughout the tradition. The Latin terms *virtus*, *pietas*, *fides*, and *gloria*, closely connected to the Greek concepts *aretē*, *eusebeia*, *pistis*, and *kleos*, are sustained well after Vergil wrote the *Aeneid*. In modified forms, they play a significant role in such Renaissance epics as the *Orlando Furioso*, *Gerusalemme Liberata*, and *Paradise Lost*, to name the most famous. Epic poets, however, wrote not simply to reaffirm traditional social values but also to subject them to scrutiny and to explore their limitations. The increased prominence of the erotic in epic from Apollonius of Rhodes onward is closely related to such a social function: the erotic becomes a means of figuring heroic values. As the major poets invest the erotic with new levels of meaning, they also make important adjustments of form. The variations and contractions of form, then, signify a difference in attitude and a change in views about the relation of the erotic to the social. As epic proceeds from Hellenistic Greece through republican and Augustan Rome into the Italian and English Renaissance, continuity of form signifies substantive difference.

In a related context, the subtle manifestations of the conflict between private desires and public responsibilities have been sensitively elaborated in a recent study of Boccaccio. Giuseppe Mazzotta has shown that the *Decameron*, which has been called a prose epic reflecting the bourgeois ethic, insistently reveals the vulnerability of social values to the intrusion of desire.[7] Sometimes Boccaccio's characters accommodate desire to societal demands. But the problems are radical: social bonds generally rely on deception or metaphors whose validity is simply unquestioned, and men's desires often emerge as an uncontrollable force, as madness. Sexuality fre-

[7]Giuseppe Mazzotta, *The World at Play in Boccaccio's* Decameron (Princeton: Princeton University Press, 1986), esp. pp. 75–104.

quently subverts social norms, and even marriage reflects an order that keeps in bounds the positive and negative forces generated by desire. In his analyses of numerous tales in the *Decameron*, Mazzotta exposes the basis for Boccaccio's dark social vision: the comforting surface that men consider as stable and permanent ultimately conceals a deeper stratum of imagination and desire. As we will see, traditional epic shares some of this skepticism. Even if poets tend to search for validity in governing social values, those discussed below also confront the violence underlying social order.

Since Homer is the source for the paradigms in this work, it is appropriate to consider briefly Greek attitudes toward love that filtered into epic. From the archaic period on, the Greeks were skeptical about the condition they called "eros." The term denotes a desire or longing for something, even a lust. Two centuries after Homer, Sappho perhaps best summarizes the contradictions inherent in the experience of love for the ancient Greeks in general.

The paradoxes underlying the erotic experience for Sappho, among other Greek writers, have been perceptively discussed by Anne Carson.[8] By nature contradictory, eros encompasses opposites, hate as well as love. It involves constant deferral. In the hymn to Aphrodite, the goddess assures Sappho in an epiphany that the one who flees will soon pursue. Sappho's most famous lyric dramatizes a "triangulation," the separation of the object of desire from the speaker by a generalized third person, a man in conversation with her beloved. The same poem also reflects that eros is most like a disease. As she gazes upon the man with the girl, the speaker experiences strong physical symptoms: sweat, ringing in the ears, paralysis of the limbs. In the experience of love, the self undergoes a radical transformation. The very boundaries of the body are dissolved: the images frequently associated with eros include melting, piercing, and stinging. Sappho, in a priamel at the opening of her poem on Anactoria, rules out traditional male values for something subjective, "she whom one loves best." The particular example that she uses to privilege delight and intimacy, Helen of Troy, reinforces

[8]Anne Carson, *Eros the Bittersweet: An Essay* (Princeton: Princeton University Press, 1986), makes the points that follow on triangulation and boundary dissolutions.

the opposition between love and the heroic ethos.[9] In essence, then, eros in Greek lyric involves change, loss, and ultimately even madness. For epic poets, Sappho's images made eros an appropriate symbol of irrationality conflicting with the requirements of steadfast labor in the heroic enterprise.

Homer, the source of the abandoned female and the night raid, presents eros less from a Sapphic or experiential perspective than in the context of the social concerns of his epics. Eros in the Homeric poems is complementary as well as antithetical to heroic aims. While specifically incorporating the abandoned female in the *Odyssey*, Homer suggests some fundamental connections between eros and violence in the heroic ethos of the *Iliad*. Since so many of the heroes competed for Helen's hand, their presence at Troy collectively reaffirms that the war is being fought for a woman. All the warriors, moreover, contend for the glory that gives their existence meaning. The connection between the two is subtly reinforced throughout the poem: in book 3 Helen weaves a tapestry in which she depicts the contests being waged over her; the old men of Troy remark that her awesome beauty makes the war understandable, though they recommend sending her back to avoid more devastation; and her position as the last speaker in the funeral rites for Hector in book 24 appropriately recalls that the great Trojan hero died for this desirable woman.[10] As the cause of the war, Helen thus links the warrior's quest for glory with a struggle that is rooted in sexuality.

The social system of Homer's epic makes the theme of eros more complex. Under the conditions of warfare, women are prizes sought by warriors in battle, the more beautiful, sexually desirable ones being the most valuable. As an expression of his powerful desire for the daughter of the priest Chryses, Agamemnon asserts that Chryseis is in no way inferior to his own wife Clytemnestra. Women as the spoils of war reinforce the high status of the warriors

[9]See Hermann Fränkel, *Early Greek Poetry and Philosophy: A History of Greek Epic, Lyric, and Prose to the Middle of the Fifth Century*, tr. Moses Hadas and James Willis (New York: Harcourt, Brace, Jovanovich, 1975), pp. 185–86.

[10]Helen's complex relation to sexuality in Homer is discussed by Linda L. Clader, *Helen: The Evolution from Divine to Heroic in Greek Epic Tradition* (Leiden: Brill, 1976).

and serve in a sexual capacity, a fact that Agamemnon callously observes when he refuses to give up the priest's daughter (1.29–31). Men need women as war prizes for status. Possession itself motivates desire. Briseis, for instance, is all the more desirable to Agamemnon because she is the concubine of Achilles, the greatest Greek warrior. Yet this woman disrupts the social system, for she is the source of contention between Achilles and Agamemnon that leads to the hero's alienation from the Greek army and devastation in his absence.

Warriors fighting defensively live with the fear that their wives, among other female relatives, may be captured in war. Even the best of the Trojan warriors, Hector, dreads the possibility of slavery for Andromache, who pleads with him not to leave her a widow and their child an orphan (6.406–39). Although he places his wife at the top of the "scale of affections," Hector cannot act upon her plea for a sensitivity to her plight by fighting defensively.[11] This most humane hero is also motivated by a sense of shame (*aidōs*) that keeps him from disappointing the expectations of the Trojans and impels him to keep winning *kleos* not only for himself but also for his father. Hector's inability to heed his wife's appeal to his affections reveals the extent to which *kleos* is a driving force in this world, overriding almost all other concerns.

The dangerous nature of female sexuality is more fully developed in the *Odyssey*, where women are frequently viewed as false and deceptive. Helen's brief appearance in book 4 is revealing: her disruptive nature surfaces even in the stories that she and her husband tell about the Trojan War. While she claims to have recognized Odysseus disguised as a battered old man at Troy, Menelaus counters her tale of loyalty by describing an incident in which she stood outside the wooden horse and cleverly imitated the voices of the wives of the warriors inside so as to make them call out in longing. Helen thus provokes sexual desire with potentially disastrous consequences for the Greek political cause. Certainly she is to some extent sympathetic here as in the *Iliad*, for she acts to quell the unhappy

---

[11]On the social implications of Hector's and Andromache's meeting in *Iliad* 6, see Marylin B. Arthur, "The Divided World of *Iliad* VI," in *Reflections of Women in Antiquity*, ed. Helene P. Foley (New York: Gordon and Breach, 1981), pp. 19–44.

feelings aroused by Telemachus's questions about his father. But by employing drugs as her method, Helen relies on an artificial remedy that only camouflages the troubled marital relations in that *oikos*.

The faithful Penelope herself uses her sexual powers in ways that might be construed as suspicious: she elicits gifts from the suitors who not only want the royal power that presumably comes with a marriage to her but also find her beauty overwhelming, and she raises their hopes for her hand by setting up the contest of the bow in book 21. She uses her cunning in the sexual sphere to trick even the hero. In order to be absolutely sure of his identity, she tells him that his bed, whose construction was their private sign and the guarantee of her fidelity, has been moved. Penelope certainly has felt doubts about the possibility of Odysseus's return and perhaps ambiguity about reuniting with the husband she knew twenty years earlier. Yet by her very caution and cunning, she reinforces the values of this epic. Unlike Helen, she has restrained her sexuality in the face of temptations and pressures by men eager for power and wealth. In particular, she protects the interests of the *oikos* by keeping things under control as well as possible until Odysseus can reestablish true order upon his return.[12]

The *Odyssey* presents three instances of females who are abandoned by the hero in his quest to return home. The goddesses Circe and Calypso reflect the dangers of entrapment, as each lures Odysseus into complacency by providing ease and pleasure with no effort but at the expense of his involvement in normal political and social affairs. With the absence of assemblies, law courts, and agriculture on the one hand, and of procreation on the other, Circe and Calypso have neither a real *polis* nor a vital *oikos*. The easy existence on both Aeaea and Ogygia reflects a stasis, a lack of growth and change in time, so important in the development of Ithacan society, where the values and responsibilities of Laertes were transferred to Odysseus, whose own son Telemachus is now coming into his own. After his experiences with these two goddesses, the hero has learned the risks of succumbing to a beautiful female offering a virtually effortless security and ease.

---

[12]For Penelope's connection to the values of the *Odyssey* through her strategies in preserving her husband's household, see Helene P. Foley, "'Reverse Similes' and Sex Roles in the *Odyssey*," *Arethusa* 11 (1978), 7–26.

The Phaeacian episode provided the archetype for the vulnerable young woman who falls in love with the hero but is left behind by him. In book 6, the princess Nausikaa encounters Odysseus after she has had a dream sent by Athena advising her that it is time to prepare her wardrobe for marriage. She is at play with her companions when she first sees this naked stranger who barely escaped death at sea. Immediately attracted to him, she is potentially a dangerous temptation. But the Phaeacians are a highly refined society, and the princess reflects their tact and sophistication. In response to his flattering speech comparing her to a tender sapling and wishing her a harmonious marriage, she reveals her ability to convey her erotic interest through indirection and advises him about successfully attaining a reception at court. Her hint about her mother's importance enables Odysseus not only to be received as a guest but also to comprehend that Arete's subtle influence extends to gift giving among the nobles at court. The clever hero then includes in his account of his adventures after the Trojan War a spicy narrative about the famous women whom he saw in the underworld and is handsomely rewarded.

In spite of the girl's attractiveness and her parents' desire to have him as their son-in-law, Odysseus wants to return to the woman whom he made his wife long ago. As a hero who has learned the value of experience, he does not choose to embark on a marriage with a young girl or to remain in a society that is, however appealing, insulated and outside the norms of human life in important ways: the Phaeacians' agriculture is not subject to seasonal restrictions; their ships seem to engage in sport rather than commerce (they operate by magical powers from Poseidon, not human skill); and their athletic contests unrelated to martial arts do not prepare them for war.[13] From Homer's perspective, the erotically motivated Nausikaa is not herself problematic; she is simply unsuited to this particular hero. Although she subtly tries to encourage him to remain by alluding to his debt to her, Odysseus responds by praising her but simultaneously rules out the possibility of a union (8.464–

---

[13]See Pierre Vidal-Naquet, "Land and Sacrifice in the *Odyssey*: A Study of Religious and Mythical Meanings," in *Myth, Religion and Society: Structuralist Essays by M. Detienne, L. Gernet, J.-P. Vernant, and P. Vidal-Naquet*, ed. R. L. Gordon (Cambridge: Cambridge University Press, 1981), esp. pp. 90–94.

68). Nausikaa is not heard from again in the remainder of the Phaeacian episode, which concludes with Alcinous providing the hero
conveyance home. This erotic incident, then, is uncomplicated: the
hero acts positively in leaving the young woman and receives no
reproach from her for his conduct.

Later epic, incorporating this figure in more highly charged
contexts, assimilates Nausikaa into two other abandoned females, Ariadne and the tragic Medea. Initially, the latter is the
central model adapted from Nausikaa, for the major stage in the
conflation of the two types is Apollonius's *Argonautica*. As his heroine is the love-struck Medea who gives Jason the magical skill necessary to obtain the Golden Fleece, the Hellenistic poet would inevitably have been influenced by the tragic playwright's account of that
character at a later stage in her relationship with the hero. This
assimilation is particularly important to epic because fifth-century
Greek tragedy created many powerful female characters as means of
reflecting upon the values of the *polis*.[14] These tragic heroines, in
other words, serve not so much to represent the condition of wom-
en per se as to expose the tensions or paradoxes of a society shaped
primarily by and for males. Euripides especially seems to have im-
bued his great female heroines with qualities that in some ways
impinge upon the male sphere: Phaedra, for instance, is extremely
concerned with her reputation as she struggles with her passion for
Hippolytus and as she ultimately decides to incriminate him by
falsifying a story of a sexual assault.[15]

Medea, the figure who concerns us here, powerfully represents
heroic values generally attributed only to males: she is clever in both
word and deed as she aggressively resists Jason's opportunistic attempt to revive his own fortunes. Creon, the king, initially refrains
from negotiating his edict of exile with her because he suspects that
he will be manipulated by her devious arguments. In her second
speech to Jason, she cunningly retracts her earlier invective for his
breach of faith by flattering him for his good sense. In her great

[14]See Froma Zeitlin, "Playing the Other: Theater, Theatricality, and the Feminine
in Greek Drama," *Representations* 11 (1985), esp. 66–68. Zeitlin specifically cites the
case of Medea and points to some of her masculine characteristics.
[15]On Phaedra's connection to *kleos*, see C. A. E. Luschnig, "Men and Gods in
Euripides' *Hippolytus*," *Ramus* 9 (1980), 89–100.

agon with the hero, she speaks out forcibly for the values that men devised to regulate political and social life: she strongly reprimands his shamelessness (*anaideia*) in contrast to proper scruples against unacceptable conduct; she emphasizes his obligations and the need for reciprocity, so important in early Greek society, for the services she rendered (enabling him to get the fleece and disposing of Pelias by a trick of false rejuvenation). Furthermore, she implies a sense of her own heroic stature by asserting that she "saved" (476) Jason, an act of the stronger on behalf of the weaker. If Jason represents perverted heroic values governed by an opportunistic desire for status, Medea is also deeply concerned about her own reputation. Her use of cunning (*mētis*) not only brings about the deaths of Glauke and Creon, who dies when he embraces his daughter dressed in the poisoned robe, but also involves the most abhorrent crime, the murder of her own children, in order to obtain the appropriate revenge upon her husband: effectively cutting off his family line and denying him the perpetuation of his *kleos*.[16]

By assimilating this tragic paradigm of the abandoned woman who is closely connected to the corruption of traditional values with the Homeric model, later epic was able to incorporate a complex analysis of the heroic values operative in its own world. Apollonius created his own powerful Medea through paradoxical allusions to both Homer's Nausikaa and Euripides' heroine. He undermines the suggestions of social integration in the portrayal of Nausikaa in the *Odyssey* and alludes to the concern for reputation and the potential for violence as well as other elements of discord in the heroine of the *Medea*. His characterization of this woman, even as she pathetically falls in love with the hero, reinforces the antiheroic vision of his epic. The erotic plays a major role in exposing the disintegration of traditional values as expediency requires.

Late republican and Augustan Roman poets added the figure of Ariadne to the paradigm, making the Nausikaa-Medea conflation even more complex. The abandoned Ariadne is a more sympathetic figure: callously deserted by the man whose enterprise she supported at the cost of betraying her family, she does not have the dark

[16]George B. Walsh, "Public and Private in Three Plays of Euripides," *CPhil.* 74 (1979), 294–309, discusses Medea's murder of her children as her most effective revenge against Jason, both to injure her enemy and to enhance her own reputation.

associations with magic nor is she tainted by the brutal murder of her own children. In poem 64, Catullus created a compelling figure who strongly maintains the importance of fidelity and affirms the values of the *domus*. While representing traditional values in a positive way, his Ariadne transforms love into hate through an increasing emotional frenzy that borders on madness. This sympathetic but troubled figure influenced both Vergil's and Ovid's versions of the abandoned female. In the *Aeneid*, Vergil constructs Dido, the most complex of all the epic heroines, by combining elements of Nausikaa, Medea, and Ariadne. Dido contains, in a precarious balance, a dedication to a civilizing enterprise, a heroic bent that encompasses a sense of her own glory, and an erotic vulnerability that has been repressed until the hero's arrival. A problematic aspect of Dido's drama is the nature of her loyalty (*fides*) to her dead husband, which conflicts with Aeneas's own fidelity to his mission and his piety as a hero. In his heroic epistles, Ovid imitates Catullus's version of the abandoned female with his own Ariadne and gives her a subjectivity that is both serious and playful. He wittily dismantles his model and creates a heroine who progressively loses her grasp on reality and moves further into her own solitude. In the process of her abandonment, she reveals the fragility of the very social values that Catullus's heroine upholds.

In the Renaissance, Ovid's version deeply influenced Ariosto's creation of the character Olimpia, who loses her grasp on reality in a different way. She is absorbed in a courtly mode of love that ultimately causes chaos for both family and society, as it operates by an artificial and unrealistic system of values. In particular, Ariosto reevaluates the concept of fidelity, upon which the other social values depend. His heroine confounds the private and social spheres in acting out her erotic desires. Finally, Milton returns principally to Vergil's Dido for his revision of the abandoned female, depicted by Eve in book 9 of *Paradise Lost*. His heroine reflects a new vision of the role of love in relation to heroic values such as piety. Male and female are now integrated in a way that overturns the earlier epic view of the weaknesses inherent in the female as an obstacle to the hero's progress and as a symbol of the corruption of social values.

While viewing the abandoned female as a major locus for the

critique of heroic values, we will see that Homer's night raid of Diomedes and Odysseus underwent a transformation in later epic that engaged eros in a dialectic with social values similar to that which occurs in the Nausikaa-Medea model. The episode of Diomedes and Odysseus in *Iliad* 10, of course, is not specifically erotic. It is, however, situated in the battle scenes of the middle books, which reflect an increasingly intense passion for slaughter and often a savage vaunting over the vanquished. This episode serves, moreover, as a powerful dramatization of the brutality and acquisitiveness potentially underlying the heroic ethic.

The initiator of this night raid, Nestor, has requested a volunteer to go off on a scouting mission to seek information about the Trojan forces after Hector has continued to devastate the Greeks. Diomedes immediately responds, reflecting his characteristic valor (*aretē*). This warrior furthermore wisely requests to have as his companion the cunning Odysseus. When they capture a Trojan spy named Dolon similarly trying to seek information about the Greeks, they shrewdly promise to spare his life in return for information yet immediately kill him upon attaining their objective. Informed by him about the arrival of Rhesus, famed for his marvelous horses, they then make quick work of the Thracian and his troops: Diomedes kills the men and Odysseus drags off the bodies so as not to scare the horses. Their duplicity with Dolon and brutal decapitation of him are morally questionable, and their success against Rhesus through stealth detracts from the glory of their deeds. Yet Homer makes Dolon unsympathetic: he is very eager for the personal glory that he hopes to obtain through capturing the horses of Achilles and shows himself desperate and cowardly when caught. This foolish man certainly represents an extreme in the materialistic side of the heroic ethic. The two Greeks, on the other hand, are not individually greedy: Diomedes intends to seek information to remedy the Greeks' defeat and accepts Nestor's offer of a reward of livestock for the exploit, and the two invoke Athena for her help with an offer to dedicate some of their booty to her.

The Doloneia reflected the less idealistic side of the heroic ethos and was a fruitful source for later poets who radically questioned heroic values. In the *Rhesus*, Euripides imitates Homer's episode so as to expose the shallow, hypocritical nature of the heroic code. The two Greek warriors are characterized as unheroic. While he omits the actual scene in which they discover and kill Dolon, Euripides emphasizes the attempts of the two men to sneak through the Trojan camp and kill Hector. Relying on deceit, they are even abetted by Athena's own trickery when she disguises herself as Aphrodite in order to help them escape. When the charioteer recounts his dream about the attack on Rhesus and his men, he describes a wolf attacking the horses, an ironic allusion to the Greeks' cunning in assuming the disguise of Dolon's own wolf costume.[17]

In this tragedy desire runs to extremes. Initially, Hector expects to attack the Greeks because he believes that total victory is within his grasp. He is then persuaded by Aeneas first to try the indirect strategy of a scouting mission. Impetuously angry when he encounters Rhesus upon the Thracian's arrival, he wishes to dismiss this ally who has arrived so late in the war. For the Trojan spy Dolon, desire is out of control. In his exchange with Hector, he crassly raises the subject of a reward, calling it a double "pleasure" (*charis*) for every deed accomplished. Dolon's rapaciousness exceeds that of his model in the *Iliad*, who accepts Hector's promise of the best horses of the Greeks. In the *Rhesus*, he rejects one gift after another offered by Hector until he finally suggests the horses of Achilles as the only suitable reward. Euripides eroticizes the quest for possessions specifically in Hector's response to Dolon's request for horses, for the Trojan leader expresses his own intense desire for the valuable prize by using the verb *eraō* ("to love") twice in one line (184).

The later adaptations of the night raid are more highly eroticized. Vergil not only views the strong drive for possessions in erotic terms but also turns the pair of warriors into lovers. This more overt eroticization of the episode may to some degree also be influenced by Homer's two close warriors, Achilles and Patroclus. Although difficult to define precisely, Achilles' bond with Patroclus does not seem to be primarily erotic but rather to be symbolic of the hero's ideal image of himself.[18] Ancient readers may well have

[17]See Vincent J. Rosivach, "Hector in the *Rhesus*," *Hermes* 106 (1978), 54–73, for a good discussion of the multiple levels of irony in this play.

[18]See W. Thomas MacCary, *Childlike Achilles: Ontogeny and Phylogeny in the* Iliad (New York: Columbia University Press, 1982), esp. pp. 127–29, on possible psychoanalytical models for Patroclus's relation to Achilles, in particular as ego ideal.

viewed this relationship as sexual,[19] but Homer does not seem to make an erotic dimension a basis for criticism of the heroic system in the *Iliad*. In the Hellenistic period, however, Apollonius in the *Argonautica* portrayed a major warrior pair, Heracles and Hylas, as an example of an anachronistic kind of liaison that needed to be replaced by a fuller integration with the female.[20]

In the Nisus and Euryalus episode in *Aeneid* 9, Vergil represented two warriors whose intensely close relationship suggests the *erastēs* and *erōmenos* of classical Greece as well as the traditional epic warrior pair. K. J. Dover and Michel Foucault have discussed homosexuality in Greece as an important period of transition for the younger man prior to his full adulthood and his assumption of the responsibilities of public life.[21] Foucault points to the importance of honor and shame in the ethic of this relationship. Youthful good looks might become a source of vainglory for the object of desire. The young man might also yield to the temptation of greed when acquiring valuable gifts from his suitors. Discretion in emotional and physical involvement was important in this relationship. The younger man in particular had to guard his conduct so as not to injure his reputation and impair his future success in public life. For his part, the older man faced the problem of excessive passion and possessiveness toward the youth. In an ideal situation, the erotic bond would ultimately be transformed into another kind of affection, *philia*, or friendship, which was an important value in Greek social and political life. While its socializing function was significant, this relationship had the potential for excess and the release of irrational

[19]W. M. Clarke, "Achilles and Patroclus in Love," *Hermes* 106 (1978), 381–96, espousing a view of homoeroticism in the *Iliad*, cites ancient writers, including Aeschylus and Plato, on the sexual side of Achilles and Patroclus's relationship.

[20]Charles R. Beye, "Jason as Love-hero in Apollonios' *Argonautika*," *GRBS* 10 (1969), esp. 45–47, discusses the traditional quality of Heracles as a hero of the type "who offers his soul to a young man," in contrast to the more progressive Jason, who moves into heterosexual relations. Heracles, however, is also significantly a father figure who has raised Hylas after killing the man's father in a struggle over cattle.

[21]K. J. Dover, *Greek Homosexuality* (New York: Vintage Books, 1980), documents the relationship with a historical emphasis. Michel Foucault, *The History of Sexuality*, tr. Robert Hurley (New York: Pantheon Books, 1978), esp. pp. 187–246, focuses on the formulation of rules of conduct and the vocabulary of honor and shame.

passions. In the *Aeneid*, Vergil implements these problems with his two characters as a means of reflecting upon the limitations inherent in the governing values of his world, for the sympathetic pair of lover-warriors reveal a passion for glory, a materialism, and a bloodlust that reaches a level of madness.

After Vergil, love continues to be a major element in the night raid, but undergoes considerable transformation. In book 10 of Statius's *Thebaid*, the warriors Hopleus and Dymas embark on a mission in the dead of night to recover the bodies of their leaders, Parthenopaeus and Tydeus. The two arrive at the scene of carnage but are intercepted by Theban troops led by Amphion. Hopleus is quickly killed. Dymas, displaying a stoic resistance in the face of external power, stabs himself with his own sword rather than yield information to the enemy. Statius plays up the selflessness of these two men. They reveal true *pietas* in their love for their leaders and uncompromising loyalty, in contrast to the general chaos and disintegration of such social values in the madness that characterizes the fight to take Thebes.[22]

Their nobility is all the more impressive in view of the problematic nature of their objects of reverence. In the Theban world, where passions have obliterated reason in the principals on the battlefield, it is not surprising that Tydeus should lose control of himself and yield to ferocity against his adversaries. Yet he goes beyond the general brutality and bloodlust when he actually cannibalizes his enemy Melanippus. The more sympathetic Parthenopaeus, the handsome son of the renowned female warrior Atalanta, is foolishly driven by an excessive love of fame. But he expresses regret for his folly on behalf of his mother, who he knows will suffer profoundly at his death. In this epic, the actions of the warriors have no positive consequences. The only glimmer of optimism that Statius reflects is oblique and tentative. The few characters who are uncorrupted, such as Hopleus and Dymas, show by their *amor*, *fides*, and *pietas* that there is still a hope, however slight, that the world can be reformed and integrity restored. A qualified optimism underlies the poet's break in the narrative apostrophizing Hopleus and Dymas

---

[22] See David Vessey, *Statius and the* Thebaid (Cambridge: Cambridge University Press, 1973), esp. pp. 92–133, on the theme of *pietas* in this epic.

with a desire that they may share the glory of Nisus and Euryalus: Statius implies a hope that his own episode may approach the poetic power of Vergil's and have a salutary effect on its readers.

Ariosto imitated both Vergil's and Statius's episodes in his version of the night raid of Cloridano and Medoro in books 19 and 20 of the *Orlando Furioso*. Love and piety again are primary forces, but the two protagonists are motivated in different directions. Like Vergil's Nisus, Cloridano is emotionally entangled with his handsome young friend. Medoro, however, resembles Euryalus in his beauty but also Dymas in his intent to find and bury the body of his beloved leader. Furthermore, the handsome youth affects other characters erotically, even among the enemy. In contrast to Vergil's and Statius's episodes, Medoro's drama ends happily through a surprising development of an erotic nature. Here, both love and piety are split in so many directions that they become private obsessions rather than social values.

Although not a subject of this book, Tasso's version of the night raid in book 12 of the *Gerusalemme Liberata* deserves mention, as that poet gave an interesting twist to the paradigm in a major Renaissance epic that influenced later works such as *Paradise Lost*. His two warriors, the pagans Clorinda and Argante, embark on a night raid in order to burn the Christians' tower. Unlike the other versions, the very objective of this expedition is destruction. When Christian forces pursue them, Clorinda is accidentally shut out of the camp by her companion and is discovered by the valiant Tancredi. Tasso emphasizes the irony of this situation because the Christian warrior is unaware that he is engaging in combat with the very woman he loves.

Amore in this case is highly problematic. Tancredi's passion for Clorinda has been an impediment to his military role as a crusader; his religious piety as well as his valor have thus been adversely affected. When she is defeated, the ardently anti-Christian Clorinda recalls the wish that her mother had long ago expressed and requests her victor to administer baptism. Through Clorinda's conversation with her guardian shortly before the night raid, the poet provides an important fact about her background: she was born white to an African queen who had experienced a kind of symbolic adultery through the story of Danae depicted in a painting in her bedroom. Clorinda is thus a troubling paradox, a figure who does not belong in Tasso's world. After performing the baptism in the daylight, Tancredi recognizes his victim. Although the hero is filled with grief, the poet implies that his act will have a positive effect. By killing his very object of desire, this man has in fact destroyed his own self-destructive, idealizing imagination.[23] Love for Tasso, then, generally conflicts with men's religious and social goals and must be eliminated or sublimated. The hero can submit to the larger community, but only at the expense of his private, subjective existence. In a sense, the night raid and the abandoned female paradigms have merged, as Tasso's female warrior is destroyed by her impetuous foray in a misguided mission but also by the very hero whose passion for her has been so intense.

[23]See Judith A. Kates, *Tasso and Milton: The Problem of Christian Epic* (Lewisburg: Bucknell University Press, 1983), pp. 93–102, on the problematic nature of Tancredi's love for Clorinda, especially its relation to the imagination.

CHAPTER I

Apollonius and Homer

ALTHOUGH APOLLONIUS extended the role of the vulnerable female by adding a tragic model to his epic paradigm, his achievement in book 3 must be viewed in relation to the complex ways by which the *Argonautica* affiliates itself with Homeric epic. For in the third century B.C., Apollonius revived a genre that had long been considered anachronistic. His older contemporary Callimachus, who helped to shape literary tastes in the Hellenistic period, strongly articulates a preference for the small-scale and the refined in literature. Besides emphasizing the "slender" style, Callimachus's surviving statements relating to literary theory imply strictures on length that speak against the scope necessary for epic.[1] Although poets in the Hellenistic period, such as Rhianus, continued to produce epic of a traditional type contrary to the prevailing aesthetic,[2] only Apollonius seems to have achieved a work of the

[1]The chief advocate of the small, well-constructed poem over the longer, more diffuse narrative, Callimachus expressed his views in the following extant works: the prologue to his *Aitia*; *Hymn* 2.105–113; and epigrams 29 and 30. For a brief, convenient summary of Callimachus's poetics, see Albin Lesky, *A History of Greek Literature*, tr. James Willis and Cornelis de Heer (New York: Crowell, 1966), pp. 710–17; more recently, John Ferguson, *Callimachus* (Boston: Twayne, 1980), esp. pp. 82–84 and 159–60. T. M. Klein, "The Role of Callimachus in the Development of the Concept of the Counter-Genre," *Latomus* 33 (1974), 217–31, considers that Callimachus created the aetiological poem specifically in contrast to what he regarded as epic, in part by turning to the ethos of smaller Greek communities.

[2]On this historical epic, see Auguste Couat, *Alexandrian Poetry under the First Three Ptolemies, 324–222 B.C.*, tr. James Loeb (London: Heinemann, 1931), pp. 347–72.

first rank, which has endured fluctuations in taste. Scholars today tend to believe that, despite the time-honored story of a quarrel between Callimachus and Apollonius, the *Argonautica* embodies a poetics compatible with the *Aitia*.[3] Playful and ironic, the *Argonautica* reflects the poet's self-consciousness about the vast distance between his own age and the heroic period represented in Homer's two great epics. Yet Apollonius seems far more cynical in his attitude toward the past and more radical in his poetic effort than Callimachus. Many recent critics have agreed that this poem is an anti-epic, pervaded by a deep pessimism.[4] For a better understanding of the nature of this work in relation to the epic tradition, one must explore further the bases of the poet's rejection of traditional heroism.

To begin, one might consider the shifts in critical evaluation of this poem. The *Argonautica* has not been so widely admired for most of this century as it was in earlier periods. Even critics who perceive considerable merit in the poem frequently find fault with its seemingly self-indulgent erudition, its lack of tight structure, and the uneven characterization of its hero.[5] The praise, by contrast, has centered on the depiction of the love-struck Medea in book 3, especially for the finely detailed psychological struggle within the young woman.[6] Too often, acknowledgment of Apollonius's achievement

[3]On the question of the quarrel between Apollonius and his "mentor" Callimachus, modern scholars have raised sound objections to the plausibility of the time-honored view. See especially Walter Wimmel, *Kallimachos in Rom, Hermes Einzelschriften* 16 (Wiesbaden: Steiner, 1960), pp. 59–70; E. L. Bundy, "The Quarrel between Kallimachos and Apollonius, I: The Epilogue of Kallimachos' Hymn to Apollo," *California Studies in Classical Antiquity* 5 (1972), 39–94; and Mary R. Lefkowitz, "The Quarrel between Callimachus and Apollonius," *Zeitschrift für Papyrologie und Epigraphik* 40 (1980), 1–19.

[4]Gilbert Lawall, "Apollonius' *Argonautica*: Jason as Anti-Hero," *YClS* 19 (1966), 121–69, has given the most cogent expression of this view; more recently, James Tatum, "Apollonius of Rhodes and the Resourceless Hero of *Paradise Regained*," *Milton Studies* 22 (1986), 255–70.

[5]K. W. Gransden, *Virgil's* Iliad: *An Essay on Epic Narrative* (Cambridge: Cambridge University Press, 1984), p. 4, for example, states that the *Argonautica*, however appealing, cannot be deemed a serious forerunner of the *Aeneid*.

[6]For example, Edward Phinney, Jr., "Narrative Unity in the *Argonautica*, the Medea-Jason Romance," *TAPA* 98 (1967), 327–41, defends Apollonius against claims that Medea's love was not "psychologically credible" and not presented in a "structurally coherent manner." He argues for a continuation of Medea's intense love in book 4 as well, but modified by tension due to fear of her father.

has skirted the problematic status of the poem as an epic by not adequately connecting book 3 to the rest of the poem. Certainly many critics, including Hermann Fränkel, Gilbert Lawall, and Charles Beye, have made more serious attempts to appreciate the *Argonautica* on its own terms and to understand how it plays on Homeric epic.[7] Because of their work, we now have a far better sense of the ironic nature of Jason as a hero, especially in comparison to Homer's Achilles. This chapter explores further the poem's expression of futility about heroic endeavor by linking the heroic to the erotic, especially through material that the poet borrows from Homer's *Iliad* and *Odyssey* and cleverly adapts for his own subversive purposes.

Modern scholars have argued that the prominence of the erotic in Hellenistic literature is related to contemporary philosophical interests. Thomas Rosenmeyer has observed that Theocritean pastoral advocates lighthearted sex in place of troubled passion, a position that has much in common with the Epicurean view of love as a "tense straining, coupled with frenzy and distress for sexual satisfaction."[8] Pastoral thus supports the goal of tranquility (*hēsuchia*) through techniques by which love is kept in a state of suspension, circumscribed, or parodied. A study of the Hellenistic epigram has further developed this view by noting the intersections of that genre with contemporary philosophy. Although both Epicureanism and Stoicism showed hostility to love as an unsettling passion, the former, like much Hellenistic poetry, advocated an idealized friendship as a means of attaining inner peace.[9]

We will briefly consider the example of Theocritus's *Idylls*, which represent some peculiarly Hellenistic approaches toward eros in lit-

---

[7]Hermann Fränkel, *Noten zu den* Argonautika *des Apollonios* (Munich: Beck, 1968), offers much sensitive and suggestive material for further work in this area. Recently, Charles R. Beye, *Epic and Romance in the* Argonautica *of Apollonius* (Carbondale: Southern Illinois University Press, 1982), has offered some brief but useful comparisons between Apollonius and Homer, especially in differentiating Jason from Achilles and Odysseus.

[8]Thomas G. Rosenmeyer, *The Green Cabinet: Theocritus and the European Pastoral Lyric* (Berkeley: University of California Press, 1969), pp. 81–85, for a discussion of Theocritus's poetic strategies for circumscribing love and maintaining the Epicurean tranquility.

[9]Daniel H. Garrison, *Mild Frenzy: A Reading of the Hellenistic Love Epigram*, *Hermes Einzelschriften* 41 (Wiesbaden: Steiner, 1978), esp. pp. 4–7.

erature. In the first *Idyll*, a shepherd named Thyrsis tells the story of Daphnis, who adamantly remains faithful to his life of chastity in nature. The youth prefers to pine away and die rather than submit to Aphrodite, who has inflicted a mutual passion on him and a maiden. As Gilbert Lawall observes, Daphnis is a tragic figure who, modeled not only on Euripides' Hippolytus but also on Aeschylus's Prometheus, is noble and heroic in the face of harsh, tyrannical forces.[10] As a gesture of friendship as well as admiration, the goatherd who listens to Thyrsis's song gives him a cup decorated with scenes from life. Lawall also notes that the physical construction of its scenes reinforces the antithesis between "passionate love (Aphrodite) and chaste innocence (Artemis)": an old man engaged in the practical matter of fishing is framed, on the one hand, by a young boy absorbed in his cricket cage even while danger lurks and, on the other, by two restless men pursuing a coy young woman. In the second *Idyll*, a young woman who seems to be independent, though of a low social status, resorts to witchcraft to bring her faithless lover back. While appearing to represent a contemporary social reality, Simaetha is a complex poetic construct. As Frederick Griffiths has shown, Theocritus has combined elements of a hetaera, naive maiden, mythical heroine, and pederast in his characterization of this young woman.[11] Her gradual disillusionment and understanding that love is a disease provide her an inner stature that transcends the absurdities of her improbable social condition. The sophisticated reader would be amused at the paradoxes of her characterization on the social level and at the literary allusiveness to Sappho and other poets that seems so incongruous to her position, but at the same time would comprehend the human experience common to all. In both poems, love is a disillusioning and disruptive force from which at best humans can emerge with a greater self-awareness.

The love theme is well recognized as Apollonius's major contribution to epic, but there has been no systematic study of the literary sources that most significantly influenced the poet's use of the erotic.

---

[10]Gilbert Lawall, *Theocritus' Coan Pastorals: A Poetry Book* (Washington, D.C.: Center for Hellenic Studies, 1967), esp. pp. 20–21.

[11]Frederick T. Griffiths, "Home before Lunch: The Emancipated Woman in Theocritus," in *Reflections of Women in Antiquity*, ed. Helene P. Foley (New York: Gordon and Breach, 1981), pp. 247–73.

Throughout the narrative, one can see that earlier Greek lyric, especially Sapphic, and contemporary innovations in that genre such as Theocritus's *Idylls* made important contributions. This chapter, however, is concerned primarily with allusions to Homeric epic, which are derived from both erotic and martial episodes in the *Iliad* and the *Odyssey*. Apollonius goes much further than the pastoral and lyric poets by examining the effects of eros on social values as well as on the psyche.

We begin with the poet's subtle insinuation of the theme in his major point of departure from Homer, the ekphrasis of the cloak that Jason wears when he visits Hypsipyle on the island of Lemnos. As scholars have often noticed, Apollonius's counterpart to the shield of Achilles in *Iliad* 18 is an ironic symbol, dismissing the earlier heroic value of military prowess for the more "civilized" qualities of charm and sexual appeal. I aim to bring out the problematic nature of the erotic in this ekphrasis: eros is not only an antithesis to traditional heroic values but paradoxically is linked to war and martial activity and even insinuates itself into the fabric of the poet's narration of the Argonautic quest. After examining the cloak in relation to the poetics and ethics of the poem, I consider another densely symbolic passage on the nature of the erotic, the visit of Hera and Athena to Aphrodite to enlist her help for Jason. There, Apollonius uses two Homeric models to dramatize the negative connotations of eros in the cloak, especially narcissism, duplicity, and a lust for power.

The final two sections examine the association of the erotic with heroism in the major human characters. First, the Lemnian episode, which does not rely on a specific Homeric model but effectively adapts Homeric similes, humorously depicts the passion of the Lemnian women for the Argonauts, especially Hypsipyle's love for Jason. But in this deceptively comic incident the poet expands on the association of the erotic with violence, which makes it antithetical to social life and to the heroic stature that Jason has been attempting to develop. This episode is closely linked with the story of Jason's involvement with Medea, whose love for the hero is the subject of the final section of this chapter. My discussion is organized around Apollonius's use of the episode of Odysseus and Nausikaa in the *Odyssey*, in an interplay with the Medea of Euripides' tragedy. The poet's deviations from his Homeric model in book 3 fully convey the problems that have been suggested in the earlier sections. As Medea is the antithesis of the civilized Nausikaa, so Jason cannot measure up to the truly cunning hero Odysseus. Conversely, allusions to the Euripidean characters in the background reinforce the antiheroic stance already implicit in the earlier Greek work.

The Cloak

As a counterpart to Achilles' shield, Jason's cloak is an emblem of the hero's prowess, or *aretē*. In the *Iliad*, the armor is an object suited for the best of all heroes, and its designs significantly mirror a comprehensive vision of the cosmos. Homer's lengthy description of the five concentric circles moves sequentially from innermost to outermost, from the heavenly bodies to the circling ocean-river that encompasses the world (18.483–608). Framed by these two rings, three inner circles form a microcosm of human life: a city at peace where marriage and litigation take place, a city at war where an assembly discusses action and an ambush is occurring; four fields where the work of the agricultural seasons is unfolded; and recreational activity in the form of a round dance. James Redfield has analyzed the balance and antithesis underlying Homer's shield, as the ekphrasis "moves from nature to culture to productivity, which is the inclusion of nature in culture; it then moves back through culture to nature."[12] By encompassing the orderly strife of the law court as well as the disorderly strife of the ambush, the shield suggests both the tension between discordant elements and their possible resolution. The potential order of that world includes relations between the sexes, encompassed by the social institution of marriage and the harmonious dance of the young men and women. Like the extended similes, the shield sets the heroic values in the poem against the larger world and implies that they are part of a totality

[12]James M. Redfield, *Nature and Culture in the* Iliad: *The Tragedy of Hector* (Chicago: University of Chicago Press, 1975), p. 188.

that ultimately limits their primacy.[13] By the end of the epic, the hero would seem to embody the potential of this shield, to transcend the narrow scope of his martial role. The order in the design of the shield, moreover, is a reflection of the geometric balance and symmetry in Homer's epic itself.[14] Both artifact and poem validate the struggles of human existence in their controlled, comprehensive structures.

Apollonius gives the cloak passage a function much different from that of Homer's shield. Ancient readers perceived in the cloak an inclusiveness encompassing "the heavenly order and human affairs."[15] Instead of pointing to the activities of the world outside of the poem, however, the seven panels allude more closely to the poem itself and, as Lawall has demonstrated, summarize its ethics: "piety, charm, the power of love, the tragedy of war, and the effectiveness of intelligence and treachery."[16] The values implicit in the cloak, furthermore, give rise to comparisons with Homer's heroes. As the panel of the Taphian raiders suggests, Jason is distanced from Achilles, for the military prowess of early heroic society does not adequately solve the problems of this world. In the poem, physical strength is the mode of Heracles: the hero who relies on force becomes absorbed in his own quest for his beloved Hylas, and by the end of this book disappears from the expedition altogether. The use of charm, sexual attractiveness, flattery, and even duplicity to attain one's ends, however, brings to mind the other great Homeric hero. In recalling characteristics of Odysseus, the poet suggests the presence of that hero as a potential model for Jason. Yet the irony of

[13]Ibid., pp. 186–87, for a contrast between the lack of productivity in the economics of combat in the *Iliad* and the self-renewing nature of the societies imaged in the similes.

[14]Cedric H. Whitman, *Homer and the Heroic Tradition* (1958; rpt. New York: Norton, 1965), pp. 87–101, devotes a chapter on the relation of Homer to geometric art in which he compares the Homeric formulae to the formalized motifs on geometric pots and the ring composition both within individual episodes and in the larger structure of the epic to the concentric-circle design in the vase paintings of the period.

[15]*Scholia in Apollonium Rhodium Vetera*, ed. Carolus Wendel (Berlin: Weidmann, 1935), on 763–64a.

[16]Lawall (above, note 4), 154. See also Donald N. Levin, "*Diplax Porphureē*," *Rivista di Filologia e di Istruzione Classica* 98 (1970), 17–36, who emphasizes persuasion and the civilized approach in his discussion of the cloak.

such an affiliation has already been implied from the beginning of the poem by Jason's dominant epithet, *amēchanos* ("resourceless"), which reverses Odysseus's *polumēchanos* ("very resourceful"). Homer's hero is a complex figure who learns through experience to temper qualities that are no longer appropriate and to employ the more ambivalent assets, such as his sexual appeal, ultimately for a social goal, the return to his *oikos* and the restoration of his kingdom.[17] Jason's ambivalent qualities, however, are employed as the need arises for attaining the fleece, to fulfill the demands of the occasion without regard to the long-term consequences.

The cloak, furthermore, alludes to a divine analogue for Jason. While Apollo is already linked to the hero by his patronage of the Argonautic mission,[18] the representation of that god here expands the association. The deity's defense of his mother Leto against the attack of the lustful Tityus dramatically illustrates his piety. As the poet indicates at the beginning of the epic, Jason's own act of piety in helping the goddess Hera across a stream when she visited earth as a mortal is one reason for her support of his mission. Similarly, he demonstrates piety toward his own mother Alcimede, whose dependence on him is made deeply poignant as the Argonauts assemble for their departure.[19] Jason's heroism thus seems bound up with piety, which may seem to be his most positive quality. Yet this virtue is also ambivalent, especially as it becomes entangled with the erotic. The poet reveals that Hera's assistance is based only secondarily on Jason's piety; her primary motivation is to avenge Pel-

---

[17]Pietro Pucci, *Odysseus Polutropos: Intertextual Readings in the* Odyssey *and the* Iliad (Ithaca: Cornell University Press, 1987), however, calls into question long-held, comfortable assumptions about this hero, especially through the interplay of Odysseus with Achilles in the *Iliad*. Pucci fascinatingly explores the significance of this new hero, who in choosing life and return over *kleos* and immortality lacks the other's immutable austerity and ironically is even governed by the undignified drives of the *gastēr*.

[18]At the beginning of the poem, Apollonius compares Jason to Apollo in a simile as the hero sets out for the Argo (1.307–10). In making a sacrifice to the god, Jason himself implies their close connection through oracles allowing him to find paths over the sea (1.359–62).

[19]The poet elaborates the farewell scene between the two at some length (1.261–305): by comparing the desolate woman clinging to her son to a girl with a harsh stepmother embracing her nurse, he indicates the psychological burden imposed on this hero in a role reversal between mother and child.

ias's insult to her dignity when he failed to offer her sacrifice.[20] Her involvement with the hero's cause then motivates her to employ drastic means to insure the Argonauts' success, in particular arranging for Medea to fall in love with Jason and to provide the magic necessary to sustain the awesome tasks of yoking the bulls and plowing the teeth. As we will see, Medea's passion causes the hero to compromise his piety after he commits himself to preserving the young woman from her father's grasp.

The design of the cloak reflects a poetics that sharply contrasts with its model in the *Iliad*. Lacking the clear structure of Homer's concentric circles, the cloak is a loose and fluid assemblage of events. It thus mirrors the episodic nature of this epic, whose structure has been called an "artificial unity" from which one could eliminate many isolated passages.[21] The individual panels even seem to allude to some of these disparate episodes within the narrative.[22] While Homer's circles provide a counterpoint to his fictional world, Apollonius's panels allude to the literary past, as the poem itself so often does. Edward George observes that "all the poet's subjects are specific mythological characters and episodes, gathered from literary tradition; none of them is an anonymous scene from literal experience of the kind that recurs in the shield of Herakles and predominates in the shield of Achilles."[23] Auguste Couat long ago recognized in the seven mythical scenes a kind of summary of cyclic epic themes.[24] The poet alludes to several subjects celebrated in the cyclic corpus: in the forging of Zeus's thunderbolt, the titanomachy in which the Cyclopes first made this weapon for the new ruler of

[20]The poet emphasizes Hera's vindictiveness as the principal reason for her support of Jason at the opening of book 1, as well as in the scene with Aphrodite at the opening of book 3. See Arthur Heiserman, *The Novel before the Novel: Essays and Discussions about the Beginnings of Prose Fiction in the West* (Chicago: University of Chicago Press, 1977), p. 13. Henri de Mirmont, *Apollonios de Rhodes et Virgile: La mythologie et les dieux dans les* Argonautiques *et dans l'*Eneide (Paris: Hachette, 1894), pp. 363–86, has some good observations on Hera's character overall in Apollonius's poem, including her persecution of Heracles.

[21]Couat (above, note 2), p. 328.

[22]See John F. Collins, "Studies in Book One of the *Argonautica* of Apollonius Rhodius" (Ph.D. diss., Columbia Univ., 1967), pp. 70–85; and Lawall (above, note 4), 154–57.

[23]See Edward V. George, "Poet and Characters in Apollonius Rhodius' Lemnian Episode," *Hermes* 100 (1972), 49.

[24]Couat (above, note 2), p. 329.

the universe; in Amphion's and Zethus's struggle to build the walls, the founding of Thebes; in the theft of Electryon's cattle, the Argos saga and the eventual birth of Heracles; in Pelops's race with Oenomaus for Hippodamia, the founding of the house of Atreus.

Several of these panels, moreover, recall an erotic context. Two of the scenes seem to allude specifically to Odysseus's seductive narrative, by which he entrances the Phaeacians in hopes of taking away gifts when he departs. In his catalogue of famous women whom he saw in the underworld, he recounts the sexual background of Amphion and Zethus, the two culture-figures who represent the polarity of might and persuasion, when describing their mother Antiope's affair with Zeus (11.260–65). In his gripping account of the punishments inflicted upon archetypal sinners, he recalls the giant Tityus who tried to rape Leto (11.576–78).[25] The panel of the Taphian raiders against the sons of Electryon contains clear verbal echoes of the Hesiodic *Shield of Heracles*,[26] specifically of bloody attack and defense operations in the long ekphrasis in which violence and slaughter predominate, as appropriate to the character of the bearer of this awesome shield. "Hesiod's" prologue to his ekphrasis includes an expanded account of Amphitryon's love for Alcmene and the revenge imposed on him, which caused his absence and enabled the philandering Zeus to visit the young wife in disguise as her husband. The sources in both Homer and pseudo-Hesiod, then, intimately link *bia*, or force, with eros.

Apollonius's description of the cloak also alludes to the erotic background of its source in Homer. The poet calls the tapestry a *diplaka porphureēn* (722),[27] a phrase which, as scholars note, echoes Homer's description of Helen's weaving in *Iliad* 3 (125–26). The dark red of Helen's robe is the color of death, appropriate to the

[25]See Apollonius of Rhodes, *Argonautiques*, Vol. 1, ed. with commentary by Francis Vian (Paris: Les Belles Lettres, 1974), pp. 258–59.

[26]Malcolm Campbell, *Echoes and Imitations of Early Epic in Apollonius Rhodius* (Leiden: Brill, 1981), p. 14, calls attention to the similarity of Apollonius's language describing the defense and attack to lines 238–41 of the Hesiodic *Shield*. If the poet acknowledges the shield as an influence here in the cloak, he seems to relegate its significance to this single expression of anachronistic values.

[27]Apollonius Rhodius, *Argonautica*, ed. Hermann Fränkel (Oxford: Clarendon Press, 1961). My quotations from the *Argonautica*, transliterated, are from this edition. The translations are my own.

nature of her subject, the bloody battle between Greek and Trojan warriors outside the walls of Troy. As we observed in the introduction, Homer recalls the erotic basis for this struggle when Helen acknowledges her role as cause of the war in her conversation with Priam. Helen has been weaving into her robe the contests being fought on her behalf. She is an ambivalent object of admiration by Trojan elders, who comment that her awesome, divine beauty makes the war understandable and yet simultaneously express the need to have her gone (3.154–58). In the so-called Teichoskopia, furthermore, Helen's catalogue of warriors on the battlefield significantly contains no mention of Achilles, the major warrior who did not compete for her hand in marriage.[28] In alluding to the origins of the war through the Trojans' admiration for her beauty and her own perspective on the battlefield, Homer makes Helen's powerful presence a means of reminding his audience that the violence is closely bound up with her sexuality.[29] Jason's cloak in the *Argonautica* is similarly *porphureos* on the borders where the scenes are woven. Violence and death underlie several of these incidents: the bloody attack of the Taphians on the sons of Electryon for their cattle; the race in which Pelops seeks to win Hippodamia through the trick of disabling Oenomaus's chariot; Apollo's act of shooting at Tityus, who attempts to rape his mother Leto. In the last two, the link between violence and erotic desire is especially graphic.

If *porphureos* hints at the erotic basis for heroic action, Apollonius goes beyond Homer by using a second, more brilliant red for the unembroidered section of the cloak. Critics have noted Apollonius's fondness for descriptions involving red, especially against a white background.[30] *Ereuthos* has special connotations in this poem, in contexts where characters feel passionate desire and act in ways that

[28]See Linda L. Clader, *Helen: The Evolution from Divine to Heroic in Greek Epic Tradition* (Leiden: Brill, 1976), pp. 7–11, especially on Helen's omission of Menelaus and Achilles from her catalogue, both of whom were not suitors for her hand.

[29]See Marylin B. Arthur, "The Divided World of *Iliad* VI," in *Reflections of Women in Antiquity*, ed. Helene P. Foley (New York: Gordon and Breach, 1981), p. 26.

[30]Edward Phinney, Jr., "Hellenistic Painting and the Poetic Style of Apollonius," *CJ* 62 (1967), 146–47, discusses passages in which Apollonius uses color and light within framed scenes, in panoramic and pastoral landscapes, and notes that he is particularly fond of the color contrast of red over a white background, one aspect of his "painter's joy in color."

have serious moral consequences. While frequently associated with erotic experience, *ereuthos* occurs in situations ranging from the loss of innocence at the inception of sexual desire to a state of violence arising from passionate emotions.[31] This word often signals an irreversible change. In one fine simile, the verb *ereuthō* conveys the flood of pent-up sexual desire in the Lemnian women eagerly awaiting Jason's arrival by comparing them to a young girl gazing at the evening star (1.774–80). In another, Apollonius compares Medea struck by Eros's shaft to a working woman kindling a fire late at night (3.293–97) and then notes the alternation of pallor and blush (*ereuthos*) on her cheeks. The young woman's next act in the narrative is to push aside her veil, a symbol of her modesty, in order to get a better glimpse of the hero (445–46). In describing Medea's agony over her passion for Jason, the poet employs the verb *ereuthō* as she loses her struggle with the social value *aidōs* ("shame"; 3.681).

More problematically, Apollonius links eros to heroic endeavor through *ereuthos*. He applies this word to Jason at the moment he seizes the Golden Fleece and thus obtains the symbol of power for which he has lusted, by noting that the fleece cast a red glow on the hero's face (4.173). This description immediately follows a simile comparing Jason to a young girl who has caught the gleam of the moon on her dress. At the climax of his success in his quest in Colchis, Jason is hereby ambivalently associated with the most erotically charged, perversely aggressive women in the poem, the Lemnians. Most strikingly, Apollonius applies this suggestive word to the scene where the hero, responding in fear to Medea's outburst, murders her brother Apsyrtus at the very temple of the goddess Artemis in order to preserve the young woman's safety and keep the

[31]Catherine C. Rhorer, "Red and White in Ovid's *Metamorphoses*: The Mulberry Tree in the Tale of Pyramus and Thisbe," *Ramus* 9 (1980), 79–88, has an excellent discussion of Ovid's use of red and white in sexual contexts in his epic. There are many similarities between the Roman and the Greek poems on the significance of red, though Apollonius seems to be more clearly interested in the moral aspects. Amy Rose, "Clothing Imagery in Apollonius's *Argonautika*," *Quaderni Urbinati di Cultura Classica* 50 (1985), 38–39, discusses the uses of red in the *Argonautica* primarily in three contexts: the good looks of youths, the blushing face of a young woman who is about to lose her sexual innocence, and the appearance of heavenly bodies. She also finds that the color describing Jason as he seizes the fleece signifies his "abandonment of the diplomatic mode."

fleece (4.474). Hero and heroine are both morally compromised in this scene, for the blood from Apsyrtus's body stains Medea's dress. While a primary example of Apollonius's artistic sensitivity to color, *ereuthos* also helps to trace the progressive moral degeneration of the two principal characters.

As a symbol of his poetics, the cloak also implicates the artist in the problematic of the erotic. Critics have frequently pointed out that the panel of the Cyclopes forging Zeus's thunderbolt evokes the *Iliad*, for the passage on the shield begins with a picture of Hephaestus laboring at his craft for the Olympians (18.372–80). Homer suggests that Hephaestus's work is analogous to his own. His depiction of the divine smith at work before and during the forging of the shield implies the poet's own tradition of oral composition, as it permits the audience to experience the continuous movement and production of the work of art. He shows that the divine artisan has complete mastery over the materials of his craft and proceeds without interruption or hesitation, with the bellows responding automatically to his commands.[32] By offering the smith god as his divine model, Homer would seem to assume a similar control over his own poetic materials and a comprehensive vision of life, which unfolds through the remainder of the epic.

Apollonius, by contrast, to some extent distances himself from the creator of the artifact itself, Athena, the counterpart of Homer's Hephaestus. Although depicting erotic material in this tapestry, the goddess later ironically admits to no understanding whatsoever of love affairs and is totally incapacitated when Hera asks for advice about helping Jason through Medea. Furthermore, the poet describes the cloak as an object already made and says nothing about the process of its creation. Instead, he transforms the passage in the *Iliad* narrating the forging of the shield into a visual image, as the first panel within the artifact itself. By representing one dynamic moment of a process in the stasis of a picture on a tapestry, he suggests a view of the artist at odds with Homer's.

The Cyclopes panel obliquely suggests Apollonius's own paradigm for the poet. Several critics have noticed, for instance, its connection with the cosmological song that Orpheus sings in order

[32]See Kenneth J. Atchity, *Homer's* Iliad: *The Shield of Memory* (Carbondale: Southern Illinois University Press, 1978), pp. 176–79.

31

to end the quarrel between Idmon and Idas earlier in book 1.[33] Focusing on the primal strife within the universe, the mythical bard ends by suggesting the advent of Zeus's rule: "While Zeus, still a child and with thoughts of a child, lived in the Dictaean cave; and the earth-born Cyclopes had not yet armed him with the bolt, both thunder and lightning; for these things bestow honor upon Zeus" (508–11). By beginning where the mythological cosmology left off, the Cyclopes panel implies that Apollonius has an analogue in Orpheus, who serves as the resident musician on the Argo. The mythical bard in book 1 does not arbitrate the quarrel but deflects the hostilities through more subtle means. As Couat notes, the content of Orpheus's song has no direct bearing on the immediate crisis but rather is meant for us as readers; it is the captivating language and cadence that soothe the irate characters.[34] Apollonius shows that the bard's effect is in fact spellbinding: "But although he had stopped, all yet strained their necks, silent in fascination, with ears perked up; such a charm of song he had left for them" (513–15). The language here is significant, as *thelktron* is commonly used for love charms as well as for music. Orpheus's song is seductive, not unlike the poet's in the *Argonautica*.

The captivating power of Orpheus's poetry may not seem so different in essence from the marvelous creations of Hephaestus, who made gold seem like dark earth on the shield (18.548–49). Yet Homer's smith god reveals a cosmic vision beyond the limited viewpoints of the human characters who necessarily operate by narrow social values. Apollonius's bard, by contrast, does not exhibit a similarly higher perspective and serves a limited function with his persuasive powers. In a revealing passage in book 2, for example, Orpheus sings a hymn of praise to Apollo, the patron divinity of the Argonauts (705–10). As critics have noted, Apollonius seems clearly to identify with the bard when he breaks off the indirect discourse and begins to invoke the god directly.[35] Yet it is important to observe that this song occurs right after a crucial point in the action, in which the Argonauts have sailed safely through the Symplegades by the decisive help of the goddess Athena. The poet's identification

[33]See Lawall (above, note 4), 154.
[34]Couat (above, note 2), pp. 335–36.
[35]See Collins (above, note 22), p. 71.

with the mythical bard at this point must be in part ironic, since the latter has failed to recognize the real source of the crew's safety and has inappropriately lavished praise on the god who has essentially done nothing for them. Orpheus's intervention in the quarrel in book 1 is also problematical, for his music temporarily allays, but does not resolve, discord. Idas in fact remains a disruptive force, voicing attitudes that challenge the more flexible views of Jason and others, who perceive the need to adapt to unforeseen circumstances with unconventional methods.[36]

Apollonius thus undermines Homer's vision of a divine counterpart for the poet with superior understanding and complete mastery over a situation. Instead, the poet-narrator mesmerizes his reader and is himself caught up in events, including the subjectivity of his heroine in book 3. Apollonius has perhaps reduced the reliability of the narrator as a reflection of the demise of the truly heroic world. The traditional epic bard rises to the demanding task of narrating the *klea andrōn*, the deeds of heroes who rose far above the status of ordinary men. This poet, however, may ironically suggest that the uncertain values and questionable ethics of the world of his epic render that kind of self-assured voice impossible.

The poet's use of the word *ereuthos* in his introduction to the cloak ekphrasis helps to reinforce this sense of a deviously erotic narrative style. As he mentions the radiance of this garment, he makes the following claim: "You would more easily cast your eyes upon the rising sun than gaze upon that brilliant red" (725–26). Since the cloak is a miniature of the poem itself, the poet here cautions the reader about the dazzling effects of the narrative. Critics have often commented on Apollonius's self-conscious awareness of the reader of his text and his adoption of certain stances, such as aloofness in the Lemnian episode.[37] Because *ereuthos* is so closely involved with passion in this poem, he would also seem to imply something about the specifically erotic nature of the narrative that he is creating. By affecting the reader with *ereuthos*, he is like an erotic agent who causes the reader to become enamored of his text and to suffer a

[36]See Hermann Fränkel, "Ein Don Quijote unter den Argonauten des Apollonios," *Museum Helveticum* 17 (1960), 1–20, on the anachronistic nature of Idas as a Homeric-style warrior relying on force.

[37]George (above, note 23), 52.

loss of innocence similar to that which the erotic victims experience.[38]

Let us consider how the cloak ekphrasis itself, as a symbol of the poem as a whole, reflects the poet's attempt to captivate through style. Here, for example, Apollonius shows the Cyclopes' labor at forging a thunderbolt that is just about completed:[39]

> By now it was almost finished, totally bright, but still it lacked only one ray, which they were beating out with iron hammers, a glowing breath of fierce fire. (731–34)

As commentators have observed, this description echoes Homer's account of Hephaestus at work when Thetis arrived. He is in the process of making twenty tripods:[40]

> These were so far completed, but the intricate ear-handles were not yet in place. He was forging them and beating out the chains. (18.378–79)

In contrast to Homer, Apollonius focuses not on the artisan but on the appearance of the object itself, the awesome effusion of light. This fascination with the effects of light was in fact shared by contemporary artists. The great Apelles in particular was said to have created strikingly dramatic effects with light in painting.[41] Pliny records the most astounding accomplishment of this artist, who

---

[38] Apollonius clearly makes the reader feel the intensity and pain of Medea's experience of falling in love in book 3, and yet at the same time keeps one distanced and almost disillusioned by the ironic interplay with the literary sources, especially in Homer and Euripides, by significant symbolic language, such as the term *ereuthos*, and by the similes, which sometimes project to the unhappy future. One is made to feel the disenchantment that Medea herself will later suffer and to sense her future vehemence.

[39] For my rendition of line 734, see Apollonius of Rhodes, *The Argonautica*, ed. with commentary G. W. Mooney (1912; rpt. Amsterdam: Hakkert, 1964), at 731–34. This interpretation takes "zdeiousan" as a participial adjective modifying "autmēn," instead of as a participle depending on "aktinos" (the reading of the Loeb). Mooney's translation makes the entire line a single vivid picture, which the poet seems to have intended.

[40] My citations from the *Iliad* come from *Homeri Ilias*, vols. 1, 2, and 3, ed. T. W. Allen (1931; rpt. New York: Arno, 1979); they are transliterated. The translations are my own.

[41] Ernst Gombrich, *The Heritage of Apelles: Studies in the Art of the Renaissance* (Ithaca: Cornell University Press, 1976), pp. 14–16.

34

"painted what cannot be painted: thunder flashes and lighting" (*HN* 35.94). Gombrich points to the great Hellenistic painter's use of *atramentum* as a technical innovation by which the artist could tone down parts of a panel and allow others to project.[42] In Apelles' painting of Alexander the Great holding a thunderbolt, the bolt would appear to leap out from the painting, thus arousing wonder in the viewer.[43] While H. A. Shapiro has even claimed that in the cloak ekphrasis Apollonius wishes to acknowledge the accomplishments of contemporary painting and sculpture,[44] the poet may be more interested in appropriating the dramatic effects of the visual arts in his own poetry.

The language of the cloak ekphrasis creates an impression of the visual effects it describes. The very structure of the Cyclopes panel reflects the process of production as it enters the last stage, for it directs the reader's attention to the blast of the final ray. After referring to the bolt as *pamphainōn* ("all-bright"), the poet conveys its incomplete state by an effective enjambment: "miēs d'eti deueto mounon / aktinos" (732–3), the final word drawing the eye to the unfinished shaft. The last four words graphically convey the appearance of the shaft itself: it is a "glowing" ("zdeiousan") "breath" ("autmēn," the final word) of "vehement fire" ("maleroio puros"). The effective word position of "autmen"; the transferral of *zdeio*, "to boil," from its usual association with water so as to conjure up an image of a hot glow; the epic resonance of *maleroios*, a word which connotes a dreadful power, frequently used by Homer and always in reference to fire—all make the reader feel the impact of

[42]Ibid., p. 17.

[43]Pliny (*HN* 35.92) notes that the effect was all the more amazing because Apelles used only four colors. A beautiful extant painting in the house of the Vettii at Pompeii may be a copy of Apelles' masterpiece, as suggested by the red shading of the chest and the well-executed face resembling portraits of Alexander; see Paolino Mingazzini, "Una copia dell'Alexandros Keraunophoros di Apelle," *Jahrbuch der Berliner Museen* 3 (1961), 7–17.

[44]H. A. Shapiro, "Jason's Cloak," *TAPA* 110 (1980), 263–86, develops many connections to contemporary art in Apollonius's cloak, but considers them as tributes that have no primary bearing on the poem itself. This view seems too narrow, for the rhetorical device of ekphrasis is clearly already linked in the *Iliad* to the ethics and poetics of the epic, a fact which would hardly have escaped the astute, self-conscious Apollonius. On the connections to contemporary art, see also T. B. L. Webster, *Hellenistic Poetry and Art* (New York: Barnes and Noble, 1964), p. 160.

this last ray of Zeus's terrifying weapon. As a Hellenistic writer experimenting widely with the effects of language, Apollonius goes far beyond Homer in making his audience participate in the event at hand.

The third panel, which represents Aphrodite gazing into the shield of Ares, epitomizes the poet's ability to infuse the erotic into his poem as a symbol of its poetics and ethics. A famous passage in the *Odyssey* seems to have influenced this scene, for its content is reminiscent of the vignette in book 8, in which the bard Demodocus tells how the goddess was once caught in her adultery with Ares through the clever stratagem of her husband Hephaestus (8.266–66).[45] Here Apollonius shifts the focus to the goddess alone and her self-absorption as she gazes at her own image in Ares' shield, which she is using as a mirror. This shield is presumably in her possession because she has just made love to her paramour. The earlier poet shows the lovers humiliated and the adulterer Ares forced to pay the *moichagria*, or fine, which was actually imposed on Greeks for this crime. The comic incident in the *Odyssey* has a narrative function, since it draws a significant contrast between the intelligence of Hephaestus and the handsome appearance of Ares that is relevant to the quarrel between Odysseus and the Phaeacian Euryalus, who later makes amends for his rudeness; it may also foreshadow the hero's own caution when he returns to Ithaca, where his wife has been wooed by a flock of determined suitors.[46] In that poem, the social values that define human life are thus upheld and order restored, at least temporarily in the divine sphere but more stably in Odysseus's kingdom. The Hellenistic poet, however, images an incident of illicit love that is successful. Social order here, and later within the narrative, is undermined.

If Apollonius knew the original of a famous Pompeian wall painting of Thetis in Hephaestus's workshop,[47] he changed the significance of the reflection: the sea goddess gazes at the shield in anticipa-

[45]See Collins (above, note 22), p. 73.

[46]See Bruce K. Braswell, "The Song of Ares and Aphrodite: Theme and Relevance to *Odyssey* 8," *Hermes* 110 (1982), 129–37, on the relevance of the story to the behavior of the young Phaeacian to Odysseus; see also Agathe Thornton, *People and Themes in Homer's* Odyssey (London: Methuen, 1970), p. 45, for a possible link to Odysseus's own later caution.

[47]Shapiro (above, note 44), 281–82.

tion of its completion, but the love goddess engages in a self-indulgent gesture. We are meant to imagine Aphrodite's fascination with the precision of her image, her beauty faithfully mirrored, for the poet explicitly mentions the accuracy of the image: "Opposite her image so precise in the bronze shield" (725–26). Here, the poet reflects the interest in mirror images that so intrigued contemporary painters, even to the extent of following principles of mathematical accuracy in the appearance of an object on a reflecting surface.[48] Furthermore, he makes the reflected object seductive through the rhetoric of his description. Emphasizing the goddess's beautiful hair, he calls her *bathuplokamos*, "luxuriant-haired," an unusual word with a sensuous cadence. A pentasyllabic word, it dominates the hexameter from the caesura to the end with its noun Cythereia: "Ηεχειες d'εσκετο // bathuplokamos Kuthereia" (742), "next the luxuriant-haired Cythereia had been fashioned." This particular physical trait is again analogous to contemporary painting, including the great Apelles' representation of the goddess squeezing water out of her hair as she rose out of the sea.[49]

The poet creates this visual focus in part by his self-conscious manipulation of Homeric vocabulary. Apollonius seems to have coined the epithet *bathuplokamos*, a *hapax legomenon* in the *Argonautica* formed on the model of two Homeric adjectives.[50] Homer frequently applies *euplokamos* in the *Iliad* to goddesses such as Thetis (e.g., 5.390, 20.80); in his ekphrasis of the shield, he describes Ariadne as *kalliplokamos* (18.592). Demetrius, author of the treatise

---

[48]John Onians, *Art and Thought in the Hellenistic Age: The Greek World View, 350–50 B.C.* (London: Thames and Hudson, 1979), p. 45, observes that the Pompeian painting is carefully executed in this respect: the reflection on the shield, a close likeness, is a reversed image of the seated goddess that conforms to correct optical principles in being one-half the size of the original.

[49]Pliny (*HN* 35.91) suggests its lifelike quality by mentioning that the damage to the lower part of this painting, which Augustus had placed in the temple of Julius Caesar, only added to Apelles' fame, since no one could be found to repair it. Gombrich (above, note 41), p. 17, observes that the technique of *splendor*, or sparkling highlights, applied to the goddess's wet hair, must have brought her to life on the panel.

[50]On Apollonius's use of Homeric vocabulary, see, for example, R. W. Garson, "Homeric Echoes in Apollonius Rhodius' *Argonautica*," *CPhil.* 67 (1972), esp. 1–5; also Enrico Livrea, "Una 'tecnica allusiva' apolloniana alla luce dell'esegesi omerica alessandrina," *Studi Italiani di Filologia Classica* 44 (1972), 231–43.

On Style, which scholars generally believe to be an early third-century B.C. work, discusses the use of neologisms as a means of rivaling Homer.[51] He asserts that this skill particularly distinguishes a great poet by making him seem like one who first gave things their names, in the manner of Homer.[52] For that critic, Sappho epitomizes this magical ability: "And she weaves every beautiful word with her poetry; she herself invented some of them" (166). By using a word such as *bathuplokamos,* Apollonius appropriates one major aspect of the genius of his great predecessor, according to Hellenistic scholars. Here, this sinuous word has considerable semantic power, for it not only suggests the goddess's beautiful, luxuriant hair but also hints at her illicit activity, since her loosely flowing locks are a sign of her tryst with Ares.

The seductive appeal of this panel is reinforced by the arrangement of its elements so as to direct the reader's gaze in a linear movement. Here, the poet describes her appearance: "And from her shoulder to her left arm, the binding of her tunic had fallen loose under her breast; and opposite in the bronze shield she seemed to see her image so precise" (743–46). In the manner of a painting, Apollonius's passage reveals the specific parts of the goddess's body from her shoulder, to her left arm, to the binding of her chiton, and finally to the focal point—her bared breast, where one's attention is, if only briefly, fixed. An indication of the care with which the poet executed this little portrait is the position of "deikēlon,"("image") within the phrase "bronze mirror": "chalkeiē deikēlon en aspidi." As the phrase literally encloses the word "image," it creates the effect of a frame on the fictional scene. In addition, the poet uses a bucolic diaeresis after "aspidi," by which the break between the fourth and fifth feet corresponds with a word termination, and

[51]On the question of the date of the treatise *On Style,* see G. M. A. Grube, *A Greek Critic: Demetrius On Style* (Toronto: University of Toronto Press, 1961), pp. 39–56, who argues for a date of composition about 270 B.C., as opposed to a much later date, because of the author's familiarity with early third-century writers, his knowledge of Aristotle, his views on third-century oratory, and his attitude toward Demosthenes. George Kennedy, *The Art of Persuasion in Greece* (Princeton: Princeton University Press, 1963), pp. 285–86, accepts Grube's position.

[52]Demetrius, *On Style,* tr. W. Rhys Roberts (Cambridge: Cambridge University Press, 1902), discusses neologisms of two types, compounds and onomatopoeic words, in sections 91–94.

places the main pause, or caesura, after "deikēlon," thus emphasizing the two structural elements of the panel. The rhetorical illusionism of this passage in effect causes the reader to participate in Aphrodite's fixation on her own image and seductive beauty. Although informed that this mirror is actually the "swift shield" of Ares himself, we are likely momentarily to forget the suggestion of adultery underlying this scene, that Hephaestus has been cuckolded and Ares has succumbed to Aphrodite's power. But beneath the enticing surface, the poet has suggested a vision of love as narcissism and duplicity.

The cloak ekphrasis, then, hints at the pervasive role of the erotic in the poem, in large part through adaptations of Homer's two great epics. Apollonius to some extent implies his predecessor's view of the erotic underpinning of martial violence, yet takes a much more critical position. He does not suggest the possibility for the positive, mutually sustaining affection that defines Hector's and Andromache's relationship in the *Iliad*, but instead emphasizes the more disruptive sexuality found in Helen. Even in that respect Apollonius moves in a much more negative direction. Helen, the symbol of sexual passion in the *Iliad*, is also a war prize; she thus represents the heroes' desire for fame (*kleos*), a social value of positive force in Homer's world. The poet here implies that traditional values, such as piety and prowess, are compromised by the erotic. The suggestion of Odysseus as an alternative model to Achilles in the cloak, as we will see, is developed in the narrative of book 3 through allusion to a significantly erotic context, the earlier hero's encounter with the love-struck Nausikaa. Violence or disorder and the erotic are more closely bound up in this work. As the Aphrodite panel implies, narcissism and duplicity underlie the erotic. Yet the poet's cunning web also involves his own effort in this problem. The moral implications of *ereuthos* have a counterpart in the poet's seductive style, which has a deviously enchanting, potentially misleading effect on the reader of the text. If there is no longer a true heroism, neither is there a guaranteed source of immutable truth. The dazzling style of the Aphrodite panel covers over but does not completely obliterate the problem of adultery, illegitimate activity. The tension caused by this devious mode of representation will be seen in our discussions of the major erotic episodes.

The Prologue Scene of Book Three

In the prologue of book 3, where Hera and Athena visit Aphrodite at home, the poet develops the implications of the cloak more fully. He virtually provides a definition of love by emphasizing the ambivalence of the erotic and insinuating the qualities of self-indulgence and duplicity. Furthermore, the narrative implies the poet's own association with this deviousness beneath the comic surface.

In this episode Apollonius amusingly adapts Homer's *Iliad* to a contemporary literary spirit. Critics have observed that the poet alludes to two passages in the *Iliad*, Hera's visit to Aphrodite, in book 14, for her seductive embellishment so that she may divert Zeus's attention from the battlefield, and Thetis's request to Hephaestus, in book 18, for new armor for Achilles.[53] These two episodes, in which the manipulative Hera exploits her sexuality to aid the Greeks in the war and Thetis uses her influence to allow the hero to return to the fighting, are powerful moments in the *Iliad* that one would expect to form the basis of a seriously dramatic incident. Instead, this episode is colored with a very playful Hellenistic humor. As scholars have frequently noted, this scene is similar to Theocritus's *Idyll* 15, in which two ordinary women going off to a religious festival at the palace of Arsinoe engage in lively chatter about domestic affairs and other mundane events in their lives.[54]

While sustaining the light, humorous surface of the Hellenistic idyll, the poet adapts the Homeric sources for a more cynical effect, as he depicts the petty behavior of the goddesses toward each other. Aphrodite is resentful at the obvious reluctance of the two visitors

[53]P. G. Lennox, "Apollonius, *Argonautica* 3,1ff. and Homer," *Hermes* 108 (1980), 45–73, discusses the prologue scene at length and points out many details that ironically echo not only the two major sources but also other passages, such as the wounding of Menelaus by Pandarus in *Iliad* 4. He stresses the impact of the Homeric models in three ways: the influence of the antipathy of the goddesses in Homer, which altered for Apollonius the traditional benevolence of Aphrodite in the Argonautic myth; the crucial importance of divine aid in Jason's quest for the fleece; and the amusing tone that the poet imparts to traditional epic material. He does not, however, connect the imitation to the larger, more problematic issue of eros in this poem.

[54] Beye (above, note 7), p. 127, notes the similarity to Theocritus. Webster (above, note 44), pp. 78–79, draws an analogy to the third-century Egyptian court.

to associate with her and responds with insincere flattery. While the poet indicates that she spoke "with crooked words" ("haim-ulioisin," 51), the goddess employs deferential terms ("honored" and "preeminent") when she asks these infrequent visitors why they have now come (53–54). In *Iliad* 18, by contrast, the surprise gener-ated by Thetis's visit seems genuine, her absence explainable by her connection with the realm of the sea. Charis greets Thetis openly and courteously: "'Why, Thetis of the light robes, have you come to our house now, you who are revered and loved? For you have not come often before'" (385–86). Similarly, in *Iliad* 14 Hera has no qualms about visiting Aphrodite and even seems to respect the powers of that goddess. Furthermore, Apollonius seems to play against the character of Homer's two goddesses, for in book 14 the straightforward Aphrodite is completely willing to offer her assis-tance to Hera in the sphere of lovemaking, whereas the latter is the devious one who speaks falsely and cunningly ("dolophroneousa," 197).

As well as implying her deviousness, Apollonius suggests an un-predictability and impulsiveness in Aphrodite's character. He pro-vides no direct explanation, for instance, for the goddess's sudden willingness to help Hera. Lennox suggests a reason why Aphrodite responds positively to Hera's account of being conveyed over a swollen river by Jason when she came to earth disguised as an old woman to test human generosity: according to Hellenistic myth, Aphrodite herself had similarly been rescued by an old ferryman named Phaon, whom the goddess then rewarded with renewed youth and good looks.[55] By perceiving her own situation in Hera's, she responds unreflectively and irrationally. She does not show the practical response based on the social norms in the *Iliad*, where Hephaestus reciprocates Thetis's favor of rescuing him in his fall from Olympus.

The poet also suggestively fails to explain Aphrodite's activity before the goddesses' arrival. When the two divine guests enter, the love goddess is in a situation similar to her appearance on the cloak: "And her white shoulders on each side were covered with her hair and she was parting it with a golden comb and about to braid up the

[55]Lennox (above, note 53), 54–55.

long tresses" (45–47). Aphrodite's languid self-indulgence and her seductively loosened hair, similar to the cloak passage, suggest that she may have just had a visitor. At the beginning of the episode, the poet prominently mentions Hephaestus's name several times in his description of the palace, as if to reaffirm the identity of Aphrodite's husband. In Lennox's view, Apollonius is playing a little joke on the reader by raising expectations of adultery on Aphrodite's part, as in the song of Demodocus in *Odyssey* 8, but then showing in fact a chaste, matronly goddess who is not engaged in extramarital affairs.[56] Yet the goddess's wantonness is hinted at by the presence of her son Eros, who is generally regarded in mythology as the product of Aphrodite's adulterous union with Ares, not of her marriage to Hephaestus.[57]

The unruly, unprincipled behavior of this child identifies him as the war god's offspring as well as the love goddess's. The poet introduces Eros by a pictorial scene in which the young boy is playing dice with Ganymede and is winning unfairly. This depiction shows him as unscrupulous and possessive: "greedy"("margos") Eros, holding in his left hand all the golden dice he has won from Ganymede, stands upright, with a sweet blush ("glukeron ereuthos") glowing on his cheeks, while Ganymede sits crouching nearby, silent and downcast (119–23). The word *ereuthos*, especially in a context of corruption by an excess of desire or passion, is now directly applied to the love god himself. Here it conveys in particular Eros's desire for lucre, a manifestation of the self-interest of the erotic agent. The god's selfishness at the expense of others can also be seen in his unruly conduct, for with malicious glee he laughs loudly at Ganymede's last unlucky throw (124).

Aphrodite is similarly unscrupulous, for she uses bribery as her method of persuasion. In order to convince him to shoot his arrow and instill in Medea a love for Jason, she promises to give him the golden ball of Zeus. The goddess herself describes this very beautiful plaything ("perikalles athurma," 132) to her son: it has all-golden zones, and double seams run around each in a circle, but the stitches

[56]Ibid., 49–50.

[57]For views on the parentage of Eros in the later Greek period, see Geoffrey Grigson, *The Goddess of Love: The Birth, Triumph, Death and Return of Aphrodite* (London: Constable, 1976), pp. 68–69.

are concealed with a dark blue spiral around all; if thrown upward, like a star it sends a flaming trail through the sky (137–41). By this time the ball was regarded as a love token to charm and win over the object of desire.[58] Apollonius gives a kind of aetiology of this token. A highly desirable material object, Eros's ball suggests wealth and power: its color is that of the precious metal gold; it belonged to Zeus while he was concealed in the cave and prepared to overthrow his father Chronos as ruler of the universe; and its trail of smoke in the sky implies the powers of the sky god who can cause comets to fall as well as wield the thunderbolt.[59] Its seductive power is seen here in Eros's response: "He threw down all his toys, and pulling on both sides of her tunic here and there, seizing her on one side and the other, eagerly held on to the goddess. He begged her to give it immediately" (146–48). Like the mock drama of Hellenistic manners at the beginning, the comic vignette of the spoiled child teasing his mother for a toy is entertaining and may seem to resist serious interpretation. Yet in the context of the detailed description of the ball, it suggests a desire for self-aggrandizement that has a cynical connection to material wealth.

This scene has significant implications for the nature of the hero of this poem. Aphrodite's son Eros, according Theodore Klein, may be an analogue for Jason: as the former cheats with Ganymede, so the latter lures Apsyrtus to his death; the hero also marvels and rejoices at the sight of the Golden Fleece and is very possessive of it.[60] The poet would thus seem to diminish Jason, since he appears to be, like Eros, as Klein puts it, "selfish, wilful, and puerile." By making Eros a figure of the hero, Apollonius heightens the irony of Jason's climactic moment of heroism in book 4. We have already observed the erotic nature of the simile that depicts Jason as a young girl catching the blush of the moon on her dress as he is at last about to possess the Golden Fleece. When one considers its relation to this prologue scene, Jason's greed there appears as base as Eros's, in large

[58] Anne Carson, *Eros the Bittersweet: An Essay* (Princeton: Princeton University Press, 1986), p. 20, notes this development on the ball and the love charm.

[59] See Apollonius of Rhodes, *Argonautiques*, vol. 2, ed. with commentary by Francis Vian (Paris: Les Belles Lettres, 1980), p. 115, for the view that the ball offered to Zeus, having a cosmic nature, symbolizes the universe.

[60] Theodore M. Klein, "Apollonius Rhodius, *Vates Ludens*: Eros' Golden Ball (*Arg.* 3.115–150)," *CW* 34 (1980–81), 223–25.

43

measure a rapacious desire for material wealth and power. The poet has thus associated the erotic with a corrupted heroism.

By using Homer as a point of departure in the first part of this episode and then moving on to the very contemporary portrait of Aphrodite and Eros, Apollonius emphasizes his own very different view of the force of love. The awesome goddess of the *Iliad*, who forces her human protegé Helen to love even though she may want to resist, is here reduced to a humanlike parent who can barely make her own child do as she says but must rely on bribery. Apollonius has certainly altered Homer's view of love as an irresistible psychological force compelling an individual such as Helen or Paris to respond to his sexual nature. For this poet, Aphrodite and Eros together embody the deceptive qualities that form the experience of love. The prologue scene of book 3, as a kind of divine allegory, represents the nature and methods of love, which unfold most dramatically as the narrative progresses.[61] As Medea undergoes her erotic awakening and Jason becomes more adept at exploiting his erotic appeal, each at different moments in the narrative will be the agent and the object of bribery: Medea will promise Jason the skills needed to win the fleece, and the hero will lure the inexperienced young woman with the story of the splendid reward that Ariadne obtained after helping Theseus. The two will fully exhibit the self-seeking, manipulative characteristics in this divine tableau, including the use of an unscrupulous method such as cheating to succeed.

The poet subtly links himself with the methods of the protagonists in this prologue. As he cloaks his narrative with a comic veneer, he has much in common with Aphrodite, especially in her enticing description of the ball, which includes the simile of a star, one of Apollonius's own central images in this poem, so often employed in seductive, erotic contexts. One might also recall the invocation to the Muse Erato at the beginning of this book. The poet compares her to Aphrodite in her ability to "charm girls" (4–5). Yet

[61]Beye (above, note 7), p. 127, refers to the scene with Aphrodite and Eros as an allegory of love, showing "its narcissistic quality, its insinuating quality, the luxury of it, and most important the wayward, uncontrollable nature of desire (Eros) as it wars with the more intellectual, other-person-oriented emotion of love (Aphrodite)." However, it seems that Apollonius views both elements of the condition of love, Aphrodite and Eros, as negative in their manipulative ways and ultimately self-interested actions; he seems especially critical of their flaunting of social values.

the Muse's skill, like the poet's, is in the realm of words, the seductive powers of language. We will see that as the narrative progresses in book 3, the poet uses a different technique: epic and tragic allusions expose the characters' flaws and foreshadow the bleak consequences. But first we consider how Apollonius expands his theme into the human sphere in the first major erotic episode of this poem.

The Lemnian Episode

The Lemnian episode illustrates the ethics of the cloak by further developing the relation between eros and heroism. It has been suggested that the Aphrodite panel suggests Hypsipyle "as warrior and paramour" in this episode.[62] The Lemnians in general represent a perverse heroism: they earlier killed the male population of the island when the men rejected the women as sexual partners, and now they assume all the male activities, including an aggressive defense of the island. Jason, on the other hand, as he wears the cloak for his diplomatic mission to Hypsipyle, represents the nonmartial values implied in the embroidered panels. Although the women accommodate their new visitors to their mutual satisfaction, Apollonius deviously manipulates the narrative so as to imply the problems underlying the Lemnians' eroticism. He maintains the comic surface of the book 3 prologue scene here, too, in part by adapting and humorously displacing Homeric similes. Although we cannot be certain if he had a specific literary source, he may well have been influenced by Euripides' tragedy and Aristophanes' comedy on the subject of the Lemnian women.[63] Our extant references to this myth suggest an essential concern to express deep tensions between the sexes that are ultimately resolved so that normal social life may be resumed.[64]

[62]Collins (above, note 22), p. 83.

[63]Little is known about these two plays. For the chronology and basic relation to the corpus of each poet, see Lesky (above, note 1), pp. 390–91 and 427.

[64]See Walter Burkert, "Jason, Hypsipyle, and New Fire at Lemnos: A Study in Myth and Ritual," *CQ* 20 (1970), 1–16, on the significance of the myth of the Lemnians, especially in relation to ritual, in which fire implies renewal after a period of abnormal life, the separation of the sexes suggests purification, and the presentation of a garment ends the war of the sexes.

Apollonius, however, by his subtle undermining of the Lemnians suggests that these problems are not ultimately neutralized.

A tension on the theme of eros exists in the very structure of this episode. By contrasting narrative and speeches against each other, the poet implicitly opposes the male view to the female view. His summary of the Lemnian disaster to the reader, an animated, highly rhetorical account, serves as a contrast to Hypsipyle's first address to Jason. Assuming the male perspective, he defends the men's rejection of their wives by explaining why they developed a great love for their concubines. He emphasizes that the women's impiety is the root of their subsequent troubles with the men:[65] "The dreadful anger of Cypris descended upon them since for a long time they had deprived her of honors" (614–15). As his narrative progresses, the poet not only reports the events but also manipulates the account rhetorically. Through an emotional apostrophe, he points to the women's excessive, irrational nature: "Oh unhappy women and insatiable in jealousy to the point of destruction!" (616). On the face of things, he seems to vindicate Hypsipyle by stating that she was the only woman to spare a man, her father (621), but then proceeds to concentrate on the fate of Thoas. What appears to be a digression on the outcome of her father's escape becomes a reinforcement of male supremacy. For after being rescued by fishermen off the island of Oenoie, Thoas produced a son by the nymph who gave her name to the land. To commemorate this regeneration, the poet informs us that the place itself was renamed Sicinus, for this male child, and lost its feminine name Oenoie (623–26).

The poet further distances the reader from the Lemnians by infusing his account of their current life with hyperbole. First, he insists that they now were simply forced to devote themselves to masculine activities, but in fact found it "easier to tend cattle, to wear bronze armor, and to plow the wheat fields than to practice the works of Athena" (627–29). By thus emphasizing how very aggressively they have usurped male occupations and have abandoned proper female activities, Apollonius hints at the desire for power that informed their earlier destructive actions. He also alludes to

[65]There has been little critical investigation of the meaning of the Lemnians' attitude toward Aphrodite; see Georges Dumézil, *Le crime des lemniennes: Rites et légendes du monde égéen* (Paris: Geuthner, 1924).

their pervasive irrationality by calling attention, for instance, to the intense fear ("deimati leugaleō") that causes the women to look constantly out to sea in anticipation of Thracian invaders (630–32). He continues the overdrawn picture when he finds them "speechless" ("aphthoggoi," 639), fearful of the approach of the Argo. Worse yet, he suggests that they are maddened, comparing them to Bacchants at the most violent moment of their ritual: "They poured forth to the beach like flesh-eating Thyiads" (635–36). The word ōmoboros ("eating raw flesh") points to the exaggerated literary portrayals of the followers of Dionysus, such as Euripides' *Bacchae*, which depict such extreme behavior as typical of dangerously subversive women. The poet, then, represents the women as utterly passionate and irrational.

In contrast to the poet's version of events on Lemnos, Hypsipyle's speech to Jason views the past from the female perspective. It has been observed that her account consists of various fabrications and outright lies.[66] Obviously, to win the confidence of the Argonauts, she cannot acknowledge the fact of the murders. Hypsipyle clearly states two falsehoods: that the Lemnian women asked the men to leave with their sons and concubines and that they now live together in Thrace. These lies are only a small part of her total story, the one beginning and the other concluding her speech. Unlike the straightforward style of her narrative as a whole, she uses poetic periphrases to describe the men's new home ("purophorous guas," "wheat-bearing fields" [796], and "arosin chionōdea," "snowy plowlands," [826]), which perhaps hint at her inability to conceive of the horrible deeds that she only witnessed. Most of her account exposes the conditions that led to the elimination of the male population on Lemnos. She focuses on the unnatural life that the women were forced to endure and by revealing their psychological plight offers a perspective totally lacking in the narrator's account.

As she speaks from the point of view of the abandoned women, Hypsipyle comments on the men's excessive behavior as they in madness ("matiē") utterly hated ("apestugon") their wives (804–5). Through the strong language conveying intense emotions that she

---

[66]For example, Donald N. Levin, *Apollonius'* Argonautica *Re-examined,* I: *The Neglected First and Second Books* (Leiden: Brill, 1971), p. 75, comments on the ambiguity and fictiveness of Hypsipyle's speech; also George (above, note 23), 59.

uses to depict the men's attitudes, Hypsipyle turns the narrator's position on the women's irrationality around. From her perspective, the men acted madly. She depicts the psychological impact of the men's neglect on all social categories of the female population: old widows, wives, daughters, sisters, unmarried maidens. Furthermore, she points to the length of the women's endurance and the ever-increasing intensity of the evil: "'For a long time we endured it, if perhaps again, though late, they might change their mind, but the evil bane always grew and doubled'" (807–9). In this context of prolonged suffering, all normal social life was overturned: lawful children were dishonored by bastards; widows and young girls alike roamed about unprotected; fathers allowed daughters to be mistreated by stepmothers; sons did not defend their mothers; and brothers did not care for their sisters (811–17). Old and young alike thus suffered emotional as well as physical injury. While she acknowledges that the women responded drastically, with overweening boldness ("huperbion tharsos," 820), Hypsipyle has offered a credible motivation.

Significantly, Apollonius avoids any direct comment on the issues underlying her speech. Furthermore, he sets her speech up for a negative reception by ambivalently prefacing it with the remark that she spoke "with crooked words" ("muthoisi haimulioisin," 792), an expression which he uses of Aphrodite in the prologue scene of book 3. Immediately after she concludes, he merely remarks that she "glossed over the fact of the murder" ("hamaldunousa phonou telos," 834). After using exaggerated pathos, parody, and sarcasm in his own account of the Lemnian women, the poet now employs the rhetorical antithesis, a silence by which he implicates Hypsipyle in the pasion and madness, even though she did not participate in the tragic events.

By using traditional Homeric similes in erotic contexts, Apollonius suggests an inversion of the normal order, the women's passion as an ironic form of epic heroism. Two extended similes borrowed from the *Iliad* are set in radically different contexts from their originals. Here, the poet compares Jason to a shining star that cloistered maidens eagerly gaze upon: "Like a bright star, which maidens closed up in newly made chambers look upon when it rises above their homes; and through the dark air it charms their eyes as it casts a fair red glow; and the maid rejoices, desiring the young man who is away among foreign people, for whom her parents keep her in her courtship" (774–80). The analogy of the hero to a star inevitably recalls the descriptions of Achilles in the *Iliad*. Homer uses the astral image when Achilles is arming as the Greeks prepare for battle with their greatest hero (19.381–82) and when he pursues Hector in their final contest (22.26–1). But the simile here radiates with irony. Whereas Achilles is active, bringing destruction upon the Trojans, Jason is passive.[67] He does not even approach the Lemnians on his own initiative but is sent by the crew; it is the women who actively seek out the fair hero for their erotic pleasure. His only adverse effect is to make the women lovesick for him. Besides underlining Jason's deficiency as a real hero, the simile suggests the disparity between the Lemnians who destroyed family bonds and the innocent maidens who are cloistered in the female quarters in preparation for their socially sanctioned marriages arranged by their fathers. By stressing the absence of the object of desire for the maid, it can only remind the reader of the reason why men have been missing in the lives of the Lemnians.

Near the end of the episode, a second Homeric simile negatively reflects the women's actions. Here, the Lemnians respond to the Argonauts' unexpected departure "as when bees buzz around fair lilies after pouring forth from their hive in the rock, and the dewy meadow rejoices throughout, and they pluck the sweet fruit, flitting from one to another" (879–82). This simile graphically portrays the women's sexuality as a hindrance to heroism. Apollonius's reader would certainly recall its background in the *Iliad* (2.87–90), where the Greek troops assemble for a political purpose in response to Agamemnon's call. The Lemnians, however, wish to impede the public activity of the Argonauts. On the one hand, there is a humorous side to this description of the women's frantic activity.[68] Yet the poet also reminds the reader of the antithesis between the chaos here and the order implied in the original: he describes the bees as "flit-

[67]On Jason's passivity in this passage, see Beye (above, note 7), pp. 90–91, who notes that Jason is here merely a sex object.

[68]See George (above, note 23), 61, on the amusing incongruity in this use of Homer's simile: the happiness of the bees in the meadow conflicts with the distraught nature of the Lemnians, and the emphasis on sound and motion makes the frantic activity of the desperate women appear ridiculous.

ting about" randomly ("pepotēmenai"), whereas in Homer they move as "nations" ("ethnea") and in unit formation, "together in clusters" ("botrudon"). Apollonius later uses the verb *pepomai* for Medea's psychological turmoil when he describes her struggling in vain with her passion for Jason. While amusing, this simile also hints that the disorder and violence underlying these erotically charged women are always potentially ready to erupt.

The farewell scene between Hypsipyle and Jason reduces both love and heroism as it shows their antithetical natures. Prefacing her remarks with tears, Hypsipyle marshals her persuasive skills to keep her lover. She extends a second invitation to Jason to rule the island after he obtains the fleece and encourages him with the assurance that he could easily gather a host of men from other cities (890–94). While acknowledging that he may not come back, she asks Jason to remember her (896–97). The echo of Nausikaa's coy request to Odysseus in the *Odyssey* (8.460–62) suggests that Hypsipyle hopes that he will remain with her. Finally, she brings up the subject of her possible pregnancy and asks Jason what she should do with the child she may bear (897–98). If Hypsipyle seems overly emotional, Jason is quite the opposite. He dutifully replies to all of her points except one: he simply ignores the request to remember her. The hero can think only of accomplishing the task set before him: "'May the gods only release me from my labors'" (903). On the subject of their child, Jason evades the reminder of their intimacy. Instead, he makes a gesture of filial piety by telling her to send the child, if a male, to his parents as a source of care and consolation for them in their old age (905–9). Finally, his very hasty departure ("and he went first of all onto the ship," 910) suggests not only his shame at Heracles' reprimands for self-indulgence at the expense of duty, but also his desire to avoid an emotional scene. Jason's act of resuming his quest is reduced to the comic: he responds in a mechanical manner to the greater hero's disapproval of his sloth.

In the Lemnian episode, then, Apollonius has reshaped an important heroic myth. By eliminating the traditional detail of the odor with which the Lemnian women were afflicted by Aphrodite, he provides no explanation for the men's abhorrence of their wives but emphasizes a more fundamental sexual hostility. He also deemphasizes the traditional theme of Hypsipyle's piety and gives no importance to the theme of female solidarity, so that the sex-starved women collectively appear ridiculous when Polyxo rises in their assembly as a Nestor-like figure (668–98). The emphasis on renewal of life in the dramatic versions is underplayed and even undermined in this episode. Later, Jason uses a purple garment of Thoas that he received from Hypsipyle as a gift of love (4.423–24) in luring Apsyrtus into his trap, at Medea's instigation. A symbol of regeneration has thus been transformed into one of deceit and death. Even though Hypsipyle actually saved Thoas, Apollonius associates only negative effects with the Lemnians: the hero's relationship with Hypsipyle is thus closely linked with his commitment to Medea, a union that he later reminds us ends in the destruction of their offspring.

The Characterization of Medea in Book Three

In his depiction of Medea's erotic awakening in book 3, Apollonius develops the love theme more deeply and links it more closely with the problem of heroism. He describes in subtle detail the young woman's struggle with her sudden passion for Jason. It is not surprising, therefore, that critics have concentrated on the sympathetic aspects of Medea's plight in book 3.[69] Yet the psychological portrayal for which Apollonius is justly so famous is closely related to epic concerns and the heroic sphere. His Medea, even in book 3, begins to show an assimilation of qualities that traditionally apply only to the male in epic. The poet consistently recalls the Phaeacian episode in the *Odyssey* yet at the same time reminds the reader of Euripides' Medea.

The tension between these two models is very strong: the highly civilized Nausikaa keeps a burgeoning sexuality under control, whereas the barbarian Medea of the tragedy is inflamed with passionate anger at Jason's desertion of her for another woman and

---

[69]The most recent articles dealing with Medea's passion emphasize the sympathetic aspects. See, for example, Graham Zanker, "The Love Theme in Apollonius Rhodius' *Argonautica*," *Wiener Studien* n.s. 13 (1979), esp. 61–68; and J. H. Barkhuizen, "The Psychological Characterization of Medea in Apollonius of Rhodes, *Argonautica* 3,744–824," *Acta Classica* 22 (1979), 33–48.

contrives a hideous revenge. Furthermore, the latter's cleverness, her *mētis* and *sophia*, at obtaining satisfaction implies that she oversteps the boundaries between male and female so carefully defined in Greek thinking. Apollonius's assimilation of elements from Greek tragedy is a major advance in epic, for the powerful, aggressive female characters in drama enabled him to reflect upon the heroic more extensively in his own narrative.[70] As a formidable woman whose heroic status must be viewed as perverse, Euripides' Medea deeply affects Apollonius's portrayal of his own heroine. The *Odyssey* passage, moreover, provided the poet with material not only to explore the character of the enamored young woman but also to reveal the hero's nature more fully, for the island of the Phaeacians is a crucial test for Odysseus's determination to end his wanderings and finally return home. Like his predecessor, Jason exploits the young woman's passion to his own advantage, but without the Homeric hero's detachment and far-ranging mind, he fails to assume a truly heroic stature.

Apollonius begins the action in Colchis by creating a scene that recalls Homer's Scheria even in details of landscape. But his version of the Phaeacian episode will be ironic, completely turning around the values of the cultivated utopian kingdom. As Beye has observed, the poet's description of the court with its bronze bulls suggests Homer's Phaeacian palace with gold and silver dogs and golden boys holding torches.[71] The Phaeacians' art visually reflects their highly civilized nature, manifested in their entertainment of the stranger, in their appreciation of Odysseus's imaginative account of his adventures after the Trojan War, and in Nausikaa's own ability to communicate her erotic desires for the hero in a subtle, tactful manner. The fire-breathing bronze bulls in Aeetes' courtyard, by contrast, symbolize tyrannical power and a lack of civilized values. Their background reinforces an association with might, for they were created by Hephaestus as a reward to Helios for helping the Olympians in the battle against the giants (3.233–34). They are also

---

[70]See Froma Zeitlin, "Playing the Other: Theater, Theatricality, and the Feminine in Greek Drama," *Representations* 11 (1985), esp. 66–68, on the use of females to represent male characteristics in Greek tragedy.

[71]Beye (above, note 7), p. 127; Mooney (above, note 39), on 3.271 also notes the allusion.

emblematic of an actual struggle within the narrative, as they foreshadow the contest that Aeetes imposes upon Jason for possession of
the Golden Fleece. Unlike the Phaeacian *objets d'art*, the Colchian
bulls symbolize the king's incessant fear of usurpation and his main-
tenance of power by means of violence.[72]

In recalling the character of Nausikaa as background for Medea,
Apollonius alludes to erotic material that sharpens the antithesis
between control and chaos. Like Nausikaa, Medea has a dream
revealing her sexuality, expressed in a desire to marry. But the
difference in details is revealing. Nausikaa's dream of marriage
raises the following points: the need to have clothes arranged as a
preparatory stage for marriage; the good reputation that she will
attain by attention to these details; the urgency of a laundering
expedition with her companions in order to facilitate the prospective
choice of a bridegroom among the many suitors already wooing
her; permission from her father for a wagon to convey them to the
washing site (6.25–40). Social order underlies even this erotic dream
of the young Phaeacian girl approaching adulthood. Her very real
concern for her good reputation shows a social maturity, since it
was considered especially appropriate for aristocratic women to
guard their *eukleia*.[73] Homer playfully shows the girl's erotic interests tempered by her sense of good form and respect for family; she
is thus a little embarrassed as she dutifully informs her father that
she needs a wagon for her chores, and he shrewdly understands her
motives (6.67). In the structure of her dream and her response to it,
Nausikaa stays within the bounds of the civilized forms of conduct
that are ingrained in her. Homer thus suggests that this young
woman will not lose control of herself but will instead be an aid to
the hero.

Medea's dream, by contrast, places her erotic awakening in a
context of solipsism and social discord. While Nausikaa has not yet

---

[72]Vian (above, note 59), pp. 23–35, makes some good points about the atmo-
sphere of fear and suspicion that Aeetes creates in his kingdom. Warned by an oracle
from Helios (3.597–600), Aeetes is especially on guard against the sons of Phrixus,
who he suspects want his throne.

[73]On women's *aretē* in the Homeric world, see Arthur W. H. Adkins, *Merit and
Responsibility: A Study in Greek Values* (Oxford: Clarendon Press, 1960), pp. 36–37.
On *eukleia* as an aristocratic concept among women in Greek tragedy, see Bernard
M. W. Knox, "The *Hippolytus* of Euripides," *YClS* 13 (1952), esp. 18.

seen the object of her desire, Medea dreams specifically about the newly arrived hero Jason. She imagines that he has come not to retrieve the Golden Fleece but to win her as his wife; she herself performs the heroic task of yoking the bulls, which Aeetes has imposed; when she is asked to choose between the strangers and her father, her decision in favor of Jason causes her angry parents to shout out in opposition (619–30). Beneath the displacement of elements common in dreams, the poet reveals some significant aspects of Medea's character:[74] an egotistical bent, as she makes herself the *raison d'être* of Jason's enterprise; a ready assumption of the male role, suggested by her sudden performance of heroic action in yoking the oxen; and her desire to reject the strong authority figure of her father. Although showing Medea's poignant struggle with her passion, the poet implies her lack of real social integration, especially in her willingness to betray her family and in her ready transformation into an aggressive agent. The elements of this dream, then, suggest that Medea will not show discretion similar to Nausikaa's but instead will embody a bizarre union of the erotic and the heroic.

Apollonius's adaptation of similes from the *Odyssey* also suggests a tension between passion and aggression in the heroine. An important passage in book 3 describes her struggle with the conflicting values of *aidōs* and *himeros*, shame and desire. As she falls on her bed in pain, the poet compares his heroine to a young widow:[75] "As when a young woman in her chamber laments her husband, to whom her brothers and parents have given her, nor does she yet mingle with all her attendants out of shame and prudence; but she sits apart in her grief: and some fate has destroyed him before they have taken pleasure in each other's charms; and her heart burning within, she silently weeps as she looks at her empty bed lest the women mock and scoff at her" (656–63).

[74]See George Devereux, *Dreams in Greek Tragedy: An Ethno-psycho-analytical Study* (Berkeley: University of California Press, 1976), esp. pp. 26–56, for a fascinating discussion of the erotic symbolism in the sexual dream of Io in Aeschylus. While I am not attempting to explain the nature of Medea's dream, there is certainly a similarity to Io's in the girl's repressed sexual state. It should be noted, however, that Medea's dream is summarized rather than directly narrated (by either poet or character).

[75]Here I do not accept Fränkel's transposition of lines but follow Seaton's arrangement in the Loeb.

Critics have commented that this simile seems paradoxical: the bride laments her dead husband, whereas Medea grieves over a man whom she has not even met and with whom she has no opportunity to unite; the bride's family gave her to the ill-fated man, whereas Medea's family would certainly not offer her to Jason; and the bride fears the reproach of her maids for appearing in public soon after being widowed, whereas Medea does not want to reveal her desires.[76] Yet the apparent incongruity of this analogy in itself is meaningful rather than gratuitous. Fränkel comments on Apollonius's subtle transferral of point of view from narrator to character in his use of Homeric models, a distinction which applies to this case.[77] The simile here seems to reflect Medea's perspective, since she has just dreamed that Jason has come to Colchis specifically to marry her. By drawing his analogy from Medea's own fantasy, the poet creates two effects for the reader: a participation in the young woman's deeply troubled state of mind and yet a realization of the inappropriateness of her desires. Finally, Medea's anxiety that her sister Chalciope may discover the real reason for her decision to help her sons reflects more than maidenly reticence. The young woman's fear of mockery suggests not simply a desire to protect her good name but even more the fierce resistance to scorn that the aggressively heroic character feels in Euripides' play.[78] By implying Medea's masculine concern for her reputation, Apollonius brings her more closely into the traditional heroic sphere. He again fuses love and the heroic in an uneasy tension, whereby the sympathetic quality of erotic suffering is qualified by misplaced male values.

[76]Jerry Clack, "The Medea Similes of Apollonius Rhodius," *CJ* 68 (1973), 311–12. For a review of the various interpretations of the widow's situation, see Anthos Ardizzoni, "Il pianto di Medea e la similitudine della giovane vedova (Apollonio Rodio III 656–73)," *Giornale Italiano di Filologia* 28 (1976), 233–40. On this passage in general, see also Paul Händel, *Beobachtungen zur Epischen Technik des Apollonios Rhodios, Zetemata* 7 (Munich: Beck, 1954), esp. 108–10.

[77]Hermann Fränkel, "Apollonius Rhodius as a Narrator in *Argonautica* 2.1–140," *TAPA* 83 (1952), 144–55, discusses point of view in the similes in the Amycus episode.

[78]For the fear of Euripides' heroine at being mocked by her enemies, see Pietro Pucci, *The Violence of Pity in Euripides'* Medea (Ithaca: Cornell University Press, 1980), esp. pp. 100, 138–40, on the ambiguity of the *thumos* that controls her response. Malcolm Campbell, *Studies in the Third Book of Apollonius Rhodius'* Argonautica (Hildesheim: Georg Olms, 1983), p. 40, refers to Medea's "sinister fear of mockery" in this scene.

Let us briefly consider the source of this simile in the Phaeacian episode. There, Odysseus, weeping in response to Demodocus's song of the wooden horse, is compared to a woman lamenting her husband who has been killed in battle:[79] "As a wife falls upon and weeps for her dear husband who has fallen before his citadel and the people while warding off the day of death from the city and his children; seeing him dying and quivering, she embraces him and wails loudly. But they, poking her back and shoulders with spears, lead her off in bondage, to have toil and misery; her cheeks are wasted away with most pitiful grief" (8.523–30). Homer's simile implies social bonds in Odysseus that contrast sharply with Medea's solipsism: the hero is like a wife weeping over her husband's corpse because he has been a nurturing, cohesive force among the Greeks; he grieves over the loss of the flower of the Greek army and the pain of separation from his comrades after the war. Superficially, the simile in the *Odyssey* also seems incongruous with the actual narrative.[80] Yet Homer appropriately stresses Odysseus's intensely emotional commitment to a social cause. In several similes, Homer portrays Odysseus in female and Penelope in traditional male roles, implying their mutual interdependence.[81] Such a flexibility represents a considerable advance from the ethos of the *Iliad*. Odysseus moves from the martial ethics of the Trojan War to a new form of heroism linked with the *oikos*. Apollonius, by contrast, reflects Medea's absorption of traditional male qualities, such as a concern for reputation, in negative terms. He shows that she does not synthesize male and female traits but rather usurps conventional heroic male egotism.

Apollonius's simile specifically mentions *aidōs*, a concept that is developed further in this passage on Medea's struggle with her de-

[79]My references to the *Odyssey*, transliterated, are from *The Odyssey of Homer*, ed. W. B. Stanford (London: Macmillan, 1965). The translations are my own.

[80]Garson (above, note 50), 8, in discussing this analogy finds that "Homer's scene of violence and hysteria occupies eight lines and accords ill with Odysseus' restrained weeping."

[81]See W. B. Stanford, *The Ulysses Theme: A Study in the Adaptability of a Traditional Hero*, 2d ed. (Ann Arbor: University of Michigan Press, 1968), esp. pp. 44–65, for Odysseus's affinity with women; and Helene P. Foley, "'Reverse Similes' and Sex Roles in the *Odyssey*," *Arethusa* 11 (1978), 7–26, for an excellent discussion of similes attributing female characteristics to Odysseus and male to Penelope.

sire. The sense of shame that keeps a person from committing an action in violation of socially acceptable standards is an important value in Homeric epic. As Redfield defines it, *aidōs* is a "responsiveness to social situations and to the judgments of others" and may be considered the "affective or emotional foundation of virtue."[82] Since *aidōs* is inherently connected to the social structure, it is an important foundation for civilized behavior and heroic activity. Paris, the cause of Troy's problems by his abduction of Helen, is the one character in the *Iliad* who conspicuously lacks *aidōs*, whereas Hector, the bulwark of Troy, is most governed by it.[83] In the *Odyssey*, the word characterizes the behavior of both Odysseus and Nausikaa in the Phaeacian episode. The former tries to conceal his tears from the Phaeacians through a feeling of shame at excessive weeping (8.221), and the latter does not mention her ideas about marriage to her father through similar scruples.

In the *Argonautica*, the poet depicts Medea's vacillation as she attempts to leave her chamber and shows *aidōs* in conflict with desire: "And when she went directly forth, shame kept her inside, and bold desire kept spurring her on, though restrained by shame" (652–53). Her struggle becomes more intense when Chalciope enters and questions her sister. Here, the inhibiting force of *aidōs* loses further ground: "And her cheeks grew red. Maidenly-shame held her back, though eager to answer. . . . At length she spoke the following with deceit, for the bold loves were driving her" (681–82, 686–87). By associating the young woman's loss of *aidōs* with the verb *ereuthō*, Apollonius implies that the moment is a critical one in the narrative for Medea, who now moves in an irreversible direction toward her own self-interest. The immediate consequence is a use of *dolos*, trickery, to deceive her sister: though it is only a pretext, she states a concern for Chalciope's sons as her motivation for helping the Argonauts against Aeetes.

In a famous passage, Apollonius describes the peaceful, quiet night with sailors scanning the heavens, travelers and warders seeking rest, and a woman whose children have died now deep in sleep (744–50). Given the exceptional nature of situations that reflect po-

[82]Redfield (above, note 12), pp. 115–16.
[83]Ibid., pp. 113–18, on the contrast between Hector and Paris in the sphere of *aidōs*. Redfield also notes Nausikaa's and Odysseus's concern for this virtue.

tential danger and turbulence instead of ordinary nocturnal rest, Medea's inability to sleep is all the more poignant and at the same time ominous. Another evocative image equates Medea's anxiety about helping Jason subdue the bulls to the agitated play of bright sunlight:

> As a sunbeam quivers upon the side of a house when it is cast up from the water, which is newly poured forth in a cauldron or perhaps a pail; and here and there on a swift eddy it darts and flickers. (756–59)

The original is Homer's description of the threshold of Alcinous's palace when Odysseus first arrives:

> There was a gleam as of the sun or of the moon beneath the high-roofed hall of great-hearted Alcinous. (7.84–85)

The Homeric passage then proceeds to describe the cause of such dazzling light effects: bronze walls, golden portals, silver posts in the bronze threshold, silver lintel and golden handle, and gold and silver dogs on either side. Significantly, the passage reflects the point of view of Odysseus observing the scene as he proceeds to the court to ask for reception as a guest and then passage home. The intelligent hero can thus surmise the kind of people he is about to encounter, for the architectural brilliance is one manifestation of the harmonious order of this advanced society on all levels.

Apollonius's simile, by contrast, depicts the lack of order within Medea. To this end, the poet emphasizes the movement of light from a particular reflecting surface. As the graphic, pictorial language enlivened the cloak scene with the Cyclopes forging the thunderbolt, so the rhetoric of this passage produces a sense of the rapid movement of light. Among several strong verbs of motion, Apollonius seems to have coined *enipallō*, a *hapax legomenon* compounded from *pallō*, "to quiver," and uses the onomatopoeic word *aïssō*, "to dart," which is mainly confined to poetry. The metaphor of a whirlwind in the noun *strophaligx*, which the scholiast notes is used for the prosaic, abstract *strophē*, also helps to convey the sense of a rapid, violent thrust. Furthermore, the poet creates a sinuous movement in the last line by repeating an *s* sound: "ōkeiē strophaliyyi tinassetai aïssousa." A possible philosophical background may contribute to the sense of disorder, for as Fränkel notes, this image was later used by Stoics to illustrate the instability of *phantasiae* in an unruly mind.[84] This interpretation is perhaps supported by another detail in the text. As Medea first glances at Jason, the poet describes her soul "creeping like a dream as it flitted about" ("pepotēto," 447). The verb recalls the Stoic use of *ptoia*, a violent fluttering of the soul, to classify eros as a disease.[85] By adapting his Homeric model in these ways, the poet has depicted a character whose inner turmoil here forebodes her later violence.

Another simile derived from the Phaeacian episode widens the gap between Apollonius's heroine and her Homeric counterpart vis-à-vis the values fostering civilized behavior. As Medea goes off to the temple of Hecate, the poet compares her to Artemis traversing the countryside with her nymphs:

> And just as by the gentle waters of Parthenius, or having bathed in the river Amnisius, the daughter of Leto stands upon her golden chariot and rides over the hills with her swift young deer and greets from a distance some steaming hecatomb. And the nymphs follow her as attendants, some assembling at the spring of Amnisius, others leaving the groves and mountain-tops with many fountains, and around her the animals fawn and whimper, trembling as she goes along. (876–84)

The model for this simile, as scholars have frequently noted, is the famous description of Nausikaa playing with her companions just before she encounters Odysseus:

> So Artemis goes showering her arrows along mountains, down lofty Taygetos or Erymanthos, delighting in mountain goats or swift deer, and the rustic nymphs, daughters of aegis-bearing Zeus, sport with her; Leto's heart rejoices, for the goddess towers over everyone and is easy to spot, though all are beautiful. (6.102–8)

Homer's simile is charming and witty. Although describing a virgin goddess, it has erotic overtones from the context of Nau-

---

[84]Fränkel, "Problems of Text and Interpretation in Apollonius' *Argonautica*," *AJPhil.* 71 (1950), 127.

[85]John M. Rist, *Stoic Philosophy* (Cambridge: Cambridge University Press, 1969), p. 26, discusses this Stoic concept.

sikaa's interest in preparing for marriage, her motivation for making the expedition with her maids. By drawing attention to the girl's grace and beauty, the simile suggests that she will be a real temptation for the sea-weary hero. Yet in its context, it affirms the social nature of the young woman, her complete harmony with her companions and participation in their recreative activity, for the princess is enjoying a game of ball with her attendant maidens after they have bathed together and shared a meal.

Apollonius's adaptation of Homer's simile achieves a somber effect. First, the poet does not point to the charm and beauty of the young woman. Instead, he may expect the reader to recall the earlier simile comparing Jason to Apollo (1.307–9), where the people are struck by the youthful, golden-haired hero as he sets off on the quest for the fleece. Ironically, in this story the hero is distinguished by good looks, and the girl does not provide the same temptation of radiant beauty as Nausikaa does with Odysseus. This simile also contrasts with the Homeric model in its social implications, for it reveals difference and separation rather than integration and harmony in the young woman. As the nymphs merely attend Artemis and the beasts cower while she goes along, so Medea's maidens follow behind and the passersby avoid her glance. The Colchian takes her maids along in order to prevent suspicion about her intended meeting with Jason, and she bribes them with promises to divide the gifts that she will receive from the Argonauts in return for helping Jason to succeed in yoking the oxen.

On another dark level of suggestiveness, this simile connects Medea with Hecate, the infernal counterpart of Artemis.[86] Since she has just invoked the goddess of magic in preparing the charm of Prometheus, a comparison with Artemis must inevitably recall not just the woodland goddess but also the deity associated with witchcraft. In mentioning the ritual element of the hecatombs, the simile itself calls attention to Medea's activity as a priestess of Hecate rather

[86]Beye (above, note 7), pp. 132–33, discusses Medea's association with Hecate, which "poses an unpredictable and potentially frightening side to her nature." On this simile, Charles R. Beye, "Jason as Love-hero in Apollonios' *Argonautika*," *GRBS* 10 (1969), 31–55, discusses the irony of the parallel with Nausikaa; see John F. Carspecken, "Apollonius Rhodius and the Homeric Epic," *YClS* 13 (1956), 77–80, for the spatial organization similar to pictorial art.

than of Artemis.[87] The poet reinforces this ironic disparity between Medea and Nausikaa as he echoes Homer's account of the Phaeacian princess and her companions frolicking about. When the young woman suggests to her maids that they should dance and gather flowers, he recalls her preparing the flowers of Prometheus for her magic potion (851–57). The very activity of picking flowers must in Medea's case represent not an innocent pastime but her activity as a priestess of Hecate.[88] The association with magic especially symbolizes Medea's alienation from true human intercourse and her alignment with forces opposed to social integration.[89] As the simile ironically makes Medea the antithesis of Nausikaa, the embodiment of grace and civility, it hints at an eroticism that is potentially destructive rather than beneficial to the hero.

As the episode unfolds, the aggressive side of Medea, which implies a perverse heroism, begins to emerge more clearly. During her meeting with Jason in the sacred precinct of Hecate, Medea seals her commitment to help Jason by taking his right hand. In Euripides' play, that gesture symbolizes Medea's assumption of a male role, which ultimately diminishes the heroic stature of Jason.[90] The tragic character thus insures a binding contract and asserts her control over events, as when she extracts a promise from Aegeus not to violate his promise to provide her safety in his court when she flees Creon's kingdom.

In her first conversation with Jason, Medea echoes Nausikaa's tactfully seductive words to Odysseus with a sinister aggressiveness. When she asks the hero not to forget her ("'remember, if you

[87]See Wendell Clausen, *Virgil's* Aeneid *and the Tradition of Hellenistic Poetry* (Berkeley: University of California Press, 1987), pp. 20–21, on Apollonius's emphasis on the ritual element that suggests Hecate as well as Artemis.

[88]Campbell (above, note 78), pp. 59–61, comments on the irony of Medea's picking flowers here, since as priestess she would presumably not normally engage in frivolous play with the other young girls.

[89]See Guido Paduano, "L'episodio di Talos: Osservazioni sull'esperienza magica nelle *Argonautiche* di Apollonio Rodio," *Studi Classici e Orientali* 19 (1970), 46–67, for an interesting, though often densely articulated, discussion of magic as a manifestation of Medea's alienation from society.

[90]Stewart Flory, "Medea's Right Hand: Promises and Revenge," *TAPA* 108 (1978), 69–74, shows that Medea's references to the right hand in Euripides' play, in contexts not normally associated with women in the fifth century, give her a larger-than-life, heroic quality.

return home, the name of Medea,'" 1069–70), her appeal suggests Nausikaa's last words to Odysseus (8.460–62). The Phaeacian's address, however, is clever and cautious. It leaves open her interest in the fascinating stranger and simultaneously suggests the possibility of reciprocation if he should leave: he can return her favor of giving him advice for a favorable reception at the court, by telling of her good deed and thereby spreading her *kleos* when he returns home. This request reflects the ideals of early Greek culture and indicates that Nausikaa values her place in her society. Nausikaa has acted only indirectly in an advisory role, but like her mother Arete, has provided valuable assistance; she therefore expects an appropriate compensation. Medea's words, by contrast, reflect a lack of propriety and a fundamentally asocial gesture, for the poet observes at this point that "*aidōs* had left her eyes" (1068). As we have already observed, that virtue measures a person's inherent respect for social values. Its loss here is significant: a vital link to societal standards has now been definitively ruptured and is not mentioned again in the poem in reference to Medea. The poet implies that she is now free to act at will, without measuring her actions against any external standards, but only with regard to her own desires and interests.

At their meeting, Jason craftily plays Odysseus to Medea's Nausikaa. As Homer's hero promised to praise the young woman for the rest of his life, Jason claims that he will spread Medea's fame abroad (992). He cleverly encourages her assistance by drawing an analogy with Ariadne's aid to Theseus. Like Aphrodite with Eros, he has his own bribe to offer as he recounts how the gods honored Ariadne for her service with a crown of stars (1001–6). In response to Medea's request for more information about Ariadne, Jason avoids any reference to the hero's abandonment of the young woman after she fled with him. Instead, he states that he would wish Aeetes to unite with the Argonauts in friendship as Minos did with the Athenian hero (1097–1101). At this point, he not only represses important facts but overtly distorts the truth, since Ariadne's father was never reconciled with Theseus. He thereby resembles Aphrodite to Hera and Hypsipyle to the Argonauts. If Jason manipulatively casts himself as Theseus, he seems unaware that the analogy to the Athenian hero bears somber implications for himself. Apollonius's reader would recall that in the myth Theseus himself suffered injury after the abandoned Ariadne cursed the faithless man; Zeus then caused him to forget to hoist the white sail as a token of his safety to his father, who then committed suicide in despair.

While she reveals that she is as enchanted with Jason's persuasive skills as with his handsome appearance, Medea cannot match Nausikaa's ability to interact with Odysseus. At the end of her meeting with the hero, for instance, Homer's character responds in a playfully suggestive manner: she refers to the men who would tease her if she appeared in company with the stranger (6.273–84). Apollonius shows how different his own heroine is when he records her reaction to Jason's flattery. At the end of their interview, she again ironically echoes Nausikaa through a second appeal for Jason to remember her (1109–10). Yet she immediately utters threats that winds may bear her across the sea to Iolkos in order to reprimand him in person about the cause of his success (1113–16). The Phaeacian's subtle reminder of the gratitude owed to her has here been transformed into a threat of grim retaliation. This response ominously forebodes much of the heroine's behavior in book 4, where she threatens to burn the Argo and even devises the plan to kill her brother rather than surrender to him. At this point, too, Apollonius comments that Hera contrived Medea's submission to Jason so that she might be a source of evil to Pelias in Iolkos (1135–36), an allusion to the latter's destruction by Medea's magic. The poet has created a character who, as Euripides showed in the later stage of her story, would be capable of performing the ultimate antisocial act, murdering her own children. The potential for this unnatural aggressiveness takes shape in book 3, as the poet transforms his character from Homer's Nausikaa into Euripides' Medea.

Throughout the poem, Apollonius relates love in complex ways to irrationality and the dissolution of social values, such as *aidōs* and *eusebeia*. Eros is thus in conflict with the demands of heroism. More insidiously, the poet shows that the hero of his epic comes to share some of the negative characteristics of eros, a manipulativeness and a lust for power. In that respect he goes beyond Homer's vision of the similarity of erotic and martial instincts as, for example, in book

14 of the *Iliad*, where Zeus's sexual appetite serves as a kind of preface to the warrior's violence on the battlefield. In this epic, eros is inherently problematic in the plot structure, but becomes even more complex when viewed in the light of Apollonius's adaptations of his Homeric models in the *Iliad* and the *Odyssey*.

In evaluating the impact of eros on the hero in this poem, it is useful to glance briefly at Heracles, a major character in book 1 until he leaves the expedition in his fruitless search for Hylas and a shadowy presence throughout the rest of the epic by virtue of the Argonauts' keen sense of his loss and the poet's allusions to his labors. In the Hylas episode, Apollonius seems to have imitated the work of his older contemporary, Theocritus. Whereas Heracles' passion is humorously depicted in *Idyll* 13, this poem emphasizes love's destructive effects. While imitating the simile of a predator attacking a flock from Theocritus's idyll, the poet applies it to Polyphemus, who likewise feels a mad panic at Hylas's disappearance (1243–47). By describing Heracles in a powerful simile of a bull tormented by a gadfly, he emphasizes the pathology of the hero's state.[91] The erotic nature of this analogy is later reinforced by a similar image of Eros inflicting Medea with passion for Jason (3.276–77). Yet Heracles' fixation does not last. His passion for the beautiful Hylas disappears when his anger has been satiated, and he abruptly returns to his absorption in his labors. The duty-bound Heracles is not permanently afflicted with erotic madness, and the poet's later references to this amazing hero underline his accomplishments through unremitting toil. He even indirectly helps the Argonauts when in book 4 they find that he has tapped a spring and thus opened a source of water for them in the Libyan desert (1441–49).

Even if Apollonius implies in the Hylas episode that the old homoerotic liaisons of the earlier heroic period are now inadequate,[92] he does not replace them with a vision of a meaningful heterosexual union. He simply leaves a void in place of the sustaining emotional bond of the traditional male relationship in epic. Jason only very briefly feels an erotic passion for Medea (3.1077–78). He is absorbed in the quest for the fleece and the task of returning home

[91]See Maria Grazia Palombi, "Eracle e Ila nelle *Argonautiche* di Apollonio Rodio," *Studi Classici e Orientali* 35 (1985), 80–81.
[92]See Beye, "Jason as Love-hero" (above, note 86).

to Greece with his crew.[93] His movement toward a fuller integration with the female results merely in a superficial accommodation, a manipulation for practical ends. To the end of the epic, this theme remains complex and disturbing. Near the conclusion of book 4, for example, an enigmatic dream with clear sexual implications is given a strictly political interpretation, which Jason offers on Apollo's inspiration.[94]

Apollonius reinforces traditional views about the excessive passion of the female, so prevalent in fifth-century Greek literature. He associates women in particular with the violation of social values and disruption of the community. In the discussion of the cloak ekphrasis, we observed how the panel of the seductive goddess Aphrodite, while engaging the reader's interest, hints at the undermining of social order through adultery. Instead of Homer's coherent cosmic design placing man's values in perspective, Apollonius's cloak ekphrasis is an emblem of duplicity and fragmentation that implies only a negative view about eros. Within the narrative proper, the Lemnians exemplify a destructive aspect of the female: the sexual jealousy which induces them to defy social bonds and destroy the very possibility of a social existence. Even though he shows them comically attempting to remedy the effects of their previous actions, the poet in many ways keeps the reader aware of their potential for disorder. In his narrative he mirrors the unnatural world where women have become masculine in nature and the heroes who arrive become effeminate and, until reproached by Heracles, lose interest in their mission. His method here sets a pattern for the devious techniques by which he undermines eros throughout the epic. A structural tension created by counterpointing male and female views and a rhetoric straining the narrative through exaggerated pathos, sarcasm, and language and imagery implying madness, mask the poet's skepticism about the erotic. Two major similes adapted from the *Iliad* reemphasize the disorder that undermines the social by making the erotic a perversion of the heroic.

In Medea's love story in book 3, Apollonius probes the relation of the erotic to the heroic more deeply. While adding a new dimension to epic by reflecting the female from within and exploring her pas-

[93]On Jason's social nature, see Paduano (above, note 89), esp. 74–75.
[94]See Heiserman (above, note 20), pp. 23–24, for a discussion of this dream.

sion with great insight and sensitivity, the poet carefully controls this new subjectivity and links it to heroic concerns. The portrayal of this character's struggle is certainly problematic, for it can easily cause the reader to empathize with the young woman's plight. In the scene of Aphrodite with Hera and Athena and then with her son Eros in the prologue of book 3, the poet suggests the qualities that define Jason's and Medea's love affair. Through an ironic adaptation of two episodes from the *Iliad*, he emphasizes the duplicity and self-interest underlying the erotic.

In the narrative of Medea's passion, Apollonius imitates Homer's Phaeacian episode so as to contrast Medea with Nausikaa and Jason with Odysseus. The similes of the lamenting bride and Artemis with her nymphs, for instance, imply self-interest and a lack of social integration, including the crucial loss of *aidōs*. Apollonius's revision of Homer's dream passage similarly reveals the young woman's sympathetic erotic struggle, but also suggests her lack of social integration, in contrast to Nausikaa's commitment to community values that enable her to be an aid to the hero. The color term *ereuthos* acquires a deepened meaning as the epic progresses. This important word, used especially in the Lemnian episode and the prologue scene of book 3, signals Medea's moral decline even as it depicts her pitiful struggle with her passion. An important addition to the major Homeric model, the echoes of Euripides' Medea further reduce the resemblance to Homer's character by recalling the aggressive male qualities of Euripides' dark heroine. If Medea is an antithesis of Nausikaa, she becomes all too similar to her sinister tragic counterpart. The implications for Jason are equally negative: he may appear to be as cunning as Odysseus, but the resemblance is merely superficial.

As the narrative progresses in book 4, the problems implied in book 3 emerge more fully. Unreciprocated by the hero, Medea's passion turns into fear and aggressiveness as she struggles to protect herself. Although she is not technically an abandoned heroine in this work, Medea fears that Jason is planning to surrender her to her brother Apsyrtus and utters recriminations that echo Euripides' heroine to her faithless husband, who has deserted her for the king's daughter Glauke. Like her tragic model, in accusing him of forgetting his oaths (*horkia*, 359) she reminds him that she abandoned her home for him (360–62) and stresses his obligations to her for obtaining the fleece for him (366–67). With increasing vehemence, she asserts the impossibility of returning to her cruel father and culminates her speech with a promise to haunt Jason as an avenging Fury (378–87). There, her outburst borders on madness, another foreshadowing of the hideous violence that will erupt in her future with Jason.

In book 4, Apollonius also adapts the Phaeacian episode in an ironic manner. He re-creates the characters of Arete and Alcinous, but now Medea plays the role of Odysseus as a suppliant to the Phaeacian queen for a safe reception.[95] To a large extent, Medea assumes the position as hero in this epic. If Jason is compared to a young woman in the moonlight when he grasps the fleece, his association with the female is negative, simply another suggestion of his failure to assume a truly heroic stature. In this context, one perceives the difference between Jason and his Homeric counterpart in the *Odyssey*. The analogies comparing Odysseus to a woman and Penelope to a man suggest their interdependence, a quality that helps the hero to restore the integrity of his *oikos* and his position as king of Ithaca. The poet furthermore shows that Medea's heroic acts are destructive to society. When she eliminates the giant Talos, an apostrophe to Zeus (1673–75) makes it clear that the loss of this ancient guardian of Crete was a misfortune rather than a blessing.[96] By putting this aggressive, passionate figure into an epic context, Apollonius magnifies his anti-epic vision and expresses the futility of any real heroism.

Apollonius's imitative techniques were influential and set some important patterns for later epic. Yet his vision is more pessimistic in the vein of Hellenistic thinking on love in general, and his interests more thoroughly aesthetic, reflecting the Alexandrian penchant for literary playfulness. His use of the epic simile contributed significantly to the dynamic of literary history. He revealed the potential for creative imitation by inverting the ethical implications of the Homeric originals and offered a model for creating a

[95]Mooney (above, note 39), on 1014, 1141, and 1170, notes several allusions to the Phaeacian episode; see also Garson (above, note 50), 6–7, on Medea's plea for rescue as an echo of Odysseus's speech at *Odyssey* 6.180–81.

[96]See Rose (above, note 31), 43, on this point about Talos.

context in which characters could be fully played out against their originals.

In re-creating contemporary artistic effects in his narrative, Apollonius developed a subtle vehicle for ethical commentary as well as psychological insights. The later poets were influenced by his brilliant deployment of light effects and of the colors red and white. In the *Aeneid*, for instance, Vergil imitates the analogy of Medea's troubled mind to the play of light from a pail, but he uses it for a very different purpose, anxiety motivated by political rather than private concerns.[97] Finally, Apollonius seems to have given epic a new kind of inclusionism, as he made tragedy serve an important structural and thematic function in the characterization of his heroine through a Euripidean model. Perhaps most effectively, Vergil deploys this technique in his portrayal of the complex character Dido, by evoking not only the epic model of Nausikaa but also the tragic paradigm of Euripides' Medea. The Roman poet uses his Hellenistic predecessor's example of setting the erotic against the social but more subtly explores the encroachment of eros upon specific social values, which nonetheless remain compelling forces in his poem.

[97]See W. R. Johnson, *Darkness Visible: A Study of Vergil's* Aeneid (Berkeley: University of California Press, 1976), pp. 85–87, on the differences between Apollonius's and Vergil's use of the light simile.

CHAPTER 2

Epic and Tragedy
in Vergil's *Aeneid*

M ORE THAN two centuries after Apollonius, Vergil revived epic as a genre that could encapsulate the whole course of Roman history and suggest some directions for the future; after a long series of civil wars the Romans welcomed a period of stability. Vergil's epic is comprehensive in scope: it moves backward in time, recounting earlier events in Aeneas's past such as the fall of Troy, and forward, flashing ahead to the city of Rome. The *Aeneid* is more deeply concerned with the significance of history than the *Argonautica*, and its use of literary models is more complex. The poet turned first of all to Homer's two epics as his primary literary sources but also incorporated allusions to a number of other heroic poems, including the *Argonautica* and Catullus's short epic, *The Marriage of Peleus and Thetis*, with its secondary story about the abandonment of Ariadne. Its inclusiveness extends to other genres besides epic. Through numerous allusions to Greek tragedy, Vergil conveys much of the sense of struggle that was involved in the long, painful foundation of Rome. Because of its interest in the irrational, Euripidean tragedy especially provided the poet with a model for criticism of time-honored heroic values.

In this account of Rome's history, the erotic assumes a role of major importance. While influenced by the Alexandrian literary interest in eros, Vergil seems to have readily drawn imaginative connections between the erotic and social issues. In the *Georgics*, his poem on agriculture written during the bitter struggle between Octavian and Marc Antony and published shortly thereafter, the image of blind passion unites the natural and human worlds. The poet connects the amorous frenzy of bulls to the madness of civil war. A famous passage describing the *amor caecus* of these animals in rivalry over a heifer (3.209–41) exemplifies irrepressible energies unable to be harnessed for constructive purposes. It recalls the powerful account of civil war, the *caecos tumultus* (1.464), including the assassination of Julius Caesar, in which right and wrong have become indistinguishable and everything is out of control, like a chariot flying out of the starting gates and unresponsive to the driver's commands (1.505–14).[1]

Vergil associates not only perverted *virtus* but *amor* with the corrupt pursuit of wealth. After exalting the glories of rustic life, he contrasts the contented man with various types engaged in destructive pursuits, including one who stirs up the seas for trade and another who would heap destruction upon a city in order to acquire bejeweled drinking cups and Tyrian purple tapestries (2.503–5). In the first example, the hypallage of "blind seas" (*caeca freta*), which conveys the unrestrained impulses of men toward greed, recalls the uncontrollable passion of the bulls and the chaos of civil war. Like his contemporary Horace in the *Epodes*, Vergil provides an eloquent voice revealing contemporary lack of restraint, most powerfully captured in the *Georgics* by the triple passions of love, greed, and warfare. Both poets stress the urgency of ending the madness of civil war and of channeling potentially destructive energies in a more positive direction for Roman society.

Recently, Daniel Gillis discussed Vergil's use of erotic language in the battle scenes in the *Aeneid* as a means of conveying his view of civil war as grotesquely perverse: "In writing of blood and its loss he is deep in the world of sexuality and procreation."[2] Not only the *virtus* of a warrior but other values cherished by the Romans, especially *pietas* and *fides*, are drawn into contexts that the poet in

[1]See, for example, Gary B. Miles, *Virgil's* Georgics: *A New Interpretation* (Berkeley: University of California Press, 1980), esp. pp. 104–9, on this section of *Georgics* 1: Vergil's reflection upon the man's refusal to accept limits, in the specific context of the contemporary chaos that included the assassination of Julius Caesar and the civil wars, is framed as a perception of the limits of the Stoic vision of life.

[2]See Daniel Gillis, *Eros and Death in the* Aeneid (Rome: L'Erma di Bretschneider, 1983), p. 32.

various ways connects to the erotic. Sometimes the link is inherent in the very nature of the material: on one level, Dido's passionate love for Aeneas is an impediment to the fulfillment of his political responsibilities, especially to found a new nation in Italy. But even in that well-known love story, the erotic acquires more significance than mere opposition between a woman's passion and a hero's sense of duty. Recent criticism of this episode has shown that Dido herself embodies a complex inclination toward the heroic as well as the more traditionally emphasized emotionality.[3] We will consider how Vergil uses the erotic in the Dido episode as a means of reflecting on heroic values, in a way that both questions and uneasily attempts to validate the crucial virtues of the poet's society. I do not discuss this incident exhaustively but instead consider Vergil's adaptation of major sources in epic and tragedy and point to some important links between the Dido episode and the social vision projected in the second half of the poem.

From there we turn to a highly admired episode in book 9, the night raid of Nisus and Euryalus, which presents a similarly complex perspective on *pietas* and *virtus*. The erotic underpinning of that episode has not been thoroughly explored: the *amor* that underlies the two young men's relationship has a destructive as well as a noble side. The poet develops the significance of the erotic by associating *amor* with *cupido*, a term for passion that in a negative sense encompasses erotic longing, greed, and other manifestations of human desire. By expanding on the implications of *cupido*, Vergil makes it a metaphor for the corrosion of the very values that seem so admirable and poignant in this story. As in the Dido episode, he renders his social criticism more suggestive by imitating Homeric epic in a complex interplay with Greek tragedy.

---

[3]The best overall studies of Dido's complex, passionate nature remain the following: Viktor Pöschl, *The Art of Vergil: Image and Symbol in the* Aeneid, tr. Gerda Seligson (1962; rpt. Ann Arbor: University of Michigan Press, 1970), esp. pp. 60–91; and Brooks Otis, *Virgil: A Study in Civilized Poetry* (Oxford: Clarendon Press, 1963), esp. pp. 65–95, on Vergil's creation of a subjective style in his portrayal of this character. More recently, Grace S. West, "Caeneus and Dido," *TAPA* 110 (1980), 315–24, has a very interesting discussion of Dido's heroic interests as one dimension of a tension between the highly aggressive and the sensitively emotional sides of her character; in particular, she examines Vergil's allusion to Caeneus in the fields of mourning in the underworld scene.

The Dido Episode

Modern critics, especially since the work of Viktor Pöschl in the late 1940s, have paid careful attention to the literary sources that went into Vergil's characterization of Dido. Their efforts have given rise to an understanding of the poet's complex assimilation of Homer's Nausikaa, Apollonius's and Euripides' Medea, Catullus's Ariadne, and even Sophocles' Ajax, to name only the most important. All the elements of Vergil's portrayal of Dido in books 1 and 4 reflect an allusiveness, often paradoxical, to major erotic heroines from epic and tragedy. Her very entrance into the epic occurs through a literary allusion, a simile comparing her to Diana:[4]

> qualis in Eurotae ripis aut per iuga Cynthi
> exercet Diana choros, quam mille secutae
> hinc atque hinc glomerantur Oreades; illa pharetram
> fert umero gradiensque deas supereminet omnis
> (Latonae tacitum pertemptant gaudia pectus). (498–502)

Just as on the banks of the Eurotas or along the ridges of Mount Cynthus Diana engages in dance, about whom a thousand Oreads flock in attendance; she bears a quiver on her shoulder and, as she walks, towers over all the goddesses. (Joy quietly gladdens Latona's heart.)

We have already considered the two Greek antecedents of this simile in the previous chapter: Apollonius borrowed the Artemis simile from Homer's Phaeacian episode to describe Medea rushing off to her assignation with Jason. Vergil, however, directly imitates the *Odyssey* passage, where Homer emphasizes Nausikaa's grace and beauty just before the princess meets the shipwrecked hero (6.102–8). While similarly focusing on beauty and harmonious participation in a group activity,[5] Vergil implies that he is taking the erotic in a more complex direction than his predecessor had. For Dido is

---

[4]Vergil, *Opera*, ed. R. A. B. Mynors (Oxford: Clarendon Press, 1969). My quotations from Vergil come from this edition, with *v* substituting for consonantal *u*. The translations are my own.

[5]On the Diana simile, see esp. Pöschl (above, note 3), pp. 63–65; Roger Hornsby, *Patterns of Action in the* Aeneid (Iowa City: University of Iowa Press, 1970), pp. 89–90; and M. K. Thornton, "The Adaptation of Homer's Artemis-Nausicaa Simile in the *Aeneid*," *Latomus* 44 (1985), 615–22.

engaged in the work of building Carthage, not in recreation as Nausikaa when frolicking with her maids on their laundry expedition. Vergil suggests Dido's energy as a leader with the verb *exerceo* ("to engage busily") and her subjects' enthusiasm with the verb *glomero*, a poetic word denoting a heaping together. The poet thus makes his first literary allusion with Dido a vehicle for a complex perspective on this character: personally attractive in her charm and sociability, she is also a political leader with important responsibilities that she had to assume after the treacherous murder of her husband.

The Diana simile furthermore adds an erotic overtone that differs from Homer's suggestion of the natural desire of the young Phaeacian princess for marriage. Vergil incorporates his description into a context in which the hero's mother Venus, disguised as a nymph-like huntress, a follower of Diana, has told her son about Dido's passionate love for her husband ("magno miserae dilectus amore," 344), and after his murder her flight from Tyre to Carthage as leader of a new people. The simile suggests Dido's aggressive determination to create a better civilization out of the chaos of the old and also relates her to Venus, thus insinuating her potential for passionate erotic feelings. In his first image of Dido, then, Vergil hints at the uneasy fusion of public and private spheres.

The poet also suggestively juxtaposes this analogy with Aeneas's fascination with the wall paintings of the newly built temple of Juno. These two moments in effect are made one by the lines that immediately precede the simile: "While Dardanian Aeneas was looking at these wondrous objects, while he was astonished and stayed fixed in rapt attention, the queen, most beautiful in appearance, proceeded to the temple with a large crowd of youths accompanying her" (494–97). Vergil seems to suggest that the scenes painted on the temple wall symbolize an important quality of the queen who commissioned these representations of the Trojan War.[6] This woman has demonstrated a heroism of her own by taking the initiative of resettling her people under extremely difficult circumstances, for her brother, the ruler of Tyre, had murdered her husband out of lust for his massive wealth. Her identification with

[6]See James Tatum, "Allusion and Interpretation in *Aen.* 6.440–76," *AJPhil.* 105 (1984), 437, on the connection between Dido and Penthesilea.

traditional heroism is implicit in the decorations on the walls of her temple to Juno, which depict the struggle of the great warriors on the battlefield at Troy: the victorious Greeks, epitomized by Achilles dragging the body of Hector around the walls of Troy and finally giving up his body to Priam for a huge ransom, and Diomedes skillfully dispatching the troops of Rhesus and carrying off his magnificent horses; the valiant Trojans, including Aeneas himself; and finally the bold Amazon Penthesilea (466–94). The paintings not only emphasize traditional forms of heroism but also give a special prominence to the aggressive female who has entered into this male sphere.

Finally, Vergil makes this simile the first of a series of significant images related to hunting and sacrifice that trace Dido's progressive movement toward disappointment in love and self-destruction.[7] As Diana the huntress, Dido is in control of her surroundings. But at the beginning of book 4, when the queen has fallen in love with the hero, Vergil describes her attempt to win over the gods through sacrificial offerings and even the unorthodox (from the Roman point of view) procedure of *haruspicium*, examining the entrails of animals (56–64). He then compares her to one of Diana's vulnerable creatures, a deer hit by a shepherd who is unaware that his shaft has reached its victim: "Just as a deer struck by an arrow which a shepherd wandering through Cretan groves has hit from afar and leaves the shaft unaware: she wanders through the Dictaean woods and groves in flight; the fatal shaft clings to her side" (69–73).

Since Apollonius had also used Homer's image of Artemis to depict his own heroine, Vergil probably assumed that his reader would recall the deer simile describing Medea in book 4 of the *Argonautica*: "Like a quick deer which the barking of dogs has terrified in the copse of a deep woods" (12–13). Apollonius attributes Medea's fear at this point to Hera's agency: she too is in large measure a victim of the gods who arrange for her to fall in love with Jason in order to aid him in his quest for the fleece. Her agony is intense and the physical symptoms acute: fire in her eyes and a fierce ringing in her ears (16–17). Medea's instability also emerges in that

[7]Eugene Vance, "Sylvia's Pet Stag: Wildness and Domesticity in Virgil's *Aeneid*," *Arethusa* 14 (1981), 127–38, discusses the role of sacrifice and notes the similarity of Dido in book 6 to the image of the wounded deer in book 4.

context, for she attempts to commit suicide for the second time but is prevented by Hera. Characteristically, Apollonius does not make this passage an example of unqualified pathos. At the beginning of book 4, for instance, he leaves open the nature of her feelings by claiming an aporia over her motivation for fleeing Colchis, whether through passion or fear.

Dido, however, is unquestionably driven by a deep love, for she tells her sister Anna of the resurgence of passion she once felt for Sychaeus (which Venus in book 1 called a *magnus amor*): "agnosco veteris vestigia flammae" (23). As critics have observed, the simile here increases the pathos of Dido's suffering because it is so sudden and to some extent outside of her control.[8] Unlike Apollonius, Vergil reveals the devastating effects of this passion not just on the physical and emotional level but also in the political sphere, for the queen becomes totally incapacitated for her responsibilities in Carthage, and work on the city then ceases (86–89).

If Apollonius implies in his deer simile that the young woman is essentially the tool of amoral divinities, Vergil makes responsibility more complex. Here the shepherd's arrow that hits the deer is symbolically a human counterpart of the divine machinery represented by Cupid's arrow. Venus carefully prepared Aeneas with relevant information about Dido's past so that he could use the knowledge of her experiences to his own advantage upon their meeting. His account of the fall of Troy (which included the painful appearance of his beloved friend Hector in a dream) and of his long wandering (in which he encountered the voice of Polydorus, who had been treacherously murdered for gold) clearly utilizes Venus's information about Dido's personal history and achieves the purpose she intended. Goddess and hero act in unison to ensure his safety at Dido's expense.

Like Hera, who protects Jason's interests, Venus keeps watch on the progress of her son Aeneas and sends Cupid in the form of Ascanius to draw Dido erotically to the hero (1.664–88). Since the goddess's motives are not only personal but also relate to the destiny of Rome, Dido is in addition the victim of historical forces beyond

---

[8]On the deer simile in book 4, William S. Anderson, "*Pastor Aeneas*: On Pastoral Themes in the *Aeneid*," *TAPA* 99 (1968), 8–9, observes that the hero, however unwittingly, is the cause of violence for the queen, in ironic contrast to his earlier appearance as a shepherd himself victimized in book 2.

her control. This aspect is made more complex, as Gordon Williams notes, by Vergil's use of language to foreshadow the treachery of Carthage, with whom Rome later fought the Punic Wars.[9] On the psychological level, Dido's vulnerability to Cupid masquerading as the hero's son suggests that her love for Aeneas is initially bound up with her maternal instincts.[10] Her inclination toward love is to some extent admirable since she longs for a child both for personal fulfillment as a woman and for the public goal of ensuring the stable rule of Carthage.

However appealing Dido may be because of her impressive public role and her capacity for love, Vergil insinuates her ambivalent connection to the civilized values governing his heroic view. Not insignificantly, he situates the first stages of her passion, Cupid's seduction and Aeneas's story of his own past, in the context of the wealth and luxury of her court. He draws attention to the magnificence of the halls: "The queen now relaxed and reclined on a golden couch in the proud halls" (697–98). The torches are fixed to golden chandeliers (726–27), and the banqueters drink from golden goblets (728–29), the queen's studded with gems (739).[11] Vergil may recall the description of the splendid Phaeacian court in the *Odyssey* but does not impart Homer's admiration for such magnificence here. The reader might furthermore recall the *Georgics* passage criticizing the man who lusts for bejeweled goblets, a symbol of decadence. The use of this image with Dido implies a similar disapproval, in effect a rejection of the earlier heroic association of status (*timē*) with wealth, which for the Homeric hero reinforced his successes on the battlefield.

[9]Gordon Williams, *Tradition and Originality in Roman Poetry* (Oxford: Clarendon Press, 1968), p. 376, discussing Venus's anxiety over the potential hostility toward Aeneas at Carthage ("indeed she fears the ambivalent house and the double-tongued Tyrians," 1.661), notes that the treacherous Carthage, Rome's great enemy, is in the background throughout this part of the poem.

[10]See Gillis (above, note 2), pp. 39–40.

[11]Charles Segal, "The Song of Iopas in the *Aeneid*," *Hermes* 99 (1971), 336–49, noting the resemblance to the Phaeacians, observes that Vergil situates the didactic song of Dido's bard in the context of the luxury of her court; he also notes that Vergil's contemporary reader would view Julius Caesar's and Marc Antony's involvements with Cleopatra in a negative light and that the reference to long winter nights in Iopas's song hints at "the long winter of idleness and luxury which Aeneas spends with Dido."

The motif of gold is highly charged in two later passages: the fatal hunting expedition when Dido and Aeneas consummate their love, and the appearance of Mercury, who admonishes the hero to leave Carthage. In the first of these passages, the poet prepares the reader in advance for the sexual consequences of this hunt by recording the conversation of Juno and Venus (90–128). His description of Dido's appearance then strikingly associates her with an excessive show of wealth:

> cui pharetra ex auro, crines nodantur in aurum,
> aurea purpuream subnectit fibula vestem. (138–9)

Her quiver was of gold, her hair was tied back with golden ornaments, and a golden broach bound her purple dress.

Vergil draws attention to the prominence of gold through sophisticated rhetorical techniques: the repetition of forms of the word *aurum*, especially the elegant anastrophe that ends the first line and begins the second, and the "golden line" separating two nouns and two adjectives by a verb, here with the words "golden" and "purple" (another sign of extravagance) juxtaposed. In the second passage, he shows the hero himself seduced into this ethos of luxury when he reflects Dido's sumptuousness of dress by wearing clothing woven with gold, "a gift which wealthy Dido had made" (263–64). In this scene Mercury scornfully calls the hero "uxorius" (266), presumably alluding to his effeminate appearance as well as to his activity of building his mistress's city. The moral overtones of both contexts reinforce the negative connotations of gold as a symbol of decadence. One may recall that Dido acquired her wealth under violent circumstances, after her husband had been murdered for his riches, and she herself stole away with it without her brother's knowledge. In book 8, the poet renounces a materialistic ethic through the mouthpiece of Evander, who admonishes the hero to accept the humble surroundings and the overall simplicity of his domain (8.362–65).

Vergil makes Dido's own attitude toward her passion highly ambivalent. He describes her anxiety over her sudden interest in the newly arrived hero in a scene that adds an important resonance of Greek tragedy to his epic models. While the situation of the love-struck heroine with her sister suggests Medea and Chalciope in book 3 of the *Argonautica*, the conversation between Dido and Anna has a tragic parallel in Phaedra's exchange with her nurse in Euripides' *Hippolytus*.[12] Like the clever nurse in the Greek play, Anna uses highly rhetorical language to persuade her sister to follow her course of action. Dido also resembles Phaedra when she reveals to Anna the shame she feels about her desires. To some extent Vergil makes both Dido and Anna more sympathetic than their Greek counterparts in their attempts to arrive at the right decision. His queen does not have the same moral pressure against the incestuous union that the tragic protagonist desires. Instead, she feels a strong bond with her first husband, to whom she has made a vow that she will never marry again. Her motivations are complex and must be considered in some detail.

Dido's decision to forego another marriage after the death of her husband Sychaeus has struck many scholars as a positive act consonant with Roman views on the privileged state of the *univira*.[13] Yet the poet implies that her persistence in remaining faithful to Sychaeus, though laudable to a point, is ultimately unnatural. Anna, who seems to understand her sister well, points to Dido's youth, her need for children, and the pleasures of love (31–33). When she asks if she will resist even a desirable love ("'placitone etiam pugnabis amori?'" 38), she implies Dido's need for an emotional and physical bond with a man. Furthermore, her practical arguments have some validity: Carthage is surrounded by enemies and as a growing city needs support (39–44). The language that Dido herself uses to convey her attitude, moreover, seems excessive. She views Sychaeus's unexpected death as a kind of personal deception ("'primus amor

---

[12]See Vergil, *The Aeneid of Virgil*, books 1–6, ed. with commentary R. D. Williams (London: Macmillan, 1972), p. 335, for some specific parallels between the two scenes. See Andrew R. Dyck, "Sychaeus," *Phoenix* 37 (1983), 239–44, for another possible tragic parallel in Sophocles' Antigone, who also has a far more idealistic outlook than her sister, a model that would add considerable pathos to Dido's situation.

[13]Richard Monti, *The Dido Episode and the* Aeneid: *Roman Social and Political Values in the Epic* (Leiden: Brill, 1981), pp. 54–55, provides a sensible discussion of the *univira* as an ideal that did not imply moral obligation for the Romans. Williams (above, note 9), pp. 380–81, presents the traditional view about the importance of this status for a woman.

deceptam morte fefellit,'" 17).[14] She then indicates that her disappointment has made her loathe the very idea of marriage: "'If I had not been thoroughly weary of the marriage bed and torch, I might perhaps have yielded to this one fault'" (18–19).

Finally, Dido's determination to remain loyal to Sychaeus is made more problematic because it involves her public image. In this scene she does not raise the issue, but Anna appeals to her general interest in glory in a comment on the advantage of a union with Aeneas: "'With the help of Trojan might, to what great heights will Punic glory rise!'" (48–49). Later, Dido acknowledges her concern with her fame in her recriminations to Aeneas when he decides to leave Carthage. She connects it specifically with her fidelity to her dead husband: "'On account of you my sense of shame was destroyed and the fame by which alone I reached the stars'" (321–23). This sense of glory is different from the general *eukleia*, or good reputation, that Nausikaa, for instance, values in the Phaeacian episode. It is more like the *kleos*, or glory, for which the epic heroes in Homer strive. Vergil, however, to a large degree takes a skeptical position on *fama* as a value that becomes a self-seeking drive in an individual at the expense of the larger social welfare and is ultimately self-destructive.[15] Dido's motivation for her vow of fidelity to Sychaeus thus seems a complex mixture of an unselfish devotion, a troubled repression of her sexuality, and a keen interest in her own glory. While her feelings for Aeneas interfere with her public role as a leader, Dido's preservation of her love for her husband is at least in part bound up with her public image, her glory.

Vergil has Dido, in her confrontation with Aeneas, raise the problem of *fides*, the important social value that guarantees the validity of oaths and contracts. Scholars have noted that as a woman facing

---

[14]Williams (above, note 12), ad loc., notes that the word *deceptus* is similarly found in many tombstone inscriptions; yet its combination with the word *fefellit* adds a strong tone. Furthermore, Dido's wish a few lines later for the earth to gape open and for Jupiter to strike her with a thunderbolt if she violates her *pudor* is exaggerated rhetoric.

[15]See Donald Earl, *The Moral and Political Tradition of Rome* (Ithaca: Cornell University Press, 1967), p. 32, for the relation between *fama* and *gloria*, and p. 73, for Vergil's critical view of *gloria*. Here, the poet seems to associate the two concepts closely in Dido's hyperbolic image of reaching the stars through her reputation for fidelity.

abandonment by her lover, Dido is very close to both Catullus's Ariadne and Euripides' and Apollonius's Medea. Her vehement reproaches resemble Medea's angry outburst at Jason both in Euripides' play when she confronts her false husband and in Apollonius's epic when she suspects the possibility of being handed over to her brother Apsyrtus. In both of those cases, however, there is an important difference to observe: the hero is violating the unquestionable obligations that he has incurred by accepting her help (and in the tragedy by actually marrying her). In her first address, however, Dido is closer to the Catullan model through her fluctuation of tone between anger and persuasion and through her emphasis on the hero's breach of *fides*. She begins her reproach by angrily addressing Aeneas as "perfide" (305), an echo of Ariadne's powerful accusation of Theseus.[16] In Catullus's poem as well as in the Greek works on Medea, there is no doubt about the accuracy of the young woman's charge because Theseus had promised to marry her after receiving her help against the Minotaur but shamelessly deserted her on his way home. We must investigate the complexity of Dido's reproach by looking more closely at the context.

The word *perfidus* here seems to reflect Dido's point of view: she believes that her relationship with the hero is to some extent a marriage and that he is unjustly deserting her.[17] Vergil also gives some credibility to the existence of a marriage, since the union was orchestrated by the marriage-goddess Juno and included symbolic elements of a formal ceremony: the lightning flashes substituting for the wedding torches and the music of the nymphs for the wedding song.[18] Yet Dido herself is ambivalent about the status of the relationship. When the poet says that she attempted to gloss over her "fault" by giving her liaison with Aeneas the "name of marriage" (172), he reflects her uneasiness about the situation: the *culpa* represents her betrayal of Sychaeus and the word *nomen* implies a "pretext" and thus casts a doubt over the extent of her belief in a real

[16]On Ariadne's powerful accusation of Theseus for violation of *fides*, see David Konstan, *Catullus' Indictment of Rome: The Meaning of Catullus 64* (Amsterdam: Hakkert, 1977), esp. pp. 42–46.

[17]Barbara J. Bono, *Literary Transvaluation: From Vergilian Epic to Shakespearean Tragicomedy* (Berkeley: University of California Press, 1984), pp. 23–24, has some good remarks on the validity of Dido's position.

[18]See Williams (above, note 12) on line 166 for these connections.

marriage. In addition, Aeneas's firm denial of any commitment to a marriage (338–39) cannot be completely fallacious and further suggests that Dido's view is only a partial truth. Both the intensity of her present passion and the depth of her guilt over betraying Sychaeus make Dido limited in her grasp of the complexity of the situation and of Aeneas's own dilemma.

But the queen seems the more pitiable as Vergil shows the hero highly flawed in his response. Aeneas's own guilt at shirking his responsibility to his son and to the future empire in Italy make his approach to the situation ethically questionable, for he initially hopes somehow to "get around" ("ambire," 283) the queen.[19] His lack of sensitivity to Dido's wish for a son who would be a reminder to her of his father and a support for her in the hero's absence suggests the shallowness of Jason, who quickly brushes off Hypsipyle's suggestion of her possible pregnancy in book 1 of the *Argonautica*. Finally, the rapidity with which he leaves, in effect sneaking off before dawn, approximates a little too closely Theseus's abandonment of Ariadne on Dia in the dead of night.

The issue of *fides* culminates in a complex passage in which Dido, certain of Aeneas's departure, utters a moving soliloquy. Vergil emphasizes the futility of her situation through an allusion to Apollonius's Medea. As he depicts the calm of the night when all creatures are at rest (522–29) except Dido, he alludes to the passage in the *Argonautica* contrasting Medea's sleeplessness with the peace of sailors, travelers, and even a mother bereft of her children (3.744–50). Medea finds a solution to her despair in the conversation with her sister, but Dido has already decided upon death as her only option. Vergil's echo thereby deepens the pathos of Dido's plight. With the pathetic question "'en, quid ago?'" (534), she poses the alternatives now left open to her. She first raises the possibility of renewing relations with her former African suitors (534–36) but rejects this option as completely unfeasible, since she is keenly aware of her earlier rejection of these rulers and previously brought up the subject of their hostility with considerable anxiety (320–21). She

---

[19]On Vergil's use of language implying deception in this passage, see Christine G. Perkell, "On Creusa, Dido, and the Quality of Victory in Virgil's *Aeneid*," in *Reflections of Women in Antiquity*, ed. Helene P. Foley (New York: Gordon and Breach, 1981), p. 364, who expands on Page's commentary.

then dismisses the possibility of following her lover to Italy, since the Trojans have shown no gratitude (*gratia*) to her and she could certainly not uproot her people a second time (537–46).

In this self-questioning, Dido echoes Catullus's Ariadne, who ironically ponders the following: a return to Crete over impassible seas; the help of her father whom she betrayed and deserted; and the faithful love of her intended husband, who now flees in the distance (64.176–83). While Ariadne angrily concentrates on Theseus's lack of *fides* and *gratia*, Dido is more ambivalent. She points to Aeneas's treachery: "'Do you not yet perceive the perjury of Laomedon's race?'" (541–42). This allusion to the original act of treachery by the Trojans when their first king dared to cheat even the god Neptune of his due is a devastating indictment of the hero and his race. In light of Aeneas's obfuscation of his role at Carthage with Dido, it is not completely without justification.[20] Yet Dido's own guilt also surfaces in this scene. She acknowledges that she succumbed too easily to her passion for Aeneas by yielding to her sister's persuasions (547–48) and by being unable to live without a life in marriage (550–51).[21] Significantly, she hints at the unfeasibility of maintaining her faith to Sychaeus by associating it with an unsocialized existence (*more ferae*). Yet she still concludes her analysis of the situation with the thought of her own lack of *fides*, her broken promise to Sychaeus (552).

In the scene in which Dido sees Aeneas's ships departing and prepares for death, her view of the violation of social values remains ambivalent. She mentions the signal value of *pietas* in a highly prob-

---

[20]Ibid., pp. 366–68, for a good discussion of Aeneas's obfuscation about the marriage issue, especially in the context of his implied pledge, "data dextera" (307).

[21]The depth of her own guilt is perhaps implied in the strange phrase, "non licuit thalami expertem sine crimine vitam / degere more ferae" (550–51), by which she seems to express a wish for a life totally outside of the demands of human life. See Vergil, *Opera* 2, ed. John Conington and Henry Nettleship (London: Bell, 1898), for a note on this passage: "She wishes she had been born to a wild life in the woods, like Camilla, without any thought of wedlock. It is not constancy to her first mate, but simply wildness, undisturbed by human passions and frailties, that is now in her mind." See also *Aeneidea*, vol. 2, ed. with commentary James Henry (1889; rpt. Hildesheim: Georg Olms, 1969), ad loc.: Vergil does not draw a contrast between a beast's life and man's in the union of the sexes but more generally opposes a wild state of innocence and simplicity with civilization and its complexities. Dido thus wishes she could have escaped both relationships that now cause her such anguish.

lematical question: "'Unhappy Dido, do impious deeds now affect you?'" (596).[22] She has certainly cast doubt on Aeneas's claim to piety when he insists that he has been ordered by Mercury to leave, for she sarcastically asserts that a messenger sent by Jove has brought "horrida iussa" to him (376–78). The hero would seem to be implicated here too. But the context draws Dido as well as Aeneas into the censure, for she is obsessively concerned about her own impiety in breaking her promise to Sychaeus. This self-reproach is in part noble but also reflects her deep-seated concern with her loss of reputation, without which she cannot face life.

In this passage, Vergil reinforces Dido's ambivalent relation to civilized values. He connects her with Hecate and the forces of magic, a subject that came up earlier when Dido told her sister about her knowledge of the powers of a Massylian witch who administers drugs to the serpent overseeing the garden of the Hesperides.[23] In this scene, Dido invokes the goddess whose powers are antithetical to the forces of civilization as she begins to call for revenge upon the hero. The excesses of her nature are here symbolized in a level of madness that surpasses all of her models, especially Euripides' Medea and Catullus's Ariadne, who in their desire for revenge show a barely restrained fury.[24] Dido herself acknowledges her state of

[22]Scholars have long debated whether Dido refers to her own impiety or to Aeneas's. Monti (above, note 13), pp. 63–68, reviewing the controversy, argues against the traditional objection to taking the phrase in reference to Aeneas because Dido could not have been affected by his wickedness until he deserted her. He notes that in the following line Dido refers to having shared her power with Aeneas, a situation related to the issue of *pietas*. She would thus imply that the possibility of impious deeds on Aeneas's part ought to have concerned her when she gave him a share in the rule. Monti seems right to stress that Dido primarily criticizes the hero's faults, but the traditional interpretation of self-reference on Dido's part is perhaps a second level of meaning, given her deep, obsessive sense of her own failure.

[23]Bono (above, note 17), pp. 24–25, views Dido's relation to magic as one indication of her link to an anachronistic mentality. In the scene referring to the powers of the Massylian witch, she specifies the poppy, a red flower that occurs later in two significant contexts of the young warrior's death on the battlefield. On Vergil's use of this image, see Robert J. Edgeworth, "The Purple Flower Image in the *Aeneid*," *Philologus* 127 (1983), 143–48.

[24]Eugene Vance, "Warfare and the Structure of Thought in Virgil's *Aeneid*," *Quaderni Urbinati di Cultura Classica* 15 (1973), 138, discusses the sexual implications of this scene. Tatum (above, note 6), 146–48, notes that both Ajax and Dido fall on a sword that was a gift from an enemy and compares Ajax's attitude toward *kleos* with Dido's toward *fama*.

mind: "'What madness now afflicts my mind?'" (595). She far exceeds her model Ariadne, since her curse not only calls for the hero's death in violent circumstances but also for perpetual hostility between the Carthaginians and Trojans. The poet, of course, increases the magnitude of Dido's curse by alluding to the long-standing enmity between Rome and Carthage when she calls for an avenger to rise from her bones.

In the passage narrating her suicide, Vergil again suggests both the inherent nobility and the irrationality of this character. Critics have long realized that in this scene the poet was influenced by Sophocles' portrayal of Ajax. Dido's death by her lover's sword is a striking reminder of the tragic hero's demise when he can no longer face the shame of his situation. Although there is an austere dignity in her tragic death, madness underlies the erotic implications of Dido's act: she symbolically experiences sexual penetration when she falls on Aeneas's sword on their bed, which is now her funeral pyre.[25] By this fusion of the sexual act with death, Vergil emphasizes the ironic waste of a potentially productive life that could have achieved so much more but, instead of procreating literally and figuratively, left only madness and hostility as a legacy.

The final appearance of Dido in the epic reinforces her ambivalence. Aeneas sees her a last time in the fields of mourning in book 6, and Dido's appearance suggests an injured beast, nursing her wound in the forest. But if she is tending the wounds of love inflicted by her encounter with Aeneas, she has also returned to her former state as wife of Sychaeus, who shares her passion (474). Furthermore, in addition to the animal image Vergil alludes to an important epic scene, the hostility of the intransigent Ajax in book 11 of the *Odyssey*. As the Trojan War hero rejects Odysseus's attempt to appease his former adversary in the contest for Achilles' arms, she refuses to

[25]Vergil has suggested the onset of madness in Dido after Aeneas rejects Anna's plea to delay his departure for a while: she imagines the voice of Sychaeus and dreams of Aeneas fiercely pursuing her in her total isolation; she is then compared to the mad Pentheus seeing double and Orestes pursued on the stage by his mother and the avenging Furies (469–73). The tension in Dido between guilt for her betrayal of Sychaeus and passion for Aeneas pervades this section, for a troubled sexuality is suggested in the reference to the repressed hero of the *Bacchae*, and impiety to a family member underlies the mention of the matricide Orestes, now plagued with guilt.

acknowledge Aeneas's justification for leaving her. While Dido's coldness stems from Aeneas's abandonment of her, she is likewise subtly connected to an unacceptable heroic stance that overvalues reputation. Although Vergil's hero does not respond adequately to Dido's plight, he does attempt to adapt to the demands of his changing world. Dido, however, is frozen in time, much like the Marpesian rock to which she is last of all compared (6.471).

To sum up, eros in the Dido episode is implicated with the social in complex ways. To some extent, her erotic passion conflicts with public concerns, and so Dido's strong feelings for Aeneas prevent her from comprehending his devotion to his political mission. Yet, more surprisingly, her great love for Sychaeus, which she preserved by rejecting another marriage, is closely tied to her public reputation, her *fama*. Thus, her *fides* in maintaining her vow also entangles self-interest with social ideals. Ironically, she also distorts this social value when she passionately censures Aeneas for violating his *fides* to her. As we observed, her claim does not completely hold up because he does not seem to have made any commitment to marriage, although he may have accepted political responsibility by helping to rule Carthage. Dido's association with wealth, furthermore, reveals another form of excessive desire that is different from the Homeric quest for status commensurate with martial accomplishments and is tainted with the violence in her previous family struggles. Finally, the confusion of private and public that the erotic involves in this episode is encapsulated in Dido's death: she sums up her life in terms of her public accomplishment of heroically founding a new city but by her suicide makes that very place vulnerable to forces of destruction. The eroticism of her suicide raises her act to the level of madness.

While readers have traditionally tended to concentrate on the first half of the poem, critics have recently paid more attention to the close connections between the last six books and the first six. K. W. Gransden exemplifies this movement to reconsider Vergil's martial books as a very complex revision of the *Iliad*; he furthermore observes that the war with the Latins is paradigmatic of the recent past of Vergil's own Rome.[26] While the *Aeneid* frequently shifts in and

---

[26]K. W. Gransden, *Virgil's* Iliad: *An Essay on Epic Narrative* (Cambridge: Cambridge University Press, 1984), esp. pp. 42–43, on Vergil's use of Iliadic conflict with a contemporary urgency.

out of political allegory alluding to the civil wars of Julius Caesar against Pompey and Octavian against Marc Antony, Vergil in general seems to imply the need for his society to assess the vengeance and violence of the past and to adopt an ethic that would insure a stable, morally grounded existence.[27]

The values that the Romans traced back to their legendary ancestors—*virtus*, *fides*, and especially *pietas*—find a difficult testing ground in these books. The hero's development can be measured to some extent by his increasingly complex relation to *pietas*, a subject of considerable debate by critics of the poem. As Michael C. J. Putnam has pointed out, Aeneas's major contests in books 10 through 12 call his deep commitment to piety into question.[28] An important example involves the noble Lausus, who tried to protect his father, the tyrant Mezentius; after killing the young man, Aeneas is recalled to the value of filial piety (10.821–24). Yet he subsequently abandons this noble reflection when he kills the boy's father and vaunts in the act (10.897–98). Even worse, he brutally slays the warrior Magus, who as a suppliant appeals to the hero's regard for his own father and son (10.524-25). In book 12, Aeneas fails to respond to Turnus's plea for mercy on the basis of paternal feelings but instead yields to *ira*, killing him when he sees the baldrick of his fallen young ally Pallas. The erotic content of this belt, which depicts the Danaids' slaughter of their husbands on their wedding night, symbolizes the frustration of the youthful vitality that might have performed constructive acts and the grotesque perversion of the marriage union that was intended to continue the family line and revitalize the race.[29] W. R. Johnson has observed that Aeneas as much as Turnus has become a victim of a "mechanical malevolence" that undermines his dignity.[30]

Vergil reflects upon the complexity of *pietas* and the other major values that Roman life was founded on in other episodes of the last

[27]On the general question of allegory in the *Aeneid*, see the brief but useful remarks of W. A. Camps, *An Introduction to Virgil's* Aeneid (London: Oxford University Press, 1969), pp. 95–104, 137–43.

[28]Michael C. J. Putnam, "*Pius* Aeneas and the Metamorphosis of Lausus," *Arethusa* 14 (1981), 139–56.

[29]On the erotic significance of the belt, see Gillis (above, note 2), pp. 102–4.

[30]W. R. Johnson, *Darkness Visible: A Study of Vergil's* Aeneid (Berkeley: University of California Press, 1976), p. 133.

six books. In the rest of this chapter we discuss the entanglement of private desires with social values in the exploits of two young, enthusiastic warriors who embark on a mission to relay information to their leader but are sidetracked by the opportunity to make a surprise attack on the enemy camp at night and fail to make their escape. While showing the potential of *pietas* for political cohesiveness, the poet also dramatizes the difficulty of achieving the ideal because of the problematic intrusion of private interests into the public sphere. In part, *pietas* and *virtus* inherently conflict with *amor*. Yet, more insidiously, the scope of passion is increased by the expressions of *cupido* that insinuate themselves into the very fabric of *gloria*, *virtus*, and even *pietas* and threaten to undermine their stability. Vergil recalls the Dido episode in his characters' private desires, such as excessive interest in wealth and an obsession with personal glory, but reveals the social implications of their desires more fully here. He conveys tension by counterpointing the more practical, realistic attitude toward heroism of Homeric epic with the skepticism of Euripidean tragedy.

The Story of Nisus and Euryalus

Vergil so emphatically invests his account of Nisus and Euryalus in book 9 with pathos that readers have traditionally responded favorably to the two ill-fated young warriors who are united by a strong bond of friendship and display a spirited courage in undertaking the dangerous expedition to report the situation at camp to Aeneas. R. D. Williams lets Heyne's judgment sum up critical opinion on the story of Nisus and Euryalus: "Episodium Aeneidis omnium facile nobilissimum."[31] Recently, however, at least one critic has found the erotic aspect of their relationship problematic and related to the tragedy of their demise. M. O. Lee discusses Vergil's complex attitude toward homoerotic relationships and finds that on the one hand the poet is keenly aware of the "obsessive and self-destructive" aspects of the bond by depicting the foul play and

[31]See Vergil, *The Aeneid of Virgil*, books 7–12, ed. with commentary R. D. Williams (London: Macmillan, 1973), on 176f.

horrible carnage but that on the other he is also sympathetic to its positive side.[32] Lee's Freudian-based criticism follows two other-works that reflect upon the complexities within this episode and portray the less positive aspects of the two main characters.[33] In a seminal study, George Duckworth observes that the protagonists' desire for military distinction provokes their excessive slaughter and their plundering; as a tragedy "which illustrates the working of free will," the story foreshadows the later actions of such characters as Pallas, Lausus, and especially Turnus.[34] While Duckworth sees the error of individuals who must pay for their actions, G. J. Fitzgerald finds a deeper ideological problem: youth seduced by patriotic values that have no solid basis.[35] Pointing to symbolic language that implies confusion and total loss of critical reflection, he concludes that the "environmental reaction" may be positive, but the reader is meant to become skeptical of such an ethic. We will see that the relation between the men's erotic bond, which is derived from Greek rather than Roman ethics, and the values that the men pursue is very complex and even more disturbing than Dido's passion in its larger implications for society.

The literary influences on the characterization of these two warriors suggest a conflict between private and public interests. Vergil's general debt to Homer's night raid of Odysseus and Diomedes in *Iliad* 10 is well known. He probably also used Homer's Achilles and Patroclus as the major paradigm for the close personal relationship of two warriors: the excesses of the lesser warrior bring about his downfall and motivate the great hero to return to battle with passionate fury. Although critics have become more aware of the influ-

---

[32]M. O. Lee, *Fathers and Sons in Virgil's* Aeneid (Albany: State University of New York Press, 1979), pp. 77–80, 109–113.

[33]For an exception, which presents a more optimistic view of the nobility of the characters in this episode, see Peter G. Lennox, "Virgil's Night-Episode Re-examined (*Aeneid* IX, 176–449)," *Hermes* 105 (1977), 331–42.

[34]George E. Duckworth, "The Significance of Nisus and Euryalus for *Aeneid* IX-XII," *AJPhil.* 88 (1967), 129–50.

[35]G. J. Fitzgerald, "Nisus and Euryalus: A Paradigm of Futile Behaviour and the Tragedy of Youth," in *Cicero and Virgil: Studies in Honour of Harold Hunt*, ed. John R. C. Martyn (Amsterdam: Hakkert, 1972), pp. 114–7. Although I agree with much of his essay, I differ principally with Fitzgerald's view of Vergil's complete and persistently ironic distance from his material in this episode.

ence of Greek tragedy on the *Aeneid*,[36] only Bernard Fenik has perceived the importance of Euripides' *Rhesus* as a major literary model for this episode. Fenik discusses the differences between the drama and the Homeric night raid and examines elements of Euripides' plot, language, and characterization that Vergil drew upon.[37] He notes that Euripides improves upon Homer by developing character and motivation more fully and by adding certain dynamic qualities to the plot, such as the disarray in the enemy camp and the discovery of the two warriors by their foe. Fenik also finds that Vergil eliminated much of the cynicism in the *Rhesus* by assuming a noncritical attitude toward the relationship between the two young men. To be sure, Vergil does not assume an antiheroic stance to the same extent that Euripides does. Yet the latter's skepticism toward heroic action may well have enabled Vergil to convey his reservations about the values driving his own warriors.

Before turning to the *Aeneid*, let us briefly review the important differences between the two Greek works. Homer reveals the ruthlessness of the martial ethic by Diomedes' murder of Dolon after Odysseus promised safety in return for information about the

[36]See, for example, W. F. Jackson Knight, *Roman Vergil*, 2d ed. (London: Faber and Faber, 1945), esp. pp. 133–40, who has very good observations on the influence of each of the three major Greek tragedians, in particular Euripides. Viktor Pöschl, "Virgile et la tragédie," in *Présence de Virgile, Actes du Colloque des 9, 11, et 12 Décembre 1976*, ed. Raymond Chevallier (Paris: Les Belles Lettres, 1978), pp. 73–79, has an excellent analysis of the influence of Greek tragedy on the Dido episode. Michael Wigodsky, *Vergil and Early Latin Poetry* (Wiesbaden: Steiner, 1972), pp. 91–97, reminds the critic of the general difficulty of being absolutely certain that Vergil is indebted to Greek tragedy rather than to Latin translations and renditions of the Greek works.

[37]Bernard Fenik, "The Influence of Euripides on Vergil's *Aeneid*" (Ph.D. diss., Princeton University, 1960): chap. 7, pp. 54–96, is an extended discussion of the echoes and parallels that Vergil employed from the *Rhesus*. Fenik begins by discussing the problem of Vergil's use of the play that we now possess under the title *Rhesus* and concludes that the specific verbal echoes of this Euripidean play are conclusive evidence that the Latin poet knew and used it. He assumes that the play is genuinely by Euripides and supports his view with some discussion of typically Euripidean irony (e.g., repetition of words meaning "to know") and the appearance of hostile and malevolent divinities. For a lengthy study of the problem of the authenticity of this play, see William Ritchie, *The Authenticity of the Rhesus of Euripides* (Cambridge: Cambridge University Press, 1964), who thoroughly examines the available external evidence as well as the internal evidence (e.g., metrics, language, style) and concludes that the work is most likely one of Euripides' earlier plays.

Trojan forces and by their surprise attack on the sleeping Thracian troops. In general, Homer's night raid illustrates the Greek heroic code in the *Iliad*, and Diomedes is a warrior who perhaps most perfectly illustrates the successful operation of this code.[38] Although Odysseus's cunning may make him a more questionable figure, in the Doloneia the two act in accordance with social norms that are ultimately validated by the end of the epic. When the heroes compete in the funeral games for Patroclus, they demonstrate strife in a socialized setting and show their capacity for generous behavior.[39] Euripides evidences a familiarity with Homer's work through frequent allusions to the Doloneia, but the *Rhesus* pessimistically expresses a sense of futility about human endeavor. There, Odysseus and Diomedes lack the status of independent agents who succeed because of their skill; instead, they receive extensive help from Athena, who even takes the form of Aphrodite in order to prevent Paris from pursuing the Greeks. The best heroes, then, have become merely pawns of the gods. The play furthermore suggests the inadequacy of logical reasoning in a world filled with unlikely events and manipulated by amoral divinities.[40] Through numerous images of sleep and dream states and language expressing chance and appearance, the *Rhesus* reflects the uncertain foundations of all human actions.

The Doloneia and the *Rhesus* imply very different views of glory as a major impetus to heroic activity. In the world of the Homeric

[38]On Diomedes' uncomplicated acceptance of the system, see Seth L. Schein, *The Mortal Hero: An Introduction to Homer's* Iliad (Berkeley: University of California Press, 1984), pp. 34–35, who places it in the context of the significant dislocation of those values in the aristeia of Patroclus in book 16 and, more important, of Achilles in book 22. Schein has an excellent discussion of Achilles' rejection of traditional values, including his painful attempt to articulate his query of the meaning of heroic glory in the embassy scene in book 9 (pp. 105–10).

[39]James M. Redfield, *Nature and Culture in the* Iliad: *The Tragedy of Hector* (Chicago: University of Chicago Press, 1975), pp. 168–69, refers to the movement "from purity through impurity to purity" enacted in the *Iliad* as the war turns harsher, culminating with Achilles' conduct with Hector's corpse and final permission for proper burial.

[40]See Euripides, *Rhesos*, tr. with introduction Richard E. Braun (New York: Oxford University Press, 1978). Braun has a useful introduction to the themes and imagery of this play (pp. 3–17). I am indebted to his discussion for my remarks immediately following on the *Rhesus*. See also Fenik (above, note 37), esp. pp. 84–93.

epic, *timē* and *kleos* are the means by which the individual in a martial-oriented society assures his status and extends his reputation into future generations.[41] *Kleos*, or "reputation," may apply to a person in general or to some particular quality that is possessed; significantly, it is awarded to a hero for accomplishing some difficult deed. Valuable possessions or prizes may have a *kleos* of their own and can bestow *kleos* upon the owner. Since *kleos* lasts beyond the grave, the poet perpetuates a person's reputation by singing of the *klea andrōn*. *Timē*, which connotes "honor," "status," or "price," is the measure of a man's worth according to his social peers; it was particularly important in an unstable world, because a man captured in battle could be ransomed at an appropriate price.

In the Doloneia, Nestor encourages a volunteer by promising *kleos* and the gift of a sheep from each of the Greek princes as a reward. There is thus a balance between social glory and material reward. Diomedes, who most thoroughly represents the values of his culture, is the first to offer his services; seeking only to have a companion in order to increase the chances of success, he immediately chooses the most cunning among the Greeks. As the two prepare to set forth, Odysseus prays to Athena for a glorious return after completing their mission (10.281–82). This desire for social glory reflects the values of a so-called shame culture, in which an individual is deterred from unacceptable conduct by fear of the disapproval of his peers.[42] The rational Greek protagonists, then, subordinate their desire for *timē* and *kleos* to the public cause of preventing Greek defeat at the hands of the Trojans; they simply expect the glory that their society naturally awards as payment for valiant actions. Unlike the Greeks, the foolish Dolon is motivated by a hubristic desire for personal glory. He dismisses Hector's offer of a chariot and two fine horses and insists upon the chariot and horses of Achilles as the reward for his spying mission. Though surprised,

[41]Redfield (above, note 39), pp. 31–35, has a very good discussion of these social terms. My definitions of *kleos* and *timē* are based on Redfield. See also Gregory Nagy, *The Best of the Achaians: Concepts of the Hero in Archaic Greek Poetry* (Baltimore: Johns Hopkins University Press, 1979), esp. pp. 40–41, 118–19.

[42]For a discussion of Homeric society as a "shame culture," see E. R. Dodds, *The Greeks and the Irrational* (Berkeley: University of California Press, 1951), esp. pp. 17–18.

Hector agrees, emphasizing the glory that the man will gain from such a prize: "'diamperes aglaieisthai'" (331), "'you will become thoroughly splendid.'"[43] Dolon clearly violates the standards of heroic society; he is excessively acquisitive and overconfident. The poet shows the utter folly of his quest for glory by depicting his desperate, futile attempts to save himself when captured by Odysseus and Diomedes (10.378–445).

Unlike Homer, Euripides takes a thoroughly skeptical position on glory in the *Rhesus*. The epic poet briefly indicates Dolon's mercenary attitude in his conversation with Hector, but the playwright elaborates the scene in which Dolon and Hector discuss the appropriate reward for the scouting mission. The Trojan leader offers the young warrior many valuable gifts before learning of his real desire. Not only does Hector agree, he also admits his own lust for the same prize: "'kai mēn erōnti g'anteras hippōn emoi'" (184), "'indeed you speak of the horses which I lust for.'"[44] Since Hector is the best of the Trojan heroes, possession of those famed horses would appropriately enhance his *timē*. But by using erotic language to describe that hero's eagerness the playwright makes his desire a passion rather than an expression of social values. The insignificant Dolon, moreover, seems all the more foolish by aspiring so high. With an unreflective enthusiasm, the chorus affirms the glory of this venture: "'ponos hod'euklees'" (197), "'this glorious endeavor.'" Thus, ignoring altogether Homer's positive references to the *kleos* of Odysseus and Diomedes, Euripides magnifies the picture of Dolon's absurd quest for material rewards. At the end of the play, he qualifies all human glory when the Muse prophesies the inglorious death of the greatest of all heroes, Achilles.

While frequently alluding to Homer and Euripides, Vergil makes glory problematic in the Nisus and Euryalus episode by associating it with erotic language and integrating it into the mutual dependence of the two lovers. Nisus is motivated primarily by his desire for

---

[43]Homer, *Iliad*, vols. 1, 2, and 3, ed. T. W. Allen (1931; rpt. New York: Arno, 1979). My references to the *Iliad* follow this edition; the original Greek is transliterated. The translations are my own.

[44]Euripides, *Fabulae*, vol. 3, ed. Gilbert Murray (Oxford: Clarendon Press, 1909). My quotations from the *Rhesus*, transliterated, follow Murray's edition. The translations are my own.

glory.[45] The young warrior acknowledges the *dira cupido* that drives him to seek opportunities for enhancing his reputation: "'My spirit has for a long time urged me to engage either in battle or in some other great deed'" (185–86). By connecting fame to *cupido*, which refers to a passionate desire, especially of sexual love, Vergil suggests that Nisus's interest in that social value is un-Homeric and more like the lust that Euripides' Dolon and even Hector feel. When Nisus mentions his plan to undertake the mission to Aeneas, he is using the public crisis as a means for glory: "'The people and the elders all demand that Aeneas be summoned and that men be sent to report the situation. If they promise the things that I ask for you (the glory of the deed is enough for me)'" (192–95). By insisting that he wants only glory for the dangerous mission, Nisus reveals that he is outside of the heroic code, especially as we see it in the *Iliad*, where material rewards are a necessary complement to the fame of a particularly impressive deed. Nisus's desire to transfer the rewards to Euryalus may to some extent imply an idealistic view of his young friend as an integral part of himself, but his desire for exclusive possession of the glory suggests a passion that overrides all else.

The problematic implications of their close relationship can be seen in the response of the younger man to his friend. Euryalus quickly reveals a thirst for glory, but is much less restrained: "obstipuit magno laudum percussus amore" (197), "he marveled, struck with the love of glory." Vergil uses strong language to convey the intensity of the youth's response: *obstipesco* denotes a state of being struck senseless with astonishment, and *percutio* implies a violent blow. Speaking in a highly rhetorical style, Euryalus betrays his excessive reaction: "'est hic, est animus lucis contemptor et istum / qui vita bene credat emi, quo tendis, honorem'" (205–6), "'here, here is a soul that scorns the light and believes that the fame which you seek is well earned at the expense of life.'" There is an element of pretentiousness in the exaggerated effect of the anadiplosis with "est," in the strong connotation of "contemptor," and in the metaphorical use of *lux* for *vita*; his reference to "'*magnanimum* Aenean et fata *extrema*'" (204, emphases mine) reinforces the impression of a

---

[45]See Duckworth (above, note 34), 131; and A. J. Boyle, "The Meaning of the *Aeneid*: A Critical Inquiry, Part II," *Ramus* 1 (1972), 113–51.

character who, perhaps because of his young age as well as his attachment to his companion, responds excessively, first on the verbal level and later in his uncontrolled slaughter and pillage.

During the mission itself, Nisus again reflects a complex entanglement of private desire with glory. On his escape from the Rutulian force, he discovers that his friend has been apprehended and ponders the right course to follow:

> quid faciat? qua vi iuvenem, quibus audeat armis
> eripere? an sese medios moriturus in enses
> inferat et pulchram properet per vulnera mortem? (399–401)

What should he do? By what force, by what weapons should he dare to rescue the youth? Or should he, ready to die, plunge into the midst of the enemy and seek a glorious death through battle wounds?

The word *pulcher* can mean "glorious" or "illustrious."[46] But the glory that Nisus might win by dying for his friend would not be proper social glory. He confuses the public sphere ("into the midst of the enemy," "battle wounds") with a private act (self-sacrifice on behalf of his friend if he cannot save him).

The last clause of Nisus's inner debate significantly echoes a passage in the fourth *Georgic*, where Vergil describes the total dedication of the bees to the welfare of the community. As a metaphor for a political unit, the bees show their collective orientation by their constant efforts for their leader. They honor him in peace and risk their lives for him in battle: "et saepe attollunt umeris et corpora bello / obiectant pulchramque petunt per vulnera mortem" (217–18), "and often they bear him on their shoulders and thrust their bodies into battle and seek a glorious death through battle wounds." The poet implies that for their total devotion to their community, the bees receive a kind of communal glory for death on behalf of

---

[46] *The Oxford Latin Dictionary*, ed. P. G. W. Glare (Oxford: Clarendon Press, 1982), gives a second meaning of *pulcher* as "splendid in respect of fame or distinction, illustrious." The context and Nisus's general thirst for glory seem to support this connotation over the more general "fair" or "noble."

their king.[47] The Romans certainly believed that a man who died fighting on behalf of his country achieved a particularly noble glory.[48] Vergil's character, however, does not truly devote himself to his leader and the Trojan community; his "beautiful death" is motivated by a great personal love for his friend. At this point, Nisus has totally lost sight of his public mission, since he could have continued on his journey to Aeneas but instead chooses to try to save his friend or to die "gloriously." At this extreme moment of crisis, Nisus still thinks essentially of his own glory. Vergil perhaps wishes the reader to see that his act is a perversion of the *Georgics* passage and the underlying Roman ethic because it is not really selfless and certainly not oriented toward the common good. It is equally far from the ethos of the relationship of Achilles and Patroclus in the *Iliad*, for after his friend's fall on the battlefield the greatest of heroes is not primarily concerned with his own *kleos*. Instead, no longer acting like a mortal, he is intent on avenging Patroclus's death and seeing him honored with a hero's funeral.

Another disturbing form of *cupido* is an excessive interest in material wealth. In the interview of the two young men with the Trojan leaders, Vergil seems deliberately to reverse Euripides' skepticism, for in contrast to the Greek chorus that refers to the lack of noble men in times of crisis, Aletes here praises the willing enthusiasm of the Trojan youth.[49] Concerned with the proper rewards for such service, the elder statesman assures them that they will be repaid not only by divine approval and personal satisfaction but also by the tangible generosity of Aeneas and Ascanius: "'What worthy rewards do I think can be paid to you, men, in return for such noble deeds? The gods and your own characters will reward you very well: then pious Aeneas will quickly provide other things and the youth Ascanius will never be forgetful of such great service'" (252–56). If Aletes is optimistic and even somewhat hyperbolic in this speech, Ascanius's response is far more extreme. He enumerates a

---

[47]For the limitations of the life of the bees, see Michael C. J. Putnam, *Virgil's Poem of the Earth: Studies in the* Georgics (Princeton: Princeton University Press, 1979), esp. pp. 254–69; and Miles (above, note 1), pp. 248–50, for Vergil's connection of the bees with monarchy, which the Romans traditionally loathed.

[48]See Earl (above, note 15), p. 32, for a very good discussion of Roman views on *gloria* in general and the appropriation of this concept by the aristocracy.

[49]See Fenik (above, note 37), p. 165.

list of very valuable objects, some belonging to his father "'cups, which my father took when he captured Arisba'" (264), "'an ancient bowl which Sidonian Dido gave'" (266), and others not even in the Trojans' possession (e.g., Turnus's horse, captive women). The expected parallel to Nestor's practical offer of sheep to the Greek volunteer does not occur here. Although scholars often note that this lavish offer of gifts reflects Ascanius's youthful enthusiasm, the poet may expect the reader to perceive a more somber note beneath the humorous depiction of character. It is particularly appropriate that Dido should be evoked here in the mention of a precious antique bowl that she had once given Aeneas. The allusion recalls her fabulous wealth, which Vergil seems to consider a major weakness in the ethic of that character. The extravagant promise of costly objects perhaps only reinforces the vainglory of the two, as it encourages the materialistic desires that lead Euryalus to the disastrous events later in the episode.

Vergil's earlier association of their close personal bond with greed in book 5 questioned the ethical implications of their behavior. In the footrace, the older youth suddenly falls and trips his opponent so that his younger friend can come in first and take the prize. The poet implies that his erotic feelings motivate Nisus's act: "Nevertheless, he was not forgetful of Euryalus, his love, for getting up through the mud, he intruded himself in Salius's way" (334–35). Homer's description of Oilean Aias (23.774–77) provides the model for Nisus's fall into the dung, but the *Iliad* passage offers no counterpart for the fallen man fouling his competitor. By Vergil's time, the racetrack seems to have provided a standard metaphor for competitive activity in life.[50] The poet here may intend this example of the race symbolically, for it foreshadows the unfortunate behavior in the night raid, where Euryalus seizes the valuable war gear from the

---

[50]Cicero, *De Officiis* 3.42, ed. and tr. Walter Miller (1913; rpt. London: Heinemann, 1961), quotes Chrysippus's use of this analogy: "'When a man enters the foot-race,' says Chrysippus with his usual aptness, 'it is his duty to put forth all his strength and strive with all his might to win; but he ought never with his foot to trip, or with his hand to foul a competitor. Thus in the stadium of life, it is not unfair for anyone to seek to obtain what is needful for his own advantage, but he has no right to wrest it from his neighbour.'" The Roman writer seems to assume a familiarity with the Greek philosopher's work and weaves the racetrack image easily into his own discussion of proper ethical conduct.

slain Rutulians: Rhamnes' *phalerae*, or decorative breast ornaments, and sword belt with golden studs (359–60), and Messapus's impressive helmet (365).

The acquisitive tendency of these two young men is a disturbing element beneath the humorous surface. Euryalus is determined to keep first prize, over objections from the unfairly defeated Salius, by a display of emotion and the appeal of his good looks: "Popular opinion favors Euryalus with his winning tears, as well as his more appealing spirit displayed in a comely body" (343–44). Nisus too asserts himself and requests a prize when Aeneas has decided to reward Salius more handsomely: "'If the defeated have such great rewards and you pity the fallen, what worthy gifts will you give to Nisus who deserved the wreath for first place with honor, had not hostile fortune interfered, as with Salius?'" (353–56). Thus, despite the playfulness of the scene, Vergil suggests the problematic entanglement of *amor* and *virtus*. Nisus's affection for the handsome Euryalus is intensely erotic and somewhat narcissistic: it leads him not only to identify with his friend's cause in the race but also, by manipulating events, to enjoy vicariously the personal glory that has slipped out of his grasp. Furthermore, the materialistic drive of these two young men results in the abandonment of ethical conduct.

The core of this episode, the attack on the sleeping Rutulians, involves another form of *cupido*, bloodlust, which is a perversion of *virtus*. Vergil's adaptation of material from both the Doloneia and the *Rhesus* conveys the irrational nature of the warriors' actions. Here, Nisus in his rampage beheads Remus after killing the man's attendants:

> tum caput ipsi aufert domino truncumque relinquit
> sanguine singultantem; atro tepefacta cruore
> terra torique madent. (332–34)

Then he cut off the head of the master himself and left the trunk gurgling with blood; the earth and the beds were soaked and made warm with dark blood.

The parallel passage in Homer states that an ugly sound arose as men were stabbed and that the earth grew red with blood:

Pitiful cries arose as the men were struck with the sword, and the earth grew red with blood. (10.483–84)

Fenik notes that the word *singultantem* seems to translate Euripides' use of *muchthismos*, by which the charioteer describes the death of Rhesus and the Thracians (789–91); both are employed in unusual contexts and have connotations of gasping and of pity.[51] But by bringing the horror of the event to the surface, Vergil even surpasses Euripides. Commentators have called attention to the harsh alliterative sounds, especially the sibilants in the phrase "sanguine singultantem." If this phrase is in bad taste,[52] the hard, strident sounds do suggest the spurt of gushing blood and the general ugliness of the scene. Furthermore, the loss of a caesura anticipated in the third foot through the elision of "singultantem" and "atro" reinforces the sense of a rapid flow of blood. Thus, more so than Homer, Vergil injects a powerful effect of revulsion into this scene.

The poet shows that this bloodlust is a passion that verges on madness. Here, he adapts an extended simile that echoes the Doloneia:

> impastus ceu plena leo per ovilia turbans
> (suadet enim vesana fames) manditque trahitque
> molle pecus mutumque metu, fremit ore cruento. (339–41)

Just as an unfed lion ranging through crowded sheep pens—for mad hunger drives him on—both gouges and drags the tender flock mute with fear; he rages with bloody mouth.

Homer's simile describes Diomedes swiftly and skillfully dispatching the enemy:

as a lion coming upon untended herds, sheep or goats, attacks them with an evil purpose. (10.485–86)

[51]Fenik (above, note 37), shows that while *muchthizdo* refers to a forced passage of air through the nostrils, other related words are used by Homer to convey grief. He suggests that Vergil recognized this second possible connotation and hit upon the word *singulto* to reproduce the two effects of Euripides' word.

[52]See Vergil, *The Aeneid of Virgil*, books 7–12, ed. with commentary T. E. Page (1900; rpt. London: Macmillan, 1967), p. 272.

This traditional epic analogue vividly describes heroic activity. While seeming to follow his model closely, Vergil makes some important changes: the notion of madness in the lion's hunger ("vesana fames"), the detail of the animal's bloody mouth, and the state of mind of the victimized flock, helpless in its terror. The poet here distances himself from the agent and empathizes with the victims. Even more significantly, he blurs the clarity of Homer's simile (which refers only to Diomedes) by failing to apply the comparison definitely to either character. Since it concludes the picture of Nisus at his deadly work, one naturally expects the simile to refer to him. However, the phrase that follows, "nec minor Euryali caedes," seems to supply the referent. Commentators and translators are uncertain as to whether the simile applies to Nisus or to Euryalus. But this syntactical ambiguity suggests that mad rage is transferred with unfortunate ease from one individual to another.

When Euryalus participates in the slaughter, one can perceive the impact of the older youth upon his young friend, who becomes even less restrained. The influence of Euripides can be noted in Vergil's description of the death of Rhoetus, for the charioteer in the *Rhesus* similarly awakes from sleep to find his king dead.[53] Here Vergil shows Rhoetus conscious of the attack:

> Fadumque Herbesumque subit Rhoetumque Abarimque
> Ignaros; Rhoetum vigilantem et cuncta videntem,
> sed magnum metuens se post cratera tegebat.
> pectore in adverso totum cui comminus ensem
> condidit adsurgenti et multa morte recepit.
> purpuream vomit ille animam et cum sanguine mixta
> vina refert moriens, hic furto fervidus instat. (344–50)

He came upon Fadus and Herbesus and Rhoetus and Abaris, who were unaware; Rhoetus was awake and saw everything but, terrified, hid behind a large bowl. Euryalus plunged his sword all the way through his chest as he was getting up and withdrew it all bloodied. The one spits up his red lifeblood and, as he dies, pours out wine mixed with blood. The other presses on eagerly with his stealthy work.

[53]See Fenik (above, note 37), pp. 72–73.

Unusual grammatical constructions and stylistic elements in this passage convey a sense of madness. In the first line, the double pair passage convey a sense of madness. In the first line, the double pair together the two members of each pair reproduce the blurred impression of a rapid, indiscriminate slaughter. After creating a striking enjambment with the word "ignaros" in the next line, Vergil immediately proceeds to qualify his statement with the words "Rhoetum vigilantem." With a bold anacoluthon, the poet retains the accusative case when he repeats Rhoetus's name (presumably to be the object of another verb), but in the next line makes Rhoetus become the implied subject of a finite verb. Page explains the difficult phrase "multa morte recepit": after burying the sword to the hilt in Rhoetus's body, Euryalus withdrew it full of blood.[54] The unusual expression "purpuream animam" may have an analogue in the Homeric *porphureos thanatos*, but Vergil brings Homer's abstraction to the level of the concrete, a disgusting combination of red wine and lifeblood. The whole passage has a nightmarish aura. Again Vergil goes beyond Euripides. Whereas the charioteer in the *Rhesus* recalls his confused sleep-state from the clarity of consciousness, the poet here describes the scene as though it were taking place in a dream. The younger man tries to emulate his friend but becomes only a grotesque parody of the noble warrior as he is driven by passionate bloodlust.

Vergil connects the bloodlust in this passage with another example of *cupido*, the rapacious grasp of plunder. The phrase "nimia caede atque cupidine" (354), which appears to be a poetic expression for "an excessive desire for killing," actually unites the lust for slaughter and for possessions. By elaborating on the belt that the younger man strips from Rhamnes, Vergil adapts a description of war gear from the Doloneia. In *Iliad* 10, Meriones gives Odysseus a helmet that had been stolen by the thievish Autolycus, who gave it as a gift to his guest Molos, who then gave it to his son Meriones. The predatory instinct of Odysseus, although potentially antisocial and self-aggrandizing, is channeled into actions for a communal enterprise.[55] A reflection of the realistic ethics of the *Iliad*, the

[54]See Page (above, note 52), pp. 272–73.

[55]Jenny S. Clay, *The Wrath of Athena: Gods and Men in the* Odyssey (Princeton: Princeton University Press, 1983), esp. pp. 69–74, discusses the social nature of Odysseus in the *Iliad* in the context of his ambiguous character in the *Odyssey*.

helmet has thus come full circle from the arch-thief who stole it to his grandson, another thief about to plunder successfully.

In Vergil's text, however, the belt has a different history. Originally given to Remulus by Caedicus, a man whose name calls to mind the verb *caedo* (to kill), the belt is closely linked with death. For the dying Remulus gave it to his grandson, who never got to keep it since he was stripped of it in war by the Rutulians ("post mortem bello Rutuli pugnaque potiti," 363).[56] Euryalus now fits into the cycle: excessively concerned with glory and war prizes, he has killed mindlessly and will soon forfeit his own life. Unlike the helmet in *Iliad* 10, the belt symbolizes a proliferation of violence passing from one generation to another. The original recipient of the belt, Remulus, may furthermore recall the founders of the Roman state, Romulus and Remus, whose struggle for power ended in the violence that marked the beginning of Rome. Vergil has thus transformed a Homeric symbol of the ambivalence of martial ethics by changing the focus to a deeper questioning of the possibility of heroism corrupted by *cupido*, man's urge for slaughter and lucre.

Vergil's description of Euryalus's death unites the erotic with the bloodlust that ends in the youth's own demise. Here Vergil compares the dying warrior to a fading flower:

> purpureus veluti cum flos succisus aratro
> languescit moriens, lassove papavera collo
> demisere caput pluvia cum forte gravantur. (435–37)

just as when a purple flower cut by a plow languishes in death, or as poppies cast down their heads with weary necks when the rains by chance weigh them down.

The second half is modeled on a passage in the *Iliad* describing the death of a young warrior named Gorgythion:

as a poppy, which has been weighed down in a garden by fruit or by the spring winds, thrusts its head to one side. (8.306–7)

[56]*Servii Grammatici Qui Feruntur in Vergilii Carmina Commentarii*, vol. 2, eds. G. Thilo and H. Hagen (Hildesheim: Georg Olms, 1961), ad loc., state that this is one of the twelve unsolvable passages in the *Aeneid* because of the ambiguous phrase "post mortem."

While Homer emphasizes the vulnerability of the youthful warrior on the battlefield, Vergil emphasizes the casualness of this event by adding the word "forte," and he further lessens the lofty epic tone by describing the flower's neck as "weary" ("lasso").[57] The first half adds an erotic suggestiveness by echoing Catullus 11, the poet's bitter farewell to his treacherous mistress Lesbia. There, the poet compares himself to a mere common plant at the edge of a meadow and his mistress to a mechanical plow mowing down anything in its path. The erotic image traditionally used for a young girl's loss of virginity has now been applied to the speaker's emotional and psychological debilitation through a woman's brutal insensitivity. Catullus's vision of an exaggerated reversal of traditional male and female roles, of *mores* totally perverted, could hardly contrast more with Homer's depiction of the heroic ethic on the battlefield. As W. R. Johnson observes, Vergil's union of the epic and lyric seems oddly mannered and produces an almost oxymoronic effect; in the tension between the two, Homer's emphasis on the nobility of the warrior's death gives way.[58] The literary background of this simile in the *Aeneid* allusively summons a context of intense passion, hinting not only at the bloodlust but also at the erotic nature of Nisus's and Euryalus's relationship. Furthermore, the word *purpureus* recalls the phrase "purpuream animam," which rather grotesquely described the death of Rhoetus. The realistic description of bloodlust is transformed into a pathetic image of the young man himself in death, as it would later with another eager youth, Pallas, who impulsively dared to engage in combat with the far superior warrior Turnus (11.68–69).[59]

Cupido even insinuates itself into the core virtue *pietas*, which assumes a highly ambivalent status in this episode. Before exploring

---

[57]Furthermore, Bertil Axelson, *Unpoetische Wörter: Ein Beitrag zur Kenntnis der lateinischen Dichtersprache* (Lund: H. Ohlsson, 1945), pp. 29–30, observes that *lassus* is a prosaic word, while *fessus* is poetic.

[58]Johnson (above, note 30), pp. 61–66, has an excellent discussion of the deaths of Nisus and Euryalus in the context of "dissolving pathos"; he compares this simile to its Homeric and Catullan predecessors and shows in subtle detail the difference between Vergil's mimesis here and Homer's in the descriptions of Gorgythion and Euphorbus in the *Iliad*.

[59]On the irony of this simile in relation to its traditional use as an image of the young woman's loss of virginity (and potential for procreation), see Gillis (above, note 2), p. 77.

the subtle connections between the warriors' *amor* and *pietas*, we will consider the sources in the *Iliad* that the poet adapted. Whereas in the *Rhesus* there are no examples of *eusebeia* toward the gods, in the Doloneia Odysseus and Diomedes initially invoke Athena at the outset of their night raid. Both offer prayers that are typical of the heroic society depicted within the poem and of their own individual characters. Odysseus recognizes the help that the goddess constantly gives in his "hard tasks": "'Hear me, oh offspring of aegis-bearing Zeus, and stand by me always in all my labors'" (10.278–79). Diomedes recalls Athena's support of his father Tydeus, who accomplished "baneful deeds" on return from a mission to Thebes; he vows a gift of a heifer for the goddess's continued support in this crisis: "'But coming back he planned very baneful deeds, with your help, divine goddess, since you stood by him in your forethought. So now willingly stand by me and guard me, I will then offer to you a broad-fronted heifer'" (10.289–92).

Homer adds a narrative comment indicating Athena's favorable response to these two Greeks, the one famed for strategy and the other for prowess: "As they spoke in prayer, Pallas Athena heard them" (10.295). By emphasizing their characters and the long history of Athena's support for them, Homer shows that Odysseus's and Diomedes's *eusebeia* is a reflection of their own behavior. Significantly, Odysseus invokes Athena a second time with a dedication of the spoils stripped from Dolon's body: "'Rejoice in these things, goddess, for we will reward you, first of all gods on Olympus. But once again lead us to the horses and the beds of the Thracians'" (10.462–64). Here too, their devotion to the goddess reflects their well-reasoned actions, since through cunning they have elicited vital information from Dolon about Rhesus and the Thracians. Afterwards, they find the Thracians and sensibly divide the task of overcoming the enemy: Diomedes slays the men and Odysseus drags away their corpses so that the horses may pass through unfrightened (10.488–93). Athena's warning for them to leave further reinforces the two men's sensible behavior.

In the *Aeneid*, Nisus calls upon a different goddess, Diana, for help: "'Be present and help me in my labor, oh goddess, ornament of the stars and Latonian guardian of the groves. If my father Hyrtacus ever bore gifts to your altars on my behalf, if I myself have honored you by my hunting or have hung trophies on your ceiling or affixed them to the temple walls, allow me now to confound this troop and guide my weapons through the air'" (404–9). Here he echoes Diomedes' prayer to Athena that refers to her protection of his father and Odysseus's second prayer that asks to find the camp of the Thracians. Yet, as he invokes the goddess only at this moment of crisis and not at the outset of his mission or at a point of preliminary success, Nisus shows himself to be unlike his Greek counterparts. The deity who presides over the woodlands is, of course, the appropriate object of worship for a hunter such as Nisus. Yet the hunters who are Diana's devotees in literature are most often virginal characters, hostile to sexual activity.[60] Nisus's connection with the austere virgin goddess is ambivalent. Dido is associated with the same goddess in book 1: the Diana simile hints at her complex relation to both public labor and erotic passion. Emotional entanglement connects Nisus and Euryalus to the passionate queen more than to their Homeric counterparts. Nisus's intense feelings surface unrestrained at this critical point. Although Diana does seem to help Nisus guide his shafts at the enemy, as the moon she also shines on Euryalus and reveals his presence to the Rutulians.[61] Unlike Athena with Odysseus and Diomedes, Diana both aids and betrays Nisus and Euryalus; she is as inconsistent with them as they themselves are in their irrational behavior.

In the first appearance of Nisus and Euryalus in the poem, Vergil suggests a paradoxical union of eros and piety. He terms their relationship a "pius amor" (5.296). This phrase captures the tension between social and private, the responsiveness of the two characters to the expectations of their leaders on the one hand and their own intensely personal relationship on the other. *Pietas*, of course, relates to social behavior, the fulfillment of obligations owed to the family, the state, and the gods. The reference to *pietas* here may even suggest that Nisus has assumed a kind of paternal responsibility for his younger friend that would thus imply the familial level of that Roman virtue. But *amor* in Vergil and other Latin writers most frequently

[60]For the associations of the hunt with a hostility to sexual activity as used in Ovid's *Metamorphoses*, see Gregson Davis, *The Death of Procris: "Amor" and the Hunt in Ovid's* Metamorphoses (Rome: Ateneo, 1983).
[61]See Lee (above, note 32), pp. 111–12.

connotes an obsessive passion.[62] The essentially private nature of *amor* is likely to interfere with the publicly oriented demands of *pietas*. W. W. Fowler's definition of *pietas* suggests its incompatibility with private emotions: "That sense of duty to family, State, and gods, which rises, in spite of trial and danger, superior to the enticements of individual passion and selfish ease."[63] Yet Vergil shows throughout the Nisus and Euryalus episode that social values are vulnerable to the incursions of such private desires. The passionate nature of Nisus's feelings for Euryalus surfaces not only when he chooses to return to find his friend and abandons his public mission but even more dramatically when he performs his final, violent actions: he lunges at Volcens and drives his sword into the man's face and then, dying, thrusts himself ("sese proiecit," 444) upon the body of his friend. The erotic implications of this act recall Dido's impassioned suicide. While familial love, especially for father and son, motivates Aeneas in his political mission, he too falls victim to this private emotion. His impulsive return to Troy for Creusa was a dangerous act which could have ended in his death and in catastrophe for the surviving Trojans. The hero's irrationality in that scene, symbolized by his labyrinthine path, has a parallel in Nisus's return for Euryalus.[64] With the example of these two young men, the poet shows the irrational, self-destructive side of *amor*.

The intrusion of the private into the social is at issue in Euryalus's conversation with Ascanius in which he requests aid for his mother in case of disaster. Moved by the young man's avowed concern for his mother, whom he has not told of his plans, Ascanius immediately thinks of filial piety: "And the image of filial piety grazed his mind" (294). Readers have frequently been impressed by the intensity of Ascanius's response to Euryalus. The very strength of his reaction

---

[62]See, for example, Archibald W. Allen, "Elegy and the Classical Attitude toward Love: Propertius 1.1," *YClS* 11 (1950), esp. 259–64; more recently, David Konstan, "Two Kinds of Love in Catullus," *CJ* 68 (1972), esp. 102–3. P. A. Brunt, "*Amicitia* in the Late Roman Republic," *Proceedings of the Cambridge Philosophical Society* 11 (1965), 1–20, has a good general discussion of the wide range of amicable relations possible in the Roman term *amicitia*.

[63]William W. Fowler, *The Religious Experience of the Roman People from the Earliest Times to the Age of Augustus* (London: Macmillan, 1911), p. 416.

[64]The intricate word placement in the passage 2.752–71 in itself mimicks a labyrinthine structure that suggests the hero's agonized quest for his wife.

encourages us to consider the context more closely. Euryalus claims that he leaves his mother without farewell because he cannot endure her tears. He reveals his anxiety by immediately justifying himself with an oath: "'May the night and your right hand be witness that I am unable to bear the tears of my parent'" (288–89).

While Euryalus suggests only that he would rather avoid a female display of emotion, Nisus earlier pointed to the obligations that the youth owed his mother. In trying to dissuade his friend from joining the expedition, he reminds Euryalus about the possibility of disastrous consequences to his mother, who did not stay behind with the other women in Sicily but continued on with the Trojans out of love for her son. As a point of filial obligation, Nisus intimates the need to consider the mother's feelings ("'May I not be a cause of such great grief to your unhappy mother,'" 216) and to remember her sacrifices on behalf of her son ("'who alone of many mothers, child, boldly followed and was not interested in the walls of great Acestes,'" 217–18). By asking Ascanius to comfort his mother, Euryalus shows that he must reject Nisus's sensitive consideration, for he cannot face his responsibility. In this light, Ascanius' immediate thought of *pietas* needs to be qualified. Although Euryalus is doubtless concerned about his mother, he fails to consider fully his familial obligations, the *pietas* that he owes under very special circumstances.

A socially vulnerable character, Euryalus's mother has the final word on piety in this episode. Interestingly, Vergil calls her only *mater Euryali*, as if to point up her social role in a genre that, because of its martial emphasis, tends to underplay the question of familial responsibility concerning the female.[65] Her lament has been justly admired for its pathos by critics from Servius onward.[66] Distinctive in style and substance, it contains echoes of Andromache's and Hecuba's laments for Hector in the *Iliad* and Electra's lament for

[65]See, however, the farewell of Jason and his mother in *Argonautica* 1 (267–305): Alcimede is an impediment to Jason as hero, and her speech, which rings with pathos, concentrates on her personal disaster of his departure. Henry (above, note 21), vol. 3, ad loc., notes (but does not elaborate) that this speech must have influenced the lament of Euryalus's mother.

[66]Servius (above, note 56), ad loc., observes that this passage fulfills all of Cicero's requirements for effectively arousing pity.

Orestes in Sophocles' play.[67] But its most important structural source is Euripides' *Rhesus*, for at the end of the play the Muse appears with the corpse of her young warrior-son and speaks of her grief to the Trojans. Like Euryalus's mother, she has lost her only child, who she acknowledges was impetuous and over-confident: "'having set out to ill-starred and wretched Troy forcefully, although I had reproached and your father had entreated you'" (899–901). She mentions several points that have intensified her grief: the trauma of conception when she was raped by the river god Strymon; her foreknowledge of her son's probable death at Troy; and her feeling of betrayal by Athena on whose city Athens she has bestowed her musical gifts. Her response is now one of bitterness: "'And as my reward for these things, I lament, holding my son in my arms'" (948–49). While reproaching the Greek goddess, she asserts that Athena will not be able to save Achilles, for whom Apollo already prepares his arrows (978–79). Her speech thus serves as a counterpoint to the prevailing male values that glorify war and heroism.

In her own bitter lament for the death of her only child, Euryalus's mother requests *pietas* from an unexpected source. She hopes that through some gesture of *pietas* she will find death at the hands of the Rutulians: "'Strike me, if there is any piety, thrust all your swords into me, oh Rutulians; annihiliate me first with the sword'" (493–94). On one level, this woman may use the "unclassical" meaning of *pietas* as "pity."[68] Given the prominent references to *pietas* in the Nisus and Euryalus episode, the poet would seem to ask the reader to think about the full significance of the word.[69] It is

---

[67]Gilbert Highet, *The Speeches in Vergil's* Aeneid (Princeton: Princeton University Press, 1972), pp. 153–55, thinks that this speech is much less restrained than its models yet not incoherent: it is almost a consolation in reverse, whereby "the bereaved mother reproaches her dead son."

[68]See W. R. Johnson, "Aeneas and the Ironies of *Pietas*," *CJ* 60 (1965), 360.

[69]The relation of *pietas* to humane conduct has long been debated in studies of Vergil. Pierre Fécherolle, "La *Pietas* dans l'*Enéide*," *Les Etudes Classiques* 2 (1933), 167–81, connects Vergil's use of *pietas* both to justice and to *douceur*, humane behavior. Camps (above, note 27), pp. 24–25, observes that an important example of Aeneas's *pietas*, burial rites, implies duty joined with human feeling. Johnson (above, note 68), 360–64, interestingly discusses ways by which Vergil creates a "tragic dialectic" by adding the connotation "compassion" to the primary notion of "duty." J. F. Burgess, "*Pietas* in Virgil and Statius," *Proceedings of the Virgil Society* 11

couched in a context in which Euryalus's mother criticizes her son's behavior and implies his failure of responsibility. Calling him *crudelis*, she asserts that he was supposed to be the consolation of her old age (481–82); that in such dangerous circumstances he should have spoken with her before leaving ("'nor did you give your wretched mother the opportunity to speak a last time with you before you went off on such a dangerous mission,'" 483–84); and that his rash act has now denied her even the consoling ritual acts of washing his corpse and closing his eyes (486–89). She simply but effectively expresses her sense of total isolation: "'quo sequar?'" (490). When she pleads for death at the hands of the Rutulians or by a thunderbolt of Jupiter, her mention of *pietas* makes the self-interest of her son's actions more powerfully felt.

The poet dramatically represents the danger of private passions bound up with the public interest through the effects of this failed expedition on both family and the larger society. Euripides shows the devastating emotional effect of Rhesus' death on his mother, but Vergil reveals that Euryalus's mother is also socially helpless in a way that could not apply to the divine Muse. Furthermore, the morale of the Trojans sinks abysmally both at the gruesome sight of the impaled heads of the two young men and at the piercing lament of Euryalus's mother: "Their spirits were shattered by this lament, and a sad groan spread through the crowd. Their strength was broken and made them useless for battle" (498–99). Nisus and Euryalus have thus impeded rather than helped the public cause. Both familial and civic *pietas* have been totally unfulfilled. As with Aeneas when he avenges the death of Pallas, the multiple conflicts of piety to country, gods, and family make it difficult to sustain this virtue in its entirety. But in this case the three levels of piety themselves are so intertwined and confused with self-interest that even the limited progress of the principal hero fails to materialize.

In complex ways, Vergil drew the erotic into his epic to question the nature of the values that defined his society. The allusions to epic

---

(1971–72), 48–61, restates the more traditional view of *pietas* as the fulfillment of obligations to family, country, and gods and rejects the additional connotation of "compassion." But, as the context in *Aeneid* 9 seems to imply, duty and humane feeling are sometimes inseparable.

and tragedy not only emphasize the incompatibility of eros and heroism but, more insidiously, reveal the encroachment of private desire upon social values. In the Dido episode, the Homeric analogue of Nausikaa serves to highlight the heroic side of Vergil's queen and her resistance, as well as her vulnerability, to love. The adaptations of the primary epic sources in Homer, Apollonius, and Catullus stress the paradoxical nature of this character. The poet shows that her admirable *virtus* is undermined by her troubled sexuality, repressed until Aeneas's arrival, when her capacity for deep feeling as well as for violent, irrational behavior surfaces. Epic allusions also provide a contrast with Dido's materialistic ethic, which Vergil finds ultimately ruinous. The tragic echoes even more problematically suggest the less positive aspect of her vow to Sychaeus, her own glory. While certainly paying tribute to the nobility of this character, Vergil reveals that her fidelity to her dead husband, so closely bound up with her concern for her reputation, is in part a narcissistic obsession. If Dido exemplifies the ambivalence of fidelity, her interchange with Aeneas exposes problems in the hero's own connection to both *fides* and *pietas*, for the poet to some extent validates Dido's censure of Aeneas's behavior at Carthage.

The Dido episode questions the integrity of public values, but the Nisus and Euryalus episode explores the wider significance of *cupido* in relation to the core values of the world of this poem. By playing his epic and tragic models against each other, Vergil dramatizes the inconsistencies within *gloria*, *virtus*, and *pietas*. The desire for glory that motivates *virtus* is particularly problematic. Allusions to Euripides' play as well as to the Doloneia show passion for glory bound up with an excessive personal desire for gain. Vergil amplifies the troubling nature of this emphasis on personal glory by showing that it is all too easily transferred to the younger warrior, who cannot control his instincts on the battleground of the night raid. In addition, Nisus's apparently noble effort to rescue Euryalus (much like his earlier action on behalf of the youth in the footrace) is intertwined with his own desire for glory.

The poet subjects *virtus* to scrutiny by associating *cupido* with erotic desire, bloodlust, and passion for gain. By adapting the Doloneia and the *Rhesus*, he reveals the madness of the men's bloodlust, *virtus* perverted. His re-creation of elements in Euripides' play to describe Nisus's murder of Remus and his attendants and Euryalus's slaughter of Rhoetus renders their actions especially revolting in their lack of restraint. Similarly, by adding details to Homer's lion simile and also by failing to supply a definite referent, he implies the easy transferral of bloodlust from Nisus to Euryalus. The description of war gear, adapted from Homer's account of Odysseus's helmet, vividly exemplifies the materialistic side of the unrestrained *virtus* that leads to disastrous consequences. The *amor* that underlies their demise reveals another aspect of corrupted *virtus*. The odd union of a flower simile from Catullus's love poetry and a young warrior's fall from Homer's narrative appropriately depicts Euryalus's death. The passion of Nisus for his friend emerges even in his final act of *virtus*, killing Volcens and then falling on Euryalus's corpse, much like Dido's passionate suicide by falling on her former lover's sword.

The pivotal value in Roman culture, *pietas* is vulnerable to the same ambivalent intrusion of private interests. The allusions to the Doloneia reveal a strong contrast to the Homeric characters' *eusebeia*. Against the background of the two Greeks' invocations to Athena, the goddess of wisdom, Nisus's expression of piety to Diana hints disturbingly at his emotional entanglement with Euryalus and the confused, irrational behavior that the two have exhibited in this episode. As in the case of Dido, the symbolic relation to this divinity suggests the conflict of private emotions with the characters' public responsibilities. Vergil's adaptation of the lament of Euripides' Muse also reinforces the ambivalence of *pietas* on the familial level. Going beyond the pathos of the situation, the poet reveals the consequences of the son's disregard for his mother and then reveals the subsequent demoralization of the troops.

In his adaptation of literary models, Vergil does not produce an ironic anti-epic in the manner of his Hellenistic predecessor, Apollonius. The poet uses the erotic as a means of exposing his characters' problematic values and self-destructive tendencies to society, and by this very gesture implies a hope that the Romans can turn the unfortunate qualities of the past around and regenerate their nation. Having reflected upon the devastations of the civil wars that he had lived through for so long, Vergil projects an attitude toward warfare that is critical but not cynical. As readers have always perceived, there are levels of contemporary allegory in the *Aeneid*. The hero himself has often been identified with Augustus, but some critics would associate almost all the major and many of the minor characters with Vergil's contemporary political figures. It is not surprising, then, that Dido has been considered as a representation of Cleopatra and even Nisus and Euryalus as the consuls Hirtius and Pansa, who valiantly lost their lives in the battle at Mutina.[70] While limited, such interpretations have their validity, especially because they suggest that the losers in contemporary political history, such as Antony and Cleopatra, were not so monstrous as the ideology of the victors would have it. Vergil's exploration of the major Roman social values reflects deeply on the consequences of the prevailing ethic, which frequently leads to the chaos of war as individuals act out their entangled private and public motives. His contemporary readers presumably would have perceived the view that a sterility pervading all levels of life was the result.

Vergil's epilogue to the Nisus and Euryalus episode embodies this vision of potential sterility. The relationship of father and son so often pathetically foiled in this poem provides a particularly poignant image of this problem.[71] The poet's very strong break in the narrative of the Nisus and Euryalus episode, his apostrophe to the two fallen warriors, brings this point home:

> Fortunati ambo! si quid mea carmina possunt,
> nulla dies umquam memori vos eximet aevo,
> dum domus Aeneae Capitoli immobile saxum
> accolet imperiumque pater Romanus habebit. (446–49)

Happy pair! If my songs have any value, no day will ever blot you out of the memory of time, as long as the house of Aeneas rests on the solid rock of the Capitoline and a Roman father holds sway.

[70]For the identification of characters in the *Aeneid* with specific historical figures, see D. L. Drew, *The Allegory of the* Aeneid (Oxford: Blackwell, 1927); more recently, R. G. Tanner, "Some Problems in *Aeneid* 7–12," *Proceedings of the Virgil Society* 10 (1970–71), 37–44.

[71]On the pathos of the father-son relationship in the *Aeneid*, see Lee (above, note 32); and Elizabeth Block, "Failure to Thrive: The Theme of Parents and Children in the *Aeneid*, and Its Iliadic Models," *Ramus* 9 (1980), 128–49.

Although they do not achieve their glorious expectations within their own society, the two flawed young men do receive the fame that only the poet can provide. It is, however, a far more qualified reward than the *kleos* that the Homeric bard bestowed upon the heroes of his song. The family image suggested by the words "domus" and "pater," here applied to the state, is a subtle reminder that Nisus and Euryalus, like Dido, have died childless and have failed to regenerate the state through sons or productive lives.

CHAPTER 3

Ovid's Ariadne and
the Catullan Epyllion

A LTHOUGH VERGIL successfully re-created the Homeric
form in the *Aeneid,* most writers of the Augustan age
seem to have considered his accomplishment an anomaly.[1] The last
of the great poets of that period, Ovid, avoided the formal unity of
the Homeric model in the *Metamorphoses.* Instead, he weaves together numerous aetiological myths that are individually self-
sufficient and so radically alters the epic genre that his poem has
defied classification.[2] Ovid uses transformation as a metaphor for
the condition of individuals who variously remove themselves from
the human sphere, especially by violating the laws of family and
society.[3] One of the dominant causes of these dehumanizing states,

[1]For example, Horace, *Odes* 1.3, a farewell to Vergil, who is about to set off to
Greece, has been interpreted by modern critics as a symbolic statement expressing
surprise and awe at Vergil's ambitious venture into epic poetry. For a summary of
recent views, see Ronald Basto, "Horace's *Propempticon* to Vergil: A Re-
examination," *Vergilius* 28 (1982), 30–43. Similarly, Propertius at 2.34.65–66 calls
Vergil's poem in progress "something greater than the *Iliad,*" yet sets this extravagant praise in the context of his own defense of writing elegy.

[2]Kenneth Quinn, *Texts and Contexts: The Roman Writers and Their Audience* (London: Routledge and Kegan Paul, 1979), pp. 68–81, gives an overview of the difficul-
ties in classifying the *Metamorphoses.* While the poem has epic meter, length, and
organization into books, it is problematic in important ways: it frequently undercuts
the high epic style; the sophisticated narrative voice is often detached from his
material; and the didactic element is made ironic by the lack of a serious subject.
Quinn thus labels the poem as "ironic epic."

[3]Catherine C. Rhorer, "Red and White in Ovid's *Metamorphoses*: The Mulberry
Tree in the Tale of Pyramus and Thisbe," *Ramus* 9 (1980), 79–88, discusses the

erotic passion, figures far more prominently in the *Metamorphoses* than in any previous heroic poem in antiquity. Modern critics have made important advances in unraveling the complex strands of this subject in Ovid's work. Although too schematic, Brooks Otis's work provides a good starting point by outlining the scope of eros in the structure and thematics of this epic work.[4]

Before composing this very innovative narrative, Ovid experimented with epic material adapted to other forms. He even invented the genre of the epistolary poem, in which legendary or mythical women write to their absent lovers. The *Heroides* offers a wealth of occasions for exploring the tension between heroic and erotic interests, as the women voice their anger and despair at losing the object of desire, often to a social or political cause. In *Heroides* 10, Ovid recreated a popular character from heroic myth and literature, the abandoned Ariadne. He presents her in the act of writing a letter urging Theseus to return to the island where he has abandoned her. Like Ovid's other epistles, this poem ingeniously blends elegiac elements with epic material. W. S. Anderson has observed that the "antique 'heroic' setting keeps these elegies from being merely comic monologues. On the other hand, the many elegiac tactics which Ovid carried over from his *Amores*, his manifest wit and his patent display of ingenuity in the manipulation of Virgilian or Homeric nuances prevent the 'heroic' situation from effacing Ovid's characteristically sophisticated note."[5] As an example of a mixed genre

---

problems that result when individuals operate outside the bounds of social laws by examining in particular the story of Pyramus and Thisbe.

[4]Brooks Otis, *Ovid as an Epic Poet*, 2d ed. (Cambridge: Cambridge University Press, 1970) devotes an entire chapter to the pathetic story of Ceyx and Alcyone (pp. 231–77) and observes that Ovid altered the traditional tale of divine vengeance for impiety (as found, for instance, in Nicander) in order to explore the human problem of loss and grief.

[5]W. S. Anderson, "The 'Heroides,'" in *Ovid*, ed. J. W. Binns (London: Routledge and Kegan Paul, 1973), p. 67. This study focuses on an analysis of the Dido epistle as an example of the techniques that characterize the *Heroides* in general. Anderson shows the psychological paradoxes of this heroine, such as her adoration of Aeneas as a god in spite of her awareness of his insensitive behavior. Most interestingly, he discusses the many ironic references to the *Aeneid* as the major source for this poem. In general, he sees Ovid's Dido, who begins by comparing herself to a dying swan, as self-consciously attempting to dramatize her situation and play up her good points. Instead of exploiting epic or tragic values in the manner of Vergil's heroine,

counterpointing radically different types of literature, this poem
foreshadows the much more sophisticated incorporation of elegiac
elements into heroic poetry in the *Metamorphoses*.[6] The heroine of
the epistle had already been incorporated into epic by Catullus, who
narrated Ariadne's plight in his mini-epic on the marriage of Peleus
and Thetis, a poem that further advanced the Hellenistic effort to
assimilate the erotic into traditional heroic material. Frequent echoes
of poem 64 show that Ovid recalls his predecessor's version of
this myth.[7] Before considering how Ovid adapted his great predecessor's epic material, let us examine Catullus's use of this myth
in his own radical revision of the epic genre.

The Literary Background

Catullus 64 epitomizes the experimentation of Latin poets in the
late republic with the miniature epic, the so-called epyllion. This
form originated in the Hellenistic period, when the predominant
school of criticism advocated a shorter, highly polished narrative
over the conventional Homeric epic, and Theocritus made it a vehicle for the subtle analysis of human emotions in several of his *Idylls*.[8]
The Roman "neoteric" poets, who wanted to break with their own

---

she argues her case and hopes to have her love reciprocated. Anderson perceptively
observes Dido's link to Ovid's sophisticated Augustan world when she expresses
skepticism about the divine sanction of Aeneas's mission and reproaches him for
possibly leaving her pregnant.

[6]On Ovid's assimilation of elegy into epic, Peter E. Knox, *Ovid's* Metamorphoses
and the Traditions of Augustan Poetry, Cambridge Philological Society Supplement, vol. 11
(Cambridge: Cambridge University Press, 1986), pp. 9–26, discusses elegiac diction, metrical style, and themes such as the lover's pride, jealousy, and revenge,
which are conveyed through specific images, such as the flame and the hunt, and
through motifs such as the vigilant doorkeeper.

[7]See J. N. Anderson, *On the Sources of Ovid's Heroides 1, 3, 7, 10, 12* (Berlin:
Calvary, 1896), pp. 78–90.

[8]The term "epyllion" seems to have been coined in the nineteenth century to
describe a type of poetry that originated in the Hellenistic period at the hands of
Callimachus and Theocritus and was cultivated by Latin poets of the late republic
and early empire. See M. Marjorie Crump, *The Epyllion from Theocritus to Ovid*
(Oxford: Blackwell, 1931), pp. 50–53, on Theocritus's role in developing the
epyllion in his Hylas poem. Also Walter Allen, Jr., "The Epyllion. A Chapter in the
History of Literary Criticism," *TAPA* 71 (1940), 1–26.

literary tradition because it seemed too rough and unsophisticated, were attracted to the innovations of the Alexandrians. In general, they stressed the following characteristics in their use of the epyllion: a well-known story from myth as subject but with an unexpected focus on more mundane, less grand details; love as the major theme, which they treated subjectively through such devices as exclamations and apostrophes by the poet; a story within a story; and a refined style employing elegant figures of speech, such as anaphora and metonymy, and unusual or unexpected diction.[9]

The most brilliant of the "new poets," Catullus developed the subjective portrayal of character in poem 64. He tells the story of Ariadne abandoned by Theseus through an ekphrasis of the tapestry covering the marriage bed of the goddess Thetis and her mortal husband Peleus. While the thematic relationship between the two stories has been much debated by scholars, the marriage of Peleus and Thetis, structurally the principal subject, serves as a frame around the long inner narrative.[10] Although within the fiction of the

[9]For a convenient summary of the characteristics of the epyllion in Roman literature of the late republic, see C. J. Fordyce, *Catullus: A Commentary* (Oxford: Clarendon Press, 1961), pp. 272–75; Gordon Williams, *Tradition and Originality in Roman Poetry* (Oxford: Clarendon Press, 1968), pp. 242–43; and Kenneth Quinn (above, note 2), pp. 73–74.

[10]Many critics have tackled this difficult question in diverse ways. Leo C. Curran, "Catullus 64 and the Heroic Age," *YClS* 21 (1969), 171–92, discusses the apparent antithesis between past and present; he ultimately concludes that Catullus's attitude is ambivalent, reflecting a nostalgia for the heroic world but comprehending its illusory nature; Michael C. J. Putnam, "The Art of Catullus 64," *Harv. Stud.* 65 (1961), 165–205, finds an important unity in the allusions throughout the poem to the poet's own values and relationships as expressed in his personal lyrics and the Attis poem; T. E. Kinsey, "Irony and Structure in Catullus 64," *Latomus* 24 (1965), 911–31, sees the primary link between the two sections as the poet's refusal to take the heroic age seriously and his desire to ironically rework an old narrative for the amusement of his audience; D. P. Harmon, "Nostalgia for the Age of Heroes in Catullus 64," *Latomus* 32 (1973), 311–31, points out discrepancies in the various sections of the poem but finds that there is a significant moral difference between the heroic world of Peleus and Theseus and the poet's own at the end of the poem; Sherron E. Knopp, "Catullus 64 and the Conflict between *Amores* and *Virtutes*," *CPhil.* 71 (1976), 207–13, finds the unity in the "inherent antagonism" between love and heroism; thus the song of the Fates at the end provides a warning to the bridal couple, Peleus and Thetis, that they could turn out as another Theseus and Ariadne or as the Achilles and Polyxena to come; David Konstan, *Catullus' Indictment of Rome: The Meaning of Catullus 64* (Amsterdam: Hakkert, 1977), emphasizes the negative aspects of the heroic system throughout the poem, especially in the figures

poem Ariadne is simply a decorative figure on a static artifact, the poet brings her to life and makes her dominate the entire poem as well as the ekphrasis. Ariadne is an intensely erotic figure: in flashing back to her desertion of family and country, the poet describes the passionate feelings that led her to such a drastic act and throughout the ekphrasis symbolizes the awesome nature of her passion through metaphors of the sea and fire. Catullus thoroughly integrates this figure into the poem; she reflects his views on the hollowness of the heroic ethic that perverts fundamental social values, especially *fides* and *pietas*. Ariadne, moreover, has a complex relation to the persona of the poet as imaginatively rendered in his polymetric lyric and elegiac poems. Michael Putnam has persuasively argued that this woman figures Catullus's own turmoil and disillusionment as represented in the poems reflecting on his relations with his mistress Lesbia.[11]

The unusual structure in this ekphrasis highlights the new kind of heroic character that Catullus has created. The frequent shifts of time from one aspect of the story to another produce a fluidity that allows the poet to focus attention on Ariadne from several perspectives, externally and internally. The narrative begins with a tableau depicting the young woman alone on the shore and looking out to sea (52–75), then moves back to the circumstances of Theseus's arrival on Crete, Ariadne's sudden passion for the handsome hero, and her desertion of family and homeland for him (76–115). It then reverts to Ariadne on the shore (116–1), at which point the heroine

---

of Theseus in the ekphrasis and Achilles at the end; and Richard Jenkyns, *Three Classical Poets: Sappho, Catullus, and Juvenal* (Cambridge, Mass.: Harvard University Press, 1982), pp. 85–150, emphasizes the poet's desire to view the age of heroes nostalgically and views the Ariadne section, the depiction of a work of art, as the focal point of a total narrative that is "a succession of high points—pictures without a frame, as it were."

[11]Putnam (above, note 10) discusses the relation between Catullus and Ariadne in the theme of betrayal by a person wanting only sexual fulfillment, in the contrast between *pietas* and sexual passion, in the lover's false words, and in the loss of the *domus*. See also Douglas F. S. Thompson, "Aspects of Unity in Catullus 64," *CJ* 57 (1961), 49–57, who discusses an erotically charged reference to Theseus's feet as a parallel to Catullus's own mention of Lesbia's *candida pes* in poem 68 and connects Ariadne's loss of Theseus, who was to be a substitute family, to Catullus's loss of his own brother, a symbol of his *domus*; and Paul W. Harkins, "Autoallegory in Catullus 63 and 64," *TAPA* 90 (1959), 102–16.

herself takes over and laments her plight (132–201). After her curse on Theseus, the narrative shifts back to the grief of Aegeus at his son's departure and instructions about hoisting the white sail, which Jupiter now causes the young man to forget (202–48). In the final scene, the poet describes the arrival of the god Bacchus, who is about to rescue the young woman (249–64). Within this loose structure, Catullus creates a strong center with Ariadne voicing her feelings and encloses it within a kind of double frame, on the outside two scenes with the abandoned woman on the beach and on the inside family scenes from both Ariadne's and Theseus's past. The chronological shifts thus set the woman's despair and passion against the hero's callous betrayal. They also suggest another consequence of heroic activity, the loss of Ariadne's *domus* through Theseus's enterprise and the destruction of the hero's own *domus* as punishment by Aegeus's suicide upon his son's return.

Catullus invests the erotic with an epic dimension in part by imitating Apollonius's *Argonautica* at several points in the ekphrasis as well as in the main story of his epyllion. In the opening lines of the poem, which describe the amazement caused by the first sea voyage, the journey of the Argonauts, he echoes the major antecedents in epic and tragedy that describe this great event in the heroic sphere. Critics have recently observed that Catullus conflates allusions to Apollonius's epic, Euripides' *Medea*, and Ennius's version of the tragedy polemically, with an understanding of the subtle variations in the tradition.[12] Such references are appropriate to a poem whose subject is the marriage of Peleus, one of the principal heroes of the Argo, but they also serve to place the story of Jason and Medea in the background from the very beginning.

This allusiveness is particularly relevant to the story in the ekphrasis. After depicting the arrival of Theseus, the poet relates Ariadne's sudden interest in the hero with many echoes of Apollonius's account of Medea's involvement with Jason. The first mention of Ariadne's reaction to the newly arrived hero emphasizes

---

[12]Richard F. Thomas, "Catullus and the Polemics of Poetic Reference (Poem 64. 1–18)," *AJPhil.* 103 (1982), 144–64, discusses Catullus's acceptance of Callimachus's version of the origin of the Argo over that of Apollonius and Ennius and considers his position on the chronology of the expedition through conflation of allusions to his predecessors.

her desire: "Hunc simul ac cupido conspexit lumine virgo / Regia" (86–87), "as soon as the royal maiden saw him with her eager eyes."[13] This description seems to conflate the Hellenistic poet's emphasis on Medea's "bright glances" ("amarugmata," 3.288) with Ennius's reference to the young woman's "cupido corde."[14] Although we cannot be certain of the full scope of Ennius's play, this echo of the tragic Medea as well as her epic counterpart forebodes the vehemence of that character. Catullus also employs the metaphor of the flame for his heroine's passion: "Nor did she turn her burning eyes away from him" (91–92). Apollonius similarly uses images of fire from the onset of Medea's passion for Jason; in the scene where she is struck with love for the hero, Eros's shaft burns deeply, "like a flame" (287). In its context, this image must be far more than a conventional metaphor for love; instead, it foreshadows an eruption of violent feelings. In his adaption of Apollonius's powerful apostrophe to Eros, Catullus increases the subjective portrayal of his heroine.[15] He addresses Cupid and Venus: "Holy child, you who mix the pleasures of men with cares, and you who rule over Golgos and verdant Idalium, on what waves of passion you tossed the girl burning in her heart and often sighing for the golden-haired stranger!" (95–98).

As we observed earlier, Vergil imitates Apollonius's apostrophe of *Argonautica* 4 in a passionate address to Dido when the queen has decided to commit suicide. The Hellenistic model is far less sympathetic to the victim of love than his imitators Vergil and Catullus. Apollonius refers to Eros as "dreadful" (*schetlios*) and decries the "baneful folly" that afflicted Medea (445–49), who has been driven to desperate straits and, fearing that Jason will strike a bargain with her brother and relinquish her, plots to murder Apsyrtus. His apostrophe reflects a very negative view of love, which has induced fear

---

[13]*Catullus*, ed. Elmer T. Merrill (1893; rpt. Cambridge, Mass.: Harvard University Press, 1977). Except where noted, all quotations from Catullus 64 are from this edition. The translations are my own.

[14]See Catullus, *The Poems*, 2d ed., ed. with commentary Kenneth Quinn (London: Macmillan, 1973), ad loc., for the possible echo of Ennius's tragedy here. Fordyce (above, note 9), ad loc., cites the allusion to Apollonius 3.286–89.

[15]Gennaro Perrotta, "Il carme 64 di Catullo e i suoi pretesi originali ellenistici," *Athenaeum* 9 (1931), 177–222 and 370–409, discusses the *Argonautica* as a significant source for Catullus's poem; see also Konstan (above, note 10), pp. 68–70.

and then aggressiveness in its victim. By recalling Apollonius's dark invocation to Eros, Catullus may to some extent set the tone for Ariadne's passionate outburst on Dia. But he expresses a far more complex attitude. The mixture of bliss and misery that he attributes to the "sacred child" reflects the poet's attitude throughout his polymetric and epigrammatic poems. Like many of those poems, Catullus 68 attempts to situate love in the larger context of a man's life. There, the poet explores his love for Lesbia by juxtaposing it with his feelings about his brother's death, all of which is placed in relation to the heroic paradigm of Laodamia's love for Protesilaus.[16] Although aware of his predecessor's skepticism about both the heroic and the erotic in human life, the Roman poet more profoundly explores the transformation of love from a pleasurable experience to a destructive emotion that can be out of control.

By omitting Apollonius's allegorical scene of Eros as a naughty and impudent young god who ruthlessly shoots his victims with his arrows of passion, Catullus heightens the powerfully elemental force of love. Appropriately, he integrates the metaphor of waves of passion into his echo of the *Argonautica*. Since the sea is a prominent element in the story of both the Argonauts and Theseus, the image acquires a particular significance in its present context. The poet first dwells on the novelty of seafaring, which caused the Nereids to marvel as the Argonauts set forth; he emphasizes the heroic nature of Theseus's journey to Crete to rescue the Athenian youths from the Minotaur in contrast with Aegeus's human grief at letting his son go; and he graphically pictures the hero's ship receding into the distance ("but the forgetful youth struck the seas with the oars as he fled," 58) as Ariadne discovers her abandonment. In this poem the sea is the locus of heroic conquest encompassing the fearless challenge of nature, the quest for glory, and the disregard of personal feelings in pursuit of public objectives. Here the poet suggests Ariadne's powerful emotions through the sea image of *fluctus*. By associating this awesome realm of nature metaphorically with his

[16]See Thomas K. Hubbard, "Catullus 68: The Text as Self-Demystification," *Arethusa* 17 (1984), 29–49, especially on Catullus's complex use of the myth of Laodamia and Protesilaus: although problematic on the theme of marital constancy and disappointed passion, it reflects a positive movement of love from the physical to the spiritual and reinforces the significance of the *domus*.

heroine, he provides an emotional female counterpoint to male heroism, the woman's total absorption in love and the transformation of that feeling to hatred.[17]

Catullus also echoes the *Argonautica* in his description of Theseus's heroic effort against the Minotaur as Ariadne waits in anxiety. He combines the physical and psychological symptoms of the heroine's passion as she watches the hero prepare for his dangerous task: "By how much more than the gleam of gold did she often grow pale, when Theseus eager to contend against the savage monster sought either death or the reward of glory!" (100–102). The last line echoes Jason's claim in the *Argonautica* "either to attain shame or great glory" when returning home with the fleece (4.205). There is considerable irony in those words, since he has just acquired possession of the fleece not through his own prowess but rather through Medea's use of magic to charm the serpent guarding it, and he is further reduced in scope by being compared to a young woman in the moonlight. In addition, the hero is very possessive about his prize and refuses to let any of the crew come near it. By echoing Jason's boastful words, Catullus's passage suggests that this hero with his great desire for glory will similarly manipulate the young woman and later betray her.

A simile adapted from Apollonius casts the hero in a negative light at his most glorious moment. The Minotaur defeated by Theseus is thus compared to a toppling tree:

> For just as a raging storm lashing the tree trunk with its blast brings down an oak which shakes its branches on the height of Mount Taurus or a cone-bearing pine with its sweating bark (the tree pulled up from its roots falls far off on its side, breaking whatever comes in its way). (105–9)

The original depicts the fall of another creature beyond the norm of human nature, the giant Talos:

> As some great pine high in the mountains which woodsmen leaving behind half-cut with their sharp axes when they return from the woods; at

[17]Catullus also uses the sea metaphorically for Ariadne's inner turbulence when he describes her looking out to sea: "et magnis curarum fluctuat undis" (62); see Putnam (above, note 10), 171–72.

first it trembles in the wind at night, then finally breaking at the stump, it comes crashing down. (4.1682–86)

Catullus has brought the first stage of Ariadne's emotional attachment to Theseus to a fitting conclusion with this adaptation of the *Argonautica*. As a variation on a typical kind of epic simile, the model refers to a very unheroic act: first, it is Medea, not Jason or any of the other heroes, who slays Talos, and second, she uses the highly dubious method of witchcraft. Catullus's echo of Apollonius's anti-heroic episode helps to remind the reader of the hero's dependence upon a woman whom he merely exploits.

Although indebted to Hellenistic literature, Catullus 64 presents a very different view of the female. The poet's empathetic style of depicting the heroine differentiates his work from Apollonius's epic: it leads the reader to identify with her plight, especially in the beginning, even though one gradually perceives that her mounting fury is a form of madness. Scholars have shown in detail that Catullus adapted Alexandrian techniques most effectively in this epyllion, especially by creating exquisite pathos for Ariadne's forlorn state in abandonment.[18] First, he describes the young woman alone on the beach in a highly pictorial manner that calls attention to the physical qualities of color and texture: her blond ("flavo") hair loosened by the absence of her finely woven ("subtilem") hairnet; her white ("lactantes") breasts no longer bound by the smooth ("tereti") chestband; her light ("levi") garment now having fallen and revealing her body (63–67). This striking picture is further enhanced by the use of exotic Greek words, such as *strophium* and *mitra*, that refer to articles of clothing that the heroine now neglects. Catullus caps the scene with the empathetic device of apostrophe:

> Sic neque tum mitrae neque tum fluitantis amictus
> Illa vicem curans toto ex te pectore, Theseu,
> Toto animo, tota pendebat perdita mente. (68–70)

[18]Jenkyns (above, note 10), pp. 116–17, however, discusses the pictorial quality of this description and finds the language too "decorative" to reflect a serious portrayal of passion. On the possible connection of the vivid style of this scene with contemporary art, see Friedrich Klingner, *Catulls Peleus-Epos* (Munich: Beck, 1956), esp. pp. 34–51.

Thus she, caring for the state of neither her hair nor her loosened tunic, was straining after you, Theseus, with her whole heart, her whole soul, and her whole mind, the wretched one.

The evocation of the absent hero makes the woman's desolation more immediate. The anaphora of the word *totus* and the evocative alliteration of *t* further emphasize the intensity of her feelings. In this vignette, then, the rhetorical devices and pictorial technique convey Ariadne's inner state of confusion and disorientation, her inability to focus on anything but Theseus's absence.

Catullus increases the complexity of his narrative by allowing Ariadne to voice her own feelings at length. When referring to her own plight, her speech contains many of the subjective devices that the poet himself uses in the narrative. A change in the tone of her lament occurs after she considers where she can go ("'Nam quo me referam?'" 177) and proceeds to rule out the various possibilities for survival. There is considerable sarcasm in her questions, as she notes that the wild sea separates her from Crete; her father will certainly not come to her rescue since she abandoned him and ran off with the man who caused her brother's death; and her *coniunx* who now flees will be of no assistance (177–87). As a model for this passage, Euripides' Medea poses the question of where she can now go (502). She, too, sarcastically notes the impossibility of returning to her father whom she betrayed or of going to the daughters of Pelias who would hardly welcome her for murdering their father (502–5).[19] Ariadne's evaluation of her situation also resembles the heroine's angry outburst in *Argonautica* 4, where fearing that Jason will abandon her, Medea asks how she can face her father (378–81).

By echoing the tragic and the epic Medea at their moments of rhetorical ferocity, the heroine lends the impression of an imminent outburst of vehement, vengeful feelings that will bring destruction to the hero. Yet she does not simply utter scathing reproaches, as Euripides' heroine does. She is able to sustain sympathy not only through the justice of her cause but also through her effective rhetoric. She evokes the desolation of her condition:

> Nulla fugae ratio, nulla spes: omnia muta,
> Omnia sunt deserta, ostentant omnia letum. (186–87)

[19]Quinn (above, note 14), on 177–87, notes the direct echo of Euripides' Medea.

There is no way of escape, no hope: everything is silent, everything
deserted; everything indicates death.

The economy of the anaphora with *nulla* and *omnia* and of the strong
asyndeton, with four connectives eliminated, makes this a powerful
statement of her lack of all possibilities for survival.

Ariadne's mounting fury strongly affects her rhetoric as she
curses the hero. Her invocation of the Furies whose "'foreheads
wreathed with snaky hair reveal the wrath breathing forth from the
breast'" (193–94) is the rhetorical culmination of her passionate
speech. The contorted style, with its *a b a b* pattern of interlocking
words ("'anguino redimita / Capillo frons'"), is more than merely a
poetic embellishment.[20] It captures her deep feelings of anger and
frustration. After acknowledging her state of fury with the metaphor of fire ("ardens," 197), she calls for the hero's destruction:

> "Sed quali solam Theseus me mente reliquit,
> Tali mente, deae, funestet seque suosque." (200–201)

> "But with such a heart as Theseus left me abandoned, oh goddesses, so
> may he bring ruin to himself and his own!"

Although correctly referring to Theseus's moral apathy in the
phrase "quali mente," she eliminates all human feelings. The last
line impresses a sense of hard finality: the strong verb *funesto* denotes
the idea of "polluting with murder," and the verse ends with an
emphatic epic-style compound connected by a double *que*.[21]

After her speech, the poet's narrative suggests the change in her
character. He depicts the young woman as unaware of the turn of
events and describes the arrival of Bacchus and his followers in vivid
language with onomatopoeia and alliteration suggesting the aural
effect of their activities. The following verses, for instance, capture
the clashing of the instruments through the prominent *t* and *c*
sounds and the onomatopoeia of "tinnitus" and "bombos":

[20]Jenkyns (above, note 10), p. 118, sees this description of the Furies as another
element of the poet's tendency to be stylistically decorative.

[21]See Quinn (above, note 14), ad loc., on the epic nature of the double *que*,
introduced into Latin literature by Ennius.

Plangebant aliae proceris tympana palmis
Aut tereti tenuis tinnitus aere ciebant,
Multis raucisonos efflabant cornua bombos
Barbaraque horribili stridebat tibia cantu. (261–64)

Some were banging on cymbals with their outstretched hands or were creating a shrill sound on smooth bronze. Many with horns blared out a raucous booming, and barbarous pipes screeched with a dreadful sound.

Using an intricate play of sound and sense in these verses, Catullus creates a cacophony that places the new arrivals in a negative light. The positive value of Ariadne's rescue seems qualified: her own troubled inner state is matched by the raucous frenzy of the new arrivals.[22] Yet the vehement outburst of anger could only forebode a future state of chaos rather than an inner peace. Ariadne's passion will now find an outlet inappropriate to the ideal vision of love that she had once anticipated.

Catullus makes the erotic theme significantly more complex by playing it against familial love. He thus gives the *domus* a new importance in heroic poetry. More than an emblem of the glory sustained by perpetuating the family line with sons who demonstrate *virtus*, it reflects an emotional bond between mother and daughter as well as between father and son. Unlike Apollonius in the *Argonautica*, the poet reveals no dissonance within the family. He makes no allusion to the discord in the house of Minos because of Pasiphae's passion for the bull. By contrast, he associates Ariadne with strong family relations, a motif which reinforces the pathos of her fate when Theseus abandons her. Here, two delicate analogies depict the tender bond between mother and daughter:

quam suavis exspirans castus odores
Lectulus in molli complexu matris alebat,
Quales Eurotae progignunt flumina myrtos
Aurave distinctos educit verna colores. (87–90)

[22]T. P. Wiseman, *Catullus and His World: A Reappraisal* (Cambridge: Cambridge University Press, 1985), pp. 179–80, comments on the implications of this bizarre scene.

she whom a pure bed exuding sweet fragrance nurtured in her mother's soft embrace, just as the waters of the Eurotas bring forth myrtles or the soft spring air creates a profusion of colors.

The adjectives *suavis* and *mollis*, two important terms in Catullan lyric connoting delicacy and tenderness, reinforce the ideal quality of maternal love.[23] The myrtle and colorful spring flowers also hint at the prospective transferral of the young girl from her father's *domus* to that of her husband, for the comparison of a young girl to such verdant plants is a characteristic of the epithalamium.[24] Catullus himself associates the myrtle of Venus and the hyacinth with the happiness of the bride Vinia in his own marriage poem.[25] The image here, however, undermines the expectation of connubial bliss and the creation of a new family, since at Theseus's arrival Ariadne is about to set off with illusory hopes of a wedding with a "suitor" who does not keep his promise to marry her. This depiction of the beloved home with the suggestion of a new family by marriage brings to epic a personal concern that runs through Catullus's lyric, narrative, and elegiac poems.[26]

The poet reinforces the importance of the theme of the *domus* by again juxtaposing the feelings of Ariadne's family with Ariadne's love for Theseus. After describing her great fear for the hero in his conflict with the Minotaur, Catullus depicts the reaction of her family when she deserts them:

> linquens genitoris filia vultum,
> Ut consanguineae complexum, ut denique matris,
> Quae misera in gnata deperdita lamentata est.[27] (117–19)

[23]David O. Ross, Jr., *Style and Tradition in Catullus* (Cambridge, Mass.: Harvard University Press, 1969), pp. 79–80, comments on *mollis* for its appropriateness to the polymetrics and *suavis* for its connotation of delicacy in neoteric poetry.

[24]See Konstan (above, note 10), p. 75.

[25]See 61.21–25, where the language suggests fecundity ("with shiny branches which the Naiads in play nourish with their dew").

[26]On the significance of the *domus* in Catullus's poetry, see Phyllis Y. Forsyth, "Catullus: The Mythic Persona," *Latomus* 35 (1976), 555–66.

[27]There is a problem with the text in this line. I do not accept Merrill's reading of *laetabatur*, which does not make the best sense with *deperdita*, but prefer Conington's emendation *lamentata est* in the *O.C.T.*, ed. Robinson Ellis (1904; rpt. Oxford: Clarendon Press, 1946).

she as his daughter leaving the presence of her father, the embrace of her sister and last of her mother, who desperately grieved over her unfortunate daughter.

The poet alludes to Ariadne's relations with her father and sister, but he portrays her mother's grief with special feeling. Catullus implies how deeply the woman is affected by the loss of her daughter by using the word *deperditus*, which denotes "ruined" or "hopelessly in love."[28] Since this tender, nurturing love contrasts sharply with the sexual *amor* that proves so destructive, Catullus makes Ariadne's separation from her *domus* all the more poignant and lamentable.

If he elevates the *domus* to a new status, Catullus reconsiders a major social value that is traditionally linked to epic poetry. The heroine herself becomes the spokesperson for the necessity of *fides* in human life by censuring Theseus for his failure in that sphere. Like the poet earlier, she refers to Theseus as *immemor*, a morally charged word that can mean "negligent" as well as simply "forgetful."[29] More specifically, she attacks him for his lack of fidelity, his violation of the *fides* that guaranteed his pledge.[30] When first addressing her false lover, she calls him "perfide" twice and observes that he bears home the perjury that will bring him to ruin (135). After this hint at a future punishment, she becomes more overtly wrathful. She claims, for instance, that because of Theseus's action women should never again believe men's promises or consider their words trustworthy ("fideles," 144) She also invokes Jupiter with a wish that this man with a handsome exterior masking sinister intentions (175–76) who has been *perfidus* had never come to her homeland. To redress the injuries that Theseus has inflicted upon her, she then invokes the trust of the gods ("caelestum fidem," 191), who are

[28]See Fordyce (above, note 9), ad loc., on the idiomatic meaning of this word as "to love to destruction."

[29]Catullus uses *immemor* with this moral connotation, for example, in poem 30, where he reproaches his false friend Alfenus.

[30]On the subject of faithfulness in Catullus's poetry, see P. McGushin, "Catullus' *Sanctae Foedus Amicitiae*," *CPhil.* 62 (1967), 85–93, who provides a good overview of the wide range of poems in which Catullus explores the loss of *fides* in relationships from friendship to marriage. The poet suggests the importance of married love as a solemn contract bound by *fides* and operating in the sphere of *pietas* not only in the formal marriage hymns but also in the poems concerning his relation to Lesbia, with whom he felt bound by a symbolic marriage.

concerned with justice. Jupiter's response is particularly appropriate: he causes Theseus to forget Aegeus's order to remove the black sail and thus makes him responsible for his father's suicide. Both Euripides' and Apollonius's Medea reproach Jason for breaking his promise, but neither raises the Greek concept of *pistis* so consistently as Catullus's Ariadne cites *fides*. Through his heroine, Catullus shows that the conventionally private erotic domain can rely on values that his society applied to social and political contexts and that were sanctioned by the king of the gods himself.[31]

In his epyllion, then, Catullus has added a new function to the erotic in epic. He shows the perversion of values that are maintained in word but not in deed by employing an archetype of the vulnerable female as the upholder of social values, especially *fides*, which is conventionally attributed to the male. The hero Theseus, by contrast, violates *fides* when he breaks his promise to marry Ariadne and *pietas* when he brings about the death of his own father. The allusions to Apollonius suggest the unhappy conclusion to the love affair of Jason and Medea, but they also strengthen the ironic view of heroism projected in the ekphrasis. Theseus seems all too like the anti-heroic Jason in the *Argonautica* and his values are similarly narrow. Catullus's emphasis on the importance of the *domus*, in part through lyrical depictions of Ariadne's familial love, not only adds a new dimension to epic but also increases the negative attitude toward traditional heroism. Theseus destroys both that family unit and his own by unwittingly sending his father to his doom.

Catullus developed the epyllion into a new anti-epic form in his ekphrasis on Ariadne. He sustains this ironic function to the end of the poem, for its closure consists of a direct attack on contemporary moral corruption, contrasted with the glorious heroic era that culminated in the illustrious offspring of Peleus and Thetis. Readers have often perceived the irony of that prophecy since the poet depicts the Trojan War hero as a brutal killer who will make mothers weep for their slaughtered sons. Both Theseus and the greater hero Achilles are destroyers of the family. The criticism of heroism im-

---

[31]See R. O. A. M. Lyne, *The Latin Love Poets: From Catullus to Horace* (Oxford: Clarendon Press, 1980), esp. pp. 24–41, on Catullus's assimilation of public values to his personal lyrics and his application of the term *foedus* to marriage for the first time in poem 64.

plied throughout the ekphrasis reinforces the profound pessimism of this poem. But his ironic use of the genre is significantly unlike Apollonius's. He does not reject the importance of the erotic in human life even though it figures into his criticism of heroism. Instead, he perceives its potential for going beyond the bounds of rationality while hinting at the positive side of the fulfillment of love. Through effective echoes of Apollonius's and Euripides' Medea, Catullus creates a highly complex heroine whose function is by no means limited to a social statement. Although she does not evoke the same negative qualities that so reduce the reader's sympathy for the Greek Medea, the dark side of her vehemence is hinted at in part through the allusions to the tragic heroine. The force of her own rhetoric and the poet's conclusion to her story keep the idea of madness just below the surface. The persona that Catullus has created in the corpus of his personal poems seems very close to Ariadne, whose feminine nature provided a means of comprehending the experience of loss and betrayal, the problem of callous, insensitive behavior, and the complex emotions that result in the "victim."

Ovid's Ariadne

Although some scholars think that the major source for *Heroides* 10 cannot be determined,[32] Ovid must certainly have considered Catullus 64 the standard for all subsequent literary versions of the myth of Ariadne. The republican poem was already a classic that influenced Vergil's depiction of Dido in *Aeneid* 4, especially in the emotional passages in which the queen considers the possibilities open to her regarding Aeneas's departure and finally curses the hero.

Those critics who accept Catullus 64 as the primary model for *Heroides* 10 differ widely on the use that Ovid made of the earlier Ariadne. Two major studies of the *Heroides* approach the Catullan

[32]See Howard Jacobson, *Ovid's* Heroides (Princeton: Princeton University Press, 1974), pp. 213–15, for a review of the controversy concerning the sources, especially the possibility of a lost Hellenistic poem.

echoes in this poem from very different perspectives. Howard Jacobson considers that the erratic nature of the poem, combining fine poetry with "overblown rhetoric and obvious artifice," is the result of the poet's desire to rival his predecessor.[33] In addition to poetic emulation, he notes the achievement of a mood of desolation, the theatrical elements of Ariadne's letter that imply a kind of role-playing, and psychological aspects such as the woman's distinction of her self from her body and her irrationality at certain points. Yet he views those qualities as incidental, not inherent to the unity of the poem. Florence Verducci, by contrast, focuses on the artifice of this poem and relates its contrived qualities to Ovid's strategy of parodying Catullus.[34] She believes that his motivation in persistently undermining Catullus arises from the overuse of Ariadne as a figure of pathos in his own time; the character is then reduced to bathos in order to expose the "unreality" and "latent sentimentality" of these post-Catullan versions. It is difficult to disagree completely with this view, given Ovid's parody of contemporary elegiac clichés, for instance, in the *Amores*. Although individual interpretations reveal Ovid's witty reshaping of the Catullan echoes, Verducci's overall view is limited: it does not relate Ariadne's language to the experience of isolation that this character endures under extraordinary circumstances.

Ovid was certainly aware of the complexity of Catullus's Ariadne, situated in the context of a major heroic event, the Argonautic quest and the eventual birth of the hero Achilles. Eliminating that broader mythical background, he also chooses a form that allows for more scope in the character's inner feelings. Through the epistolary genre, in which Ariadne is the sole voice, the poet reflects upon the effect of isolation by showing the woman writing and detailing the progressive stages of her situation. Hermann Fränkel remarks that nothing happens in the *Heroides*, where "the real events are all in the past and in the future," but that much goes on within

[33]Ibid., p. 215. Jacobson frequently alludes to Catullus in his discussion of individual points on specific passages of *Heroides* 10, but resists making any synthesis. He is somewhat critical of this poem for its overblown rhetoric, faulty logic, and gratuitous use of some of the imitations of Catullus.

[34]Florence Verducci, *Ovid's Toyshop of the Heart*: Epistulae Heroidum (Princeton: Princeton University Press, 1985), pp. 244–85.

these characters.[35] The dynamics of this poem arise from the psychology of the heroine, who through numerous verbal echoes is measured against Catullus's sublime Ariadne. Whereas the earlier heroine articulates the injustices of a competitive social ethic and an insensitivity in human relations that preoccupied the republican poet, Ovid's Ariadne represents the more general human experience of grappling with a completely unexpected event and trying, with self-interest and even self-deception, to comprehend the situation.

To appreciate more fully the gap between these two poems, let us first recall the differences between the social and political environments of the two Roman poets. Catullus viewed the contemporary aristocracy as self-serving, avaricious, and especially reprehensible in its failure to uphold the obligations incurred by *amicitia* and the patron-client relationship.[36] He marshaled some of his most venomous and even scurrilous wit against men like Piso or Clodius, who assumed heroic postures in military and political affairs but were in fact mainly self-aggrandizing. The faithlessness in love that he perceived in his own mistress Lesbia is a corollary of this social and political disintegration. His views on human relations, whether public and formal or private and informal (the world of lovers, friends, and fellow poets), validate traditional mores as the foundation of civilized life. The moral point of view that informs poem 64 through the stress on such social values as *fides* and *gratia* is lacking in *Heroides* 10.

In the political stability of the Augustan world, Ovid had less reason to be actively interested in the public affairs and personalities that engaged the sensitive and critical minds of Catullus and others of his generation. He does not attack the duplicitous, destructive

[35]Hermann Fränkel, *Ovid: A Poet between Two Worlds* (Berkeley: University of California Press, 1945), p. 45, has some good observations on the practical futility of the *Heroides* as persuasive love letters. Although emphasizing the lack of real drama or action in these epistles, he does perceive a kind of change at the end of this poem when Ariadne tries to make a form of "spiritual contact" with Theseus (p. 38).

[36]Marilyn B. Skinner, "Pretty Lesbius," *TAPA* 112 (1982), 197–208, sees Catullus's use of sexual gibes against Publius Clodius Pulcher as "a statement of apprehension over the crisis in the Roman state, focusing on the breakdown of traditional standards of fair dealing among friends and allies." She also refers to Catullus's lampoon of Piso in poem 28 as a criticism of the methods of patronage and class privilege.

values of the active, public life such as *virtus* and *gloria* or uphold other social values such as *fides*, through the persona of his heroine. By contrast, he dismisses the heroic code as inconsequential and has little faith in the traditional Roman values of his predecessor. Although aware of the limitations of social values, he looks inward at the motivations of human behavior and examines the psychology of the "victim." Ovid eliminates the grand stature of the earlier heroine, who is strongly influenced by the powerful Medea of epic and tragedy, and examines the paradoxes of her response to abandonment, in part through his use of elegiac conventions that are at odds with the sublimity of the Catullan rhetoric.

In the first part of *Heroides* 10, Ariadne's discovery of Theseus's absence, Ovid reduces the scope of the passion of Catullus's heroine. He has the young woman record, for example, precisely the way she groped for Theseus in her sleep:[37]

> Incertum vigilans, a somno languida, movi
> Thesea prensuras semisupina manus:
> Nullus erat: referoque manus iterumque retempto
> Perque torum moveo bracchia: nullus erat. (9–12)

Waking up from sleep but languid, I raised myself and moved my hands uncertainly as I tried to grasp Theseus. There was nobody; I return my hands and try again and move my arms over the bed; there was nobody!

The opaque style imitates the reality that his heroine experiences. As he describes the motion of her hands, Ovid not only has Ariadne mention her repeated efforts to touch her lover but also has her execute this thought verbally by framing the distich with the phrase "nullus erat": a circular, repetitive movement is thus mimicked. Verb tense also reflects desire, for Ariadne views the fact of Theseus's absence as an action completed in the past ("erat") yet envisions her attempt to grasp him as an action ongoing in the present ("refero," "retempto"). This use of narrative present along with the past tense perhaps suggests the heroine's need to reenact her last experience with Theseus in their final night together. By

[37]Ovid, *Heroides, with the Greek Translation of Planudes,* ed. Arthur Palmer (Oxford: Clarendon Press, 1898). My quotations from *Heroides* 10 are from this edition. The translations are my own.

employing the third person "Thesea" instead of the second person pronoun "te," she makes her lover the object for which she was searching and that she now tries to recapture in her epistle. While Verducci focuses on its discordant elements,[38] this passage has frequently been admired for its vividness. One critic has observed that these lines "brilliantly suggest first the langor [sic] of the hypnopompic state, then the sudden and emphatic wakefulness inspired by an unexpected discovery."[39] In addition to this mimesis of physical states, the language reveals the unconscious motivations of the heroine. As Ovid shows more fully in the *Metamorphoses*, language reveals the desires that characters are often unaware of or would not wish to acknowledge.[40] In her letter, Ariadne evokes the absent object of desire and recalls his presence. Catullus's heroine, by contrast, sees the ship in the distance as soon as she awakes and is quickly filled with fury (52–54).

Throughout the first part of this epistle, the poet manipulates language in ways that suggest the woman's fixation on the object she has lost and its effect on her. Here she begins to recount her search for Theseus:

> Luna fuit, specto, siquid nisi litora cernam;
>   Quod videant, oculi nil nisi litus habent. (17–18)

There was a moon. I look to see if I can discern something except shore;
but as far as my eyes can see, they find nothing except shore.

The emphasis in this passage has shifted from touch to vision, a motif that assumes thematic significance in the course of this epistle. Ariadne stresses this faculty by using three different verbs of seeing (*specto*, *cerno*, and *video*). The verbal echo of the phrase "nisi litora" in "nisi litus," which occupies the corresponding position in the pentameter, intimates her sense of an endless expanse of shore.

[38]Verducci (above, note 34), p. 249.

[39]D. W. Vessey, "Humor and Humanity in Ovid's *Heroides*," *Arethusa* 9 (1976), esp. 96–97.

[40]See, for example, Charles Altieri, "Ovid and the New Mythologists," *Novel* 7 (1973–74), 31–40, who discusses Ovid's use of language in the *Metamorphoses* as mediating interior and exterior, self and other; Gregson Davis, *The Death of Procris: "Amor" and the Hunt in Ovid's* Metamorphoses (Rome: Ateneo, 1983), pp. 37–38, on Apollo's speech to Daphne concealing his predatory nature.

Ovid alludes to Catullus's poem by playing on the motif of vision but eliminates the intensity of passion that is transformed to hatred in his predecessor's heroine. After climbing to a precipice from which she could get a good view out to sea, Ariadne is at once unwilling to acknowledge the truth of the situation: "When I saw or as if I thought that I saw" (31).[41] Her physical response reflects her disbelief: first she becomes numb and then is roused to call out to her lover (32–36). This description of Ariadne's incredulity echoes Catullus's poem, where the heroine is similarly unwilling to believe her eyes: "Nor yet does she believe that she sees what she actually sees" (55). Although stunned and momentarily filled with disbelief, she immediately exhibits an unrestrained passion, "indomitos furores" (54). Ovid's heroine, by contrast, becomes totally disoriented and clings to hope and even delusion.

In referring ironically to the attitude toward nature in Catullus 64, Ovid has his heroine evoke pathos but also reflect her self-deception. Ariadne thus describes herself calling out to the hero on the beach:

> Interea toto clamanti litore 'Theseu':
> Reddebant nomen concava saxa tuum,
> Et quotiens ego te, totiens locus ipse vocabat:
> Ipse locus miserae ferre volebat opem. (21–24)

Meanwhile, the hollow rocks returned your name to me as I shouted "Theseus" along the entire shore. And as often as I called you, the place itself called out; the very place wished to bear aid to an unhappy woman.

Much like a character from elegy, the young woman sees herself through a pathetic fallacy as the object of nature's active support, echoing her calls for her lover. She describes this benevolent response of the natural world with an alliterative *t* sound, which evokes the very name that she keeps calling. The abandoned woman laments that she has lost the center of her existence, and her language reinforces her keen sense of longing and desire to regain that object. The text thus implies Ariadne's wish to restore order in her

[41]This is the reading accepted by Palmer, though the manuscripts are at variance on the second half of this line.

disintegrating world.[42] Catullus's heroine, by contrast, expresses her awareness that nature is indifferent to her by affirming that it is useless to lament to the ignorant breezes, "'which endowed with no feelings can neither hear words uttered nor return them'" (165–66). She clearly understands the futility of her situation and, while bitter, maintains control over her responses. Within a few verses, she invokes Jupiter with a wish that the hero had never come to her homeland. Aware that there is no possibility of Theseus's return, she seeks a means of getting even with him. Whereas Catullus's Ariadne transforms desire into a passion for revenge, Ovid's is still absorbed in a vain longing for her lover.

By adapting an epic simile from Catullus, Ovid has Ariadne convey the immediate effect of losing her last link with her lover when Theseus's ship disappears from view. The young woman thus compares herself to a raving Bacchant and an immobile rock:

Either I wandered alone with loosened hair, just as a Bacchant aroused by the Ogygian god. Or looking out to sea, I sat coldly on a rock and was myself as much a stone as the very seat itself. (47–50)

Catullus similarly describes Ariadne in poem 64:

She looks out just like the stone image of a Bacchant; alas, she looks out and tosses upon great waves of agony. (61–62)

The earlier simile encapsulates the woman's feelings as she stares toward the water and sees her lover fleeing. The poet represents his heroine's psyche by the evocative exclamation "eheu" and by the sea image (for her inner turmoil). By splitting Catullus's simile into two parts, Ovid dismantles the powerful image of an internal state, trapped and seething in passion.[43] His simile concentrates on physi-

---

[42]See John Brenkman, "Narcissus in the Text," *Georgia Review* 3 (1976), 293–327, for a very densely articulated but provocative study of the Echo and Narcissus episode in the *Metamorphoses*. There he applies the Derridean theory of language and desire to Ovid's text by discussing the representation of voice-consciousness in the story of Echo and the reflected image in opposition to speech in the drama of Narcissus.

[43]Verducci (above, note 34), p. 251, finds that the comparison to a Bacchant refers to Ariadne's loosened hair, not her emotional state, and considers her analogy of the stone on which she sits far less successful than the more figurative *saxum effigies* of art in Catullus.

cal appearance, juxtaposing motion and rigidity. It also differentiates her from her model in regard to her feelings for Theseus: it may
imply despair (in the woman's frantic running) or fear (in her frozen
position on the rock), but it indicates nothing about deep erotic
passion. This double analogy symbolizes the disorientation of a
distraught woman who can react only in contradictory ways. The
image of instability brings the first stage of Ariadne's experience of
abandonment to a conclusion and projects the psychological disintegration that she reveals in the rest of the letter.

The second part of *Heroides* 10 corresponds to Ariadne's powerful, bitter presentation of the options left open to her in Catullus 64.
She now begins to consider the future and fears for her safety:

> What can I do? Where can I go alone? The island is barren of cultivation. I
> see no activities of men or of animals. The sea girds the entire border of
> the land: nowhere is there a sailor, no ship about to set forth through
> dangerous routes. Imagine that companions and winds and ship are
> granted to me. Where should I go? My father's land forbids my approach.
> If I should glide over calm seas in a lucky ship, if Aeolus should moderate
> the winds, I will be an exile! (59–66)

As the consequence of betraying her father, she now perceives that
she will be an exile, forever alienated from the land that produced
and nurtured her. The anxiety that this awareness provokes affects
her letter, for the young woman at this point abandons the epistolary form proper and begins to weave in and out of attention to her
addressee and the issue of his abandonment of her.

This self-examination closely echoes Catullus 64. Yet instead of
expressing dismay at her emptiness and fear of exile, Catullus's
character perceives the consequences of her involvement in
Theseus's heroic enterprise with a bitter wit and rules out the
sources of refuge that might have been available. First, she cannot
go home because she has no way of getting there: no route will
afford her a crossing back to Crete. Next, she emphasizes the impossibility of returning to her father because she willingly abandoned him and helped to cause her brother's death. Finally, she
sarcastically mentions Theseus's "faithful love" and alludes to his
promise to marry her by calling him *coniunx*, "husband" (177–87).
While acknowledging her own flaws, she decries the hero's more

serious moral culpability and builds up steadily to the climactic passage of her curse.

As Ovid's heroine considers the consequences of her situation, she to some extent displaces the hero as her center. Whereas her model speaks to the point, she loses her focus, and her rhetoric drifts off. The shifting of time that occurs in this flow of private feelings reflects her loss of a rational, coherent perspective; it is very different from the chronological fluidity by which Catullus highlights the important events in his heroine's story. As Ovid's Ariadne begins to envision her future, her psychological disorientation generates varied, sometimes conflicting responses in poetic modes such as elegiac and invective. The variety of styles mirrors fragmentation and instability and suggests the impossibility of the kind of monolithic response that Catullus represented.

In an allusion to the earlier Ariadne, she first dwells upon her anxieties and creates a succession of dramatic vignettes. She observes that she is now beset by mental terrors worse than physical dangers: "A thousand images of dying rush to my mind. And death offers less of a threat than the delay of death" (81–82). At this point, the abandoned woman no longer refers to the realities that she earlier recalled but to the configurations of her troubled mind. Catullus's heroine succinctly mentions being prey to animals: "'On behalf of this service, I will be given to the beasts to mangle'" (152). Ovid's Ariadne, on the other hand, creates a dramatic scene as she conjures up the approach of wild animals, including wolves, lions, and seals. She imagines, for example, the approach of wolves:

> Iam iam venturos aut hac aut suspicor illac,
> Qui lanient avido viscera dente, lupos; (83–84)

Now, now I fear that wolves are about to come from here or there to tear me apart with ravenous mouth.

The emphatically heavy rhythm consists of five spondees in the hexameter and dramatically conveys a sense of the victim's dread at the aggressor's approach. The hypallage of "avido dente" targets the main feature of the terrifying animal; this graphic phrase, furthermore, surrounds the word "viscera," which she fears may be attacked. The postponement of the name of the beast ("lupos") until the very end of the verse heightens the suspense. After continuing to describe her fear of these wild creatures (85–88), Ariadne moves further into her solitude and ponders the future, which she contrasts with an idealized vision of the past.

Ovid echoes moments of the intense passion of his Catullan model only to dissolve them. When Ariadne returns to the addressee of her letter, she reflects her increasing loss of a coherent, rational perspective. She expands upon the Catullan Ariadne's reference to Theseus's "'hard heart'" (138): "You have borne flint and adamant stone there. You have a Theseus which can even surpass flint" (109–10). In an amusing adaptation of the topos of the hero with a heart of iron or stone, she makes the very name of the hero the term for a substance that can challenge the most impervious rocks. Yet this sharp sarcasm immediately yields to a muted elegiac lament, which begins with an evocative question: "Crudeles somni, quid me tenuistis inertem?" (111), "Cruel spirits of sleep, why did you keep me unconscious?" The verse is permeated with a plaintive assonance of *i* and *e* sounds and with a hard *c* sound reinforcing the anaphora of "crudelis." By personifying this natural state (and the elements of wind in the following lines), Ariadne envisions them as conscious participants in her destruction. She then recalls the hero's role in her plight:

> Dextera crudelis, quae me fratremque necavit,
> Et data poscenti, nomen inane, fides.
> In me iurarunt somnus ventusque fidesque. (115–17)

Cruel right hand, which killed my brother and me, and the pledge given to me when I asked for it but now an empty word. Sleep, winds, and trust all swore against me.

By addressing Theseus indirectly through the metonymy of "dextera crudelis" and the word "fides," she recalls her Catullan model's emphasis on the hero's violation of *fides*, but expresses a very different point of view about that social virtue. As we have observed, after referring several times to her lover's breach of faith, the earlier heroine invokes the *fides* of the gods, especially Jupiter who protects the inviolability of oaths.[44] That divinity's response to Ariadne's prayer validates her censure of Theseus and reinforces the sacredness of the virtues that preserve human social intercourse. The heroine of the epistle earlier referred to *fides* in a similar spirit. Reproaching her lover for his perjury, she expressed the traditional view that *fides* cannot be dismissed at will. If Theseus had killed her as well as the Minotaur, then at least he would not be guilty of a violation of trust: "Esset, quam dederas, morte soluta fides" (78), "The oath which you had made would have been dissolved by death." Now, however, the young woman views *fides* as an empty form, "nomen inane."

Whereas Catullus's heroine evokes the virtue of fidelity in order to expose Theseus's moral failure and bring about his punishment, Ovid's perceives it simply as another impermanent, relative value in an unstable world. There is in fact no center of gravity in this poem on the question of ethical conduct. Although her predecessor actually called upon Jupiter through the Eumenides to avenge Theseus's breach of *fides*, she does not seem to expect the aid of divine justice and even expresses her fear of "divine images" ("simulacra deorum," 95), presumably phenomena such as thunder and lightning which the gods might inflict upon her. In contrast to Catullus's heroine, her faith in the stability of traditional values dissolves in the course of her letter.[45]

Ovid clearly recognized the significance of the family in Catullus's poem, which poignantly recalls the nurturing maternal bond. The *domus* in poem 64, seen both through Ariadne with her mother and Theseus with his father, forms a contrast to corrupt heroic values. Catullus's delicate descriptions of Ariadne's previous domestic life subtly contrast the benevolence of familial relations with the brutality of sexual love. Ovid's character, by contrast, persistently evokes an idealized vision of her family but with no awareness of the moral issues. Here, for instance, she creates a

[44]On general Roman views of the sacred nature of *fides* from its early history in association with Jupiter, see Georges Dumézil, *Archaic Roman Religion*, tr. Philip Knapp (Chicago: University of Chicago Press, 1970), esp. pp. 198–99. On its significance in practical Roman life, see Donald C. Earl, *The Moral and Political Tradition of Rome* (Ithaca: Cornell University Press, 1967), pp. 26–27.

[45]Similarly, at lines 141–42 Ariadne relinquishes two major concepts of service and reward (*meritum* and *gratia*), a reciprocation essential to the heroic value system.

funereal elegy in which she imagines what her death will be like: "Therefore, as I am about to die, will I not see my mother's tears, and will there be no one to close my eyes with her hands? Will my unfortunate spirit wander on foreign winds, and will a friendly hand not rub with oil my limbs when laid to rest? Will sea vultures stand over my unburied bones? Is this a burial worthy of my services?" (119–24). She focuses on the lack of traditional rituals permitting the transition of the individual from life to death: the lament of female relatives, especially the mother, the closing of the eyes in the rite signaling entrance into the eternal darkness of death, and the anointment of the corpse by a dear one.[46] As a result, her soul will not gain entrance into the underworld but will instead be forced to wander about perpetually. An even worse projection about her physical state culminates this passage, for she fears that her body will be left as carrion to birds, a hideous antithesis of the proper rites accorded to the dead.

This lament about her death echoes the following passage in Catullus's poem: "'I will be given as prey to the birds and when dead will not be buried and will not have earth thrown over my body'" (152–53). Catullus's character, by contrast, does not dwell upon alienation from her family as the consequence of her decision to help the hero and flee with him. Since she also alludes to her own betrayal of her father and half-brother, she seems to understand the consequences of her actions. She concentrates all her energy on Theseus's failure to compensate her for the extraordinary help she gave at such a cost to herself. In *Heroides* 10, however, Ariadne sentimentally idealizes her family relations while ignoring the implications of her own betrayal.[47] In evoking the pathos of her fate, she creates some poignant images but completely loses sight of the ethical questions inherent in them.

In another shift of mood, Ariadne censures the hero's inhu-

---

[46]On the importance of burial rites in Roman society, including the ritual act of closing the eyes, see Harold W. Johnston, *The Private Life of the Romans* (1903; rpt. Freeport, N.Y.: Books for Libraries Press, 1972), pp. 326–31.

[47]See also her reference to Minos as "iusto parenti" (69), which must be ironic in the context of Theseus's expedition even if Ovid is making an oblique allusion to the Cretan king as judge in the underworld; and the sentimental references to her "brother," the Minotaur: "Me quoque, qua fratrem, mactasses, improbe, clava" (77) and "quae me fratremque necavit" (115).

manity, an important issue which echoes the Catullan heroine. She makes one of her strongest reproaches by questioning Theseus's parentage: "Your father is not Aegeus, nor are you the son of Aethra, daughter of Pittheus: your parents were rocks and the sea" (131–32). Like Dido who similarly vilified Aeneas, Ariadne imitates the powerful accusation of her Catullan model: " 'What lioness bore you at the foot of a barren rock? What sea churning with whirling waves cast you forth? What Syrtis, what ravenous Scylla, what gaping Charybdis?' " (154–56).

This reproach has literary antecedents as far back as the *Iliad*, where Patroclus renounces Achilles' lack of pity for the suffering Greek troops.[48] The image traditionally indicates an alienation from the object of reproach with a tragic finality, as in the case of Dido and Ariadne in Catullus. Yet Ovid's heroine immediately qualifies the accusation of total inflexibility, for after this bitter analogy, she does not sustain her anger but immediately softens her tone with a plaintive address to her absent lover: "If only the gods had caused you to see me from the top of the stern: my sad appearance would have moved you to pity" (133–34). With the earlier Ariadne and Dido, the line between passionate love and intense hatred is very thin. When the former reproaches Theseus for not taking her with him, at least as a slave who would bathe his feet if not as his wife (158–63), she only thinly veils the depth of her erotic passion.[49] Her curse is generated by intense desire now turned to hatred. In Ovid's text the heroine's movement from rage to pathos demonstrates her inability to sustain any one mood. Anger dissolves as rapidly as it appears and finds no outlet in action against the false lover.

As her letter draws to a close, Ariadne reveals her retreat from reality and withdrawal into her own imagination. A final delusion is her effort to manipulate the faithless hero by picturing herself in a retrospective glance at her earlier condition. Once again, she returns

[48]On Patroclus's denial of Achilles' parentage, see Robert Finlay, "Patroklos, Achilleus, and Peleus: Fathers and Sons in the *Iliad*," *CW* 73 (1980), 267–73, who discusses Patroclus's association with patriarchal values in his reproach to the hero.

[49]See Justin Glenn, "Ariadne's Daydream (Cat. 64.158–63)," *CJ* 76 (1980), 110–16, for a good discussion of the erotic overtones of Ariadne's reference to servile duties that she would be willing to perform; he reveals the nature of Ariadne's desires by analyzing the significance of feet in erotic contexts in Greek and Latin literature, including Catullus's own poem 68.

to the rock image: "Now see me not with your eyes but with your mind, as you can, clinging to a rock which the waves beat" (135–36). By this injunction to Theseus, Ariadne recalls her previous description of herself sitting on a rock but in a way that reveals her distance from reality. She may naively imply that Theseus looked back and saw her and that he retained the image.[50] Rhetorically, she now turns her earlier depiction of the scene into a device for persuasion in the manner of an elegiac poet.

Absorbed in the pathos of her own situation, she employs poetic similes as persuasive devices. She describes her physical condition in an attempt to evoke pity: "See my hair let down in the manner of the bereaved and my tunic saturated by tears as if by rain. My body shudders like a cornfield dashed by the north winds, and the letter slips as my hand trembles" (137–39). Perhaps overdrawn, her images imply death and dissolution. As well as overtly referring to mourning the dead, she also suggests the picture of a Homeric or Vergilian warrior falling on the battlefield in the image of the grain field battered by the winds. She then mentions her trembling hand: "Litteraque articulo pressa tremente labat" (140). This image may well call attention to the improbability of the fiction of this heroine composing a letter in her abandonment.[51] Yet the metrical effects also mimic Ariadne's sense of instability and fragility through the jolting elision of "litteraque articulo" and the correspondence of the second syllable of "labat" with the final half-foot of the pentameter, which reinforce the effect of a faltering hand.

Her final appeal to Theseus reinforces her total absorption in the pathos of her condition. At this point, she no longer thinks at all of the hero's obligations to her. In contrast to Catullus's character who steadfastly maintains the hero's debt, the *praemia* which he owes to her, she now dismisses the service (*meritum*) that she performed and the *gratia* that one expects in the epic value system (141–42). Her appeal instead is through an attempt to convey her flagging energy and spent emotions: "I stretch to you these hands, weary from beating my mournful breast, unhappily across the vast seas. I sadly

[50]See Ovid, *Heroidum Epistulae XIII*, ed. with commentary Evelyn S. Shuckburgh (London: Macmillan, 1879), ad loc.

[51]Verducci (above, note 34), p. 253, makes the point about the absurdity of the fiction.

show to you the hair, which I have not yet torn out; I beg you on behalf of the tears which you have caused" (145–48).

There is certainly humor in the exaggerated picture of her hair previously disheveled but now considerably thinned out. Yet if her attempt to elicit pity through the wretched condition of her body is not entirely successful, it accurately represents her irrational state. Furthermore, by metaphorically stretching her hands out across the sea, she recalls her initial reaction to Theseus's departure, where she made a point of mentioning her hands vigorously waving a sign to Theseus as she saw his ship departing (39–40). Now she can reach her lover only in her mind through the language of her delusion. Having retreated into her own subjective reality, Ariadne can act as though Theseus may indeed return. If love has not completely disappeared from her consciousness, passion has been superseded.[52] The loss of traditional values and the fear of imminent death underlying so much of her discourse inform her final plea to Theseus: he can carry away her bones rather than take her back as wife or mistress. So ends her letter. In contrast to Catullus 64, there is no final curse, no vengeance. Appropriately, the poet gives no hint of any future rescue by Bacchus as Catullus does at the conclusion of his ekphrasis. The myth of Ariadne in this case does not require a denouement with the advent of a god or a realistic possibility of the hero's return because of her missive: her essence is a voice that is not rooted in any stable reality.

In *Heroides* 10, Ovid's use of Catullus 64 implies the precariousness of the values that the earlier poet defended as essential for a sound, cohesive society. Catullus's Ariadne, so much like an idealized hero herself, is here diminished. There are no heroic figures in Ovid's poem. We perceive Theseus only through Ariadne's eyes, and her own vision is ultimately self-directed, oriented toward the

---

[52]Jacobson (above, note 32), pp. 225–26, observes that Ariadne is more concerned with life than love, though he puts too great an emphasis on her real understanding that her love is dead and cannot possibly be revived. See also E. A. Schmidt, "Ariadne bei Catull und Ovid," *Gymnasium* 74 (1967), 489–501, for the view that Ariadne remains fixed on her love for Theseus. Fränkel (above, note 35), pp. 226–38, shows the personal significance of the theme of exile in the *Metamorphoses*, where Ovid's own exile is perhaps alluded to with powerful images of fragmentation in the story of Hippolytus (15.493–546).

terrifying possibilities that await her, physically and emotionally: immediate torments, exile from her homeland, and ultimately death. Many of the inconsistencies and paradoxes of her epistle result from the shifts in her response to the situation. As her erratic state of mind unfolds, her connection to traditional social norms gradually dissolves. Ovid's rhetorical undermining of Catullus 64 coincides with a radically different perspective on human social nature and the integrity of human character.

Although the *Heroides* stands on its own merits poetically, the epistles have affinities with Ovid's ironic epic. The *Metamorphoses* shows the poet's skepticism about heroism in the psychological flaws impeding the characters' social roles, in the lack of a strong central focus moving toward a particular goal, and in the pervasive undermining of the historical significance of the Trojan War and the legendary story of the founding of Rome, upon which the Augustan Age had built its own ideology.[53] The poet specifically undercuts the myth of Theseus by dismissively summing up the whole story of the hero's conquest of the Minotaur through the young woman's help, his abandonment of her on Dia, and her rescue by Bacchus in fourteen lines (8.169–82). After reducing the content of *Heroides* 10 to four words by referring to Ariadne as "desertae et multa querenti," he devotes half of this passage to the impact of Bacchus's arrival on her. Whereas Catullus suggested the sinister qualities of the god and his unruly throng, Ovid expresses a fascination with an astrological phenomenon, the metamorphosis of Ariadne's crown into a constellation. In the *Metamorphoses*, both the traditional hero and the lofty heroine of Catullus's epyllion are diminished.

Ovid integrates the psychological realism of *Heroides* 10 more fully into his narrative poem by exploring the psyche in broader contexts. Although influenced by Apollonius in his depiction of Medea's love for Jason, he takes a very different approach from his epic predecessor. In the young woman's monologue, which echoes book 3 of the *Argonautica*, Ovid reveals the process of delusion by which she leads herself into her fatal action. Her self-deception through language sets this Medea apart from her model and makes

[53]Charles Segal, "Ovid: Metamorphosis, Hero, Poet," *Helios* 12 (1985), 49–63, has a good discussion of the characteristics of the *Metamorphoses* that undermine the traditional heroic ethic.

her one of many characters in the *Metamorphoses* who bring about their own demise. At the beginning of book 7 (1–73), this heroine uses language in a way that promotes her increasingly distorted view of the real situation. Although she believes that she is rational, she moves more deeply into a kind of madness. By repeatedly playing on the notion of *crudelis*, she manipulates the meaning of the word for her own purposes. Significantly, she confuses appearance and reality by equating Jason's handsome exterior with a nobility of character and by subverting moral dicta decreed by social and religious laws through recourse to a "deus intra." In *Heroides* 10 Ovid dissociated the erotic heroine from an inherent tie to social values: here he depicts even more fully the precariousness of such values as individuals act upon their own desires.

Among Greek and Roman poets, Ovid perhaps most affected the course of the erotic in heroic poetry. He differs significantly from Apollonius and Vergil, for whom the vulnerable female and the erotic in general are closely linked to male values, often as one form of a problematic heroism. He moves beyond Catullus as well, for in his epyllion the republican poet to some extent used the female symbolically to expose the perversion of social values and to reflect upon the tensions that afflicted his own existence. Still viewing the erotic in primarily negative ways, Ovid does not use the female to express male values but rather explores the problems of passion that affect individuals in various situations. Although he certainly deals with character types and reflects preconceptions about the female, Ovid is fundamentally interested in the human psyche and its adverse effect on action.

The women in the *Metamorphoses* who are frequently the victims of male aggression reveal the nature of their trauma in highly individual ways. Io's transformation into a heifer, for instance, is symbolic of her response to her first sexual experience as the object of Jupiter's lust. Yet by making an effort to identify herself to her father by scratching her name in the sand, she reveals an attitude that differs from that of other raped virgins in the poem. Daphne's metamorphosis into a laurel tree, by contrast, symbolizes her intense fear of sexuality, an unwillingness to participate fully in the human experience. Yet the reverse is also true in the cases of Echo, Salmacis, Myrrha, and Byblis. The victim of Juno's vengeance for aiding

Jupiter in his love affairs, Echo surmounts the extremely difficult limitation of being able to express herself only by repeating the last words of another's speech. She skillfully adapts Narcissus's statements in ways that perfectly reflect her own feelings, both her desire for the handsome youth (in contrast to his total resistance to love for anyone but himself) and her pity for him as he pines away. By presenting a psychologically realistic portrayal of the experience of abandonment in *Heroides* 10, Ovid created a prototype of these more complex women and men in the *Metamorphoses*, whose passions are met with the resistance of their objects of desire or who justify their desires in a complex process that very often involves self-deception through language.

CHAPTER 4

Ariosto and Roman Epic Values

Orlando Furioso, the successor of Boiardo's *Orlando Innamorato*, is deeply rooted in the tradition of chivalric romance. Yet the genre of this engaging narrative, debated even in Ariosto's own day, has remained a subject of controversy. Patricia Parker discusses romance in this poem and focuses on *errore* as a central metaphor that includes the search for the erotic object as a major facet of the endless quest of romance, the "labyrinth of desire" which encompasses so many fruitless pursuits and mistaken perceptions.[1] Moreover, she approaches the poem as epic by subtly analyzing allusions to the *Aeneid* as evidence of Ariosto's deliberate "deviation" from Vergil and to the *Metamorphoses* as evidence that the poet profited from Ovid's ironic transformations of his great predecessor. This poem seems to fluctuate between the attractive vagaries of chivalric romance and the historical consciousness of formal epic.[2]

[1]Patricia A. Parker, *Inescapable Romance: Studies in the Poetics of a Mode* (Princeton: Princeton University Press, 1979), esp. pp. 40–44, discusses Ariosto's varied uses of "error," which increase the significance of wandering in romance: on the error of love, she cites the poet's creation of the palace where each individual seeks the image of his own desires; the reader and the poet are also included in this narrative labyrinth. Parker has some brief but astute remarks on the poet's "deviation" from Vergil, in part by playing up the "romantic" elements of the *Aeneid*, and discusses Ariosto's use of Ovid's own revision of his predecessor.

[2]See David Quint, "The Figure of Atlante: Ariosto and Boiardo's Poem," *MLN* 94 (1979), 77–91, for the interesting thesis that after the destruction of Atlante's palace Ariosto abandons Boiardo's romance, with its failure to acknowledge temporality and mortality, and turns to epic historicity.

Albert Ascoli has recently contended that Ariosto purposefully uses his chivalric material sometimes for aesthetic indulgence, sometimes for ethical criticism, to reveal that the two functions are not only inherently at odds with each other but also self-contradictory.[3] Throughout the *Furioso*, the poet reflects his profound understanding of the central intellectual concerns that engaged Renaissance minds, such as identity and madness, as much as he indulges in a playful escapism. As Ascoli points out, Ariosto implicitly takes part in the debate on man's unified selfhood in the *Furioso*; in particular, he responds to Pico's *Oration on the Dignity of Man*, which stresses the importance of freedom, will, and rhetoric, by questioning the formation of an integrated self through education.

Ariosto disagrees with many humanistic views and takes a skeptical position on the values that inform Renaissance notions of society. It is a commonplace that the erotic interferes with the social goals of the warriors in this poem; as the extreme case, Orlando's love for Angelica leads to a frightening madness that removes the hero from the human sphere altogether. On the surface, Ariosto's versions of the abandoned heroine and the night raid do not fit into the conflict between public and private interests. Yet the clever poet implements his classical sources in subtle ways that question their underlying premises of the fundamental values of social life. Moreover, he often renders the material with an Ovidian irony that might be interpreted as mere playfulness rather than as a commentary on the futility of the traditional confidence in a humanistic view of human dignity. In his versions of both the abandoned female and the night raid, Ariosto reveals the deceptive surface of his poetic world. The protagonists in both elicit a sympathetic response in the reader, yet their actions also open up the possibility for a more detached, critical evaluation based on the nature of the social values that they espouse.

[3]Albert R. Ascoli, *Ariosto's Bitter Harmony: Crisis and Evasion in the Italian Renaissance* (Princeton: Princeton University Press, 1987), has fine discussions of the ways in which the poem is divided against itself through its portrayals of the central concerns of the Renaissance, especially the dialectical interplay between education and madness, in part through the figure of Heracles, and the exploration of identity in the split between name and being.

In his story of Olimpia, Ariosto offers a fresh interpretation of the abandoned Ariadne figure. He weaves together allusions to the two major Latin poets whose versions we have examined, suggesting that he was attuned to the various transformations and reinterpretations. Madness crept into Catullus's version of this heroine and an instability and irrationality into Ovid's, and we can to some extent predict the direction that the ironic Ariosto might take. Yet, he complicates the model considerably by dwelling on the young woman's active role before her abandonment. The problem of responsibility for one's actions is an underlying issue in the narrative.

In the story of Cloridano and Medoro, the poet associates the warrior pair with the classical virtues of piety and fidelity. He adapted allusions to Vergil's night raid in ways that shift the emphases on love and the traditional heroic values. Furthermore, he uses Statius's version, which emphasizes the personal nature of piety, as a second model. One can easily view this episode, too, as outside of the classical debate on the signal social values, an example of the poet's uncomplicated empathy with a youthful heroic effort. But Ariosto, by increasing the significance of love in this episode and by assimilating social values to the private desires of the individual, encourages a reconsideration of the piety and fidelity in the two Roman models.

The Metamorphosis of Ariadne

In canto 10 Ariosto seems to emphasize the pathos of the victim of betrayal in love in his version of the classical Ariadne. His character Olimpia has endured a long struggle to be united with her hero Bireno and thus seems all the more sympathetic when he deserts her. She first appears in the preceding canto, where she tells Orlando of her efforts to rescue her lover Bireno from the harsh tyrant Cimosco; the latter has imprisoned him in retaliation for the murder of his son Arbante, whom Olimpia was forced to marry after a long struggle in which her father and brothers were killed. After Orlando valiantly opposes the ruthless Cimosco and liberates Bireno, the two lovers are reunited; they get married and then begin a sea voyage to his homeland of Zeeland. On the journey Bireno, who has fallen in love with a beautiful captive, the young daughter of Cimosco, hastily abandons Olimpia and leaves her on a deserted island.

Much like the classical Ariadne, Olimpia awakes to find herself alone and laments her plight. Her despair is especially intense since, like Ariadne, she has made enormous personal sacrifices on behalf of her lover. Even more, she has proved herself over a long period of time before being united with Bireno. She thus represents the signal virtue of fidelity, which distinguishes the noblest female characters in Ariosto's poem and gives them a heroic stature.[4] Some critics have in fact felt that the poet added this episode to the third edition of his work (1532) as an attempt to redress the misogynistic overtones of such later stories as the *femine omicide* in cantos 19 and 20.[5]

Although Olimpia exhibits constancy toward Bireno in all her actions, she differs significantly from other female characters, such as Isabella and Fiordiligi, who prove themselves faithful under the most adverse circumstances. The very concept of fidelity shifts between its private, erotic associations in romance and the more public, social view in epic. The *fides* of Catullus's Ariadne or Vergil's Dido is rooted in the Roman notion of the sacredness of a contract. In the *Aeneid*, the hero seems to have made some commitment to Dido's new city, if not to the woman herself, when he accepted a share in the rule of Carthage. The fidelity that Olimpia emphasizes is far more subjective and highly problematic. I will show that the genuine pathos of her situation is qualified by the limitations of the character herself.

The poet introduces Olimpia in canto 9 as a woman saturated with literary precepts derived from the traditions of Ovidian and courtly

[4]On the *virtus* of women in Ariosto's poem, see Georges Güntert, "Le imprese di Isabella d'Este Gonzaga e l'*Orlando Furioso*," in *Il Rinascimento: Aspetti e problemi attuali*, ed. Vittore Branca, Claudio Griggio, et al. (Florence: Olschki, 1982), pp. 445–54; in relation to more general Renaissance views on women's duties and virtues, see Pamela J. Benson, "A Defense of the Excellence of Bradamante," *Quaderni d'Italianistica* 4 (1983), esp. 136–41.

[5]See Giuseppe dalla Palma, "Dal secondo al terzo *Furioso*: mutamenti di struttura e moventi ideologici," in *Ludovico Ariosto: Lingua, stile e tradizione*, ed. Cesare Segre (Milan: Feltrinelli, 1976), pp. 98–99; C. P. Brand, *Ludovico Ariosto: A Preface to the "Orlando Furioso"* (Edinburgh: Edinburgh University Press, 1974), pp. 176–77, observes that the faithful Olimpia replaces the faithless or wicked women of the early cantos, such as Angelica, Dalinda, and Alcina; Cesare Segre, *Esperienze ariostesche* (Pisa: Nistri-Lischi, 1966), p. 32, also comments that Ariosto completes his "gallery" of female characters with the tragic nature of Olimpia's story.

love poetry. She reveals no awareness of the inappropriateness of these sentiments, even though she relates the progressive stages of her love for Bireno in retrospect, after the disaster to her family and country. As a consequence of her ill-founded attitudes and actions, the woman abandoned by her lover becomes a very remote descendant of the classical heroine. By closely reproducing Ovid's version of Ariadne in *Heroides* 10, Ariosto signals that he is re-creating a particular version of the abandoned female. We should perhaps be alert to ironic, essentially unheroic, implications of this choice. The specific echoes of *Heroides* 10 in fact suggest that the poet grasped much of Ovid's own wit and reevaluation of Catullus's version. Through allusions to Catullus and Vergil, Ariosto does not create a complex character embodying important tensions between social values so much as a figure blinded by the many contrived literary conventions that she has assimilated.

Ariosto introduces Olimpia into the poem by allowing her to tell her own story to Orlando in canto 9 and thus to reveal her character directly. She relates the pertinent facts: she fell in love with a visiting count and then rejected her father's attempts to arrange a marriage with the son of the neighboring king of Frisia. As a result of her persistence, the angry king Cimosco attacked Holland and killed her two brothers and her father and continued to besiege her country until the populace finally handed her over. To avenge the death of her kin, she pretended to be willing to marry Arbante but then arranged to have him murdered on their wedding night. Since Cimosco had left to fight the forces of Bireno, whom Olimpia had summoned for help, she was able to escape punishment at his hands but did not know that her lover had been captured (9.22–43).

Throughout this account of her fidelity to Bireno, the poet suggests that Olimpia's behavior is governed by literary precepts and shows her familiarity with the Ovidian and courtly love tradition. When she describes falling in love with Bireno, she uses the military metaphor exploited by Ovid in the *Amores* and later appropriated by the courtly tradition, which emphasized imprisonment.[6] She thus sees herself as a captive in the battle of love: " 'con poca guerra me gli

---

[6]On the derivation of this courtly metaphor from Ovid, see C. S. Lewis, *The Allegory of Love: A Study in Medieval Tradition* (1936; rpt. London: Oxford University Press, 1959), pp. 6–7.

fer captiva'" (9.23.5), "'he conquered me with scarcely a struggle.'"[7] She also echoes the notion of the lover's exterior as a reflection of his inner self, for she is all the more certain of Bireno's
affection because of his appearance of love ("'quel ch'apparea
fuori,'" 9.23.6).[8] The young woman then affirms her belief in her
lover's sincerity with an emphatic pronouncement:[9]

> "io credea e credo, e creder credo il vero
> ch'amassi et ami me con cor sincero." (9.23.7–8)

"I believed and do believe, and I believe that I believe the truth that he
loved me and still loves me with a sincere heart."

As Caretti points out, Ariosto here echoes a line from the episode of
Pier delle Vigne in *Inferno* 13.[10] Dante's verse itself recalls the contorted style of delle Vigne, a poet of the Sicilian school known for
twisted constructions, bizarre conceits, paradoxes, and antitheses.[11]
The source pointedly suggests the self-deception of Dante's character, who needs to convince his examiner of his fidelity to the emperor
so that, like many of the sinners confined to Inferno, he may redeem
his damaged reputation.[12] In the *Furioso*, the effect is similar: the
language belies the spontaneity that the speaker presumes. The poet
implies that Olimpia has absorbed the style of erotic poetry such as
delle Vigne's and that she lacks the self-awareness to perceive the
artificiality of her speech and the limitations of her point of view.

[7]Ludovico Ariosto, *Orlando Furioso*, ed. with commentary Lanfranco Caretti
(Turin: Einaudi, 1971). All quotations from the *Furioso* are from this edition. Except
where noted, the translations are from Ludovico Ariosto, *Orlando Furioso*, tr. Guido
Waldman (New York: Oxford University Press, 1974).

[8]See Maurice Valency, *In Praise of Love: An Introduction to the Love-Poetry of the
Renaissance* (New York: Macmillan, 1958), pp. 44–48, for a discussion of the importance of a man's bearing and behavior as the new standards for nobility in courtly
love poetry and romance.

[9]The translation is my own in order to render the Italian literally in this context.

[10]Caretti (above, note 7), ad loc., cites the allusion to *Inferno* 13. Vincent Cuccaro,
The Humanism of Ludovico Ariosto: From the "Satire" to the "Furioso" (Ravenna:
Longo, 1981), p. 207, also notes the allusion; in his brief discussion of Olimpia, he
observes that she is affected by courtly mannerisms.

[11]For a brief summary of Pier delle Vigne's literary style, see C. H. Grandgent,
ed., *La Divina Commedia di Dante Alighieri* (Boston: D. C. Heath, 1933), pp. 116–17.

[12]On Dante's use of Pier delle Vigne, see Leo Spitzer, "Speech and Language in
Inferno XIII," in *Dante: A Collection of Critical Essays*, ed. John Freccero (Englewood
Cliffs, N.J.: Prentice-Hall, 1965), pp. 78–101.

Ariosto, of course, has many of his characters use language that is demonstrably literary. Bradamante, for instance, utters Petrarchan conceits in soliloquies when she is most frustrated about the possibility of finding her beloved Ruggiero. Yet the language that she employs is an appropriate vehicle to reflect the depths of despair and torment into which she has been thrust.[13] Her use of a literary style, then, is not so much formulaic as it is a mode of psychologically credible self-representation. She is, furthermore, not limited to a specific literary discourse but expresses herself in a variety of forms that seem suitable to the occasion.

When Olimpia presents her background to Orlando by referring to the period in which Bireno was delayed in Holland, her use of metaphorical language seems contrived. She plays on the connotations of "contrary" for adverse winds and antithetical desires, and creates a hyperbolic image of time: "'In the course of those days, during which contrary winds kept him with us—'contrary' to the others, that is, not to me, for to the others those days extended to forty, while to me they were but a minute, so quickly did they go winging past.'" (9.24.1–4).

In accordance with the emphasis on secrecy in the tradition of erotic poetry, Olimpia notes that the two made their declarations of love and plans for marriage without the knowledge of her relatives or anyone else at court.[14] Furthermore, she maintains total silence about her engagement even while her father is negotiating with Cimosco for a marriage to his son. It is only when the deal is almost concluded that she speaks out in protest and refuses to accept Arbante. She

---

[13]Interestingly, when Bradamante's mother refuses to allow her to marry Ruggiero, Ariosto portrays her inner struggle as she contemplates her dilemma of choosing between filial piety and her own desires. Both her agony and her human frailty are made credible. On the one hand, she acknowledges clearly and sensibly her duty as a "good daughter" of "good parents," yet on the other, she perceives herself as a "slave" of Love, who will show "furore" if she "offends" him (44.42–44). Certainly, Bradamante uses some of the same literary clichés as Olimpia, but she shifts between a conversational tone and a more literary language. Furthermore, as she does not echo specific literary works, she does not leave the impression of being too derivative or parodic. Olimpia, by contrast, pervasively relies on literary clichés, and her echoes of Ovid, Catullus, and Vergil are consistently made ironic by the deviations from their models.

[14]On the importance of secrecy in courtly love, see Valency (above, note 8), pp. 169–70.

explains that she could not have broken her promise to her lover and would not have been willing to, since "'Love would not have let me be so fickle'" (9.26.3–4); her explanation is also founded on Ovidian and courtly precepts. As the principal god of the erotic literary tradition, Love is thus the power that dominates and controls the actions of the lover, especially in the sphere of fidelity.[15]

Olimpia reveals that her very manner of speech is controlled by the literary precepts in which she has immersed herself, and she shows no awareness of the consequences of such conditioning. By allowing his heroine to narrate unreflectively the tremendous destruction resulting from her actions, the poet implies that her obsession with fidelity is the product not of an amusing game but rather of a system that is totally out of touch with reality and incapable of functioning in a real social context. Olimpia's behavior as dictated by her erotic ideals causes great devastation after she forces her father to withdraw from the marriage negotiations at the last minute. She persists even after her father and brothers are killed, and the citizens of her country then suffer greatly at Cimosco's hands. Most strikingly, her cold-blooded murder of Arbante suggests an unnatural level of violence, for she foils the desires of her new husband by summoning from hiding an agent who splits open the man's head with an axe. Olimpia, it would seem, prefers to take any course of action, no matter how morally repugnant, rather than to submit to a change in the plans that she has made for union with Bireno.

The poet plays Olimpia's blind naiveté against the realistic politics of Machiavellian characters: the vicious Cimosco, who has been called an exemplar of the *volpe*, *lione*, and *lupo*, and the opportunistic Bireno, the *sciacallo*.[16] The power of authority, a pervasive theme in Ariosto's additions to the third *Furioso*, is especially malevolent here, since Cimosco is said to be the first to employ firearms in

---

[15]See Lewis (above, note 6), pp. 18–22, 32. Ovid, in *Amores* 1.1, humorously but vividly depicts Cupid forcing him to stop writing epic and instead to devote himself strictly to matters of love and love poetry.

[16]Dalla Palma (above, note 5), pp. 103–4, discusses the problem of authority and cites relevant scholarly work on the question of Machiavelli's influence on this episode.

battle.[17] The brutal tyrant is particularly treacherous as he exploits this force from ambush without warning and almost manages to fell the great warrior Orlando himself (9.73–79). The narrator even comments that only Cimosco's extreme agitation or God's wish to preserve His faithful servant could have kept the cannon from killing the knight as well as his horse (9.76). Here the very foundation of chivalry, its military function in society, is threatened by the invention that would render its battle tactics useless. By contrast, Olimpia's obsession with chivalry's private values must then seem all the more self-indulgent and egocentric.

As a preface to the story of Olimpia's abandonment, Ariosto plays up the courtly nature of his heroine by adeptly employing an ironic narrative persona. He addresses a particularly female audience that would be familiar with and sympathetic to the literary conventions that Olimpia espouses. By this point in the work, it is obvious to the reader that the poet frequently underscores these addresses to his courtly audience with considerable irony. The poet-narrator emphasizes Olimpia's fidelity and the *prove* by which she manifests her love. When he informs the *donne* that Bireno did not requite Olimpia's affection after such great constancy, he advises them to be on guard against the entreaties of lovers. He situates the concept of fidelity in a context of chivalric romance rather than epic by using language and images rooted in that tradition. In particular, he applies the metaphor of servitude to describe the woman who succumbs to the persuasion of a suitor and gives up the distance or cool indifference that was expected of the courtly object of desire.[18]

To manipulate his audience further, Ariosto uses a simile to describe the successful young lover who quickly tires of the woman he has obtained: "As a huntsman who pursues a hare in the cold as in the heat, over hill and dale, but no longer prizes it once he has it in the bag, and hastens off the moment he sights a new quarry fleeing

---

[17]See C. D. Klopp, "The Centaur and the Magpie: Ariosto and Machiavelli's *Prince*," in *Ariosto 1974 in America: Atti del congresso ariostesco, dicembre 1974*, ed. Aldo Scaglione (Ravenna: Longo, 1976), pp. 69–84, on the innovation that the poet as well as the contemporary political writer passionately opposed.

[18]On the generally unattainable nature of the lady in courtly love, see Richard Barber, *The Knight and Chivalry* (London: Longman, 1970), pp. 77–79.

from him" (10.7.5–8).[19] The poet singles out handsome young men in particular as proving fickle once they have made their "catch," suggesting such contemporary discussions of love as book 4 of the *Courtier*, in which another courtly audience listens to precepts relating to the erotic state.[20] By evoking an audience of women who are well versed in the symbolism of courtly love, Ariosto ironically calls attention to the literary tastes of his readers and their potential complicity in the mannerisms and conventions of his naive character.

In the next part of Olimpia's story, her abandonment by Bireno, Ariosto portrays a woman who responds to her predicament in literary formulae and clichés. The clever poet, however, allows uncritical readers—perhaps some of the ladies at the court of Ferrara who were so fond of love poetry—to interpret this episode in a straightforward way as a pathetic example of betrayed love.[21] He imitates one of the most admired poems about betrayal and abandonment in Ovid's *Heroides*, Ariadne's letter to Theseus.[22] This particular myth may have had a special appeal to Ariosto's immediate audience at Ferrara, since Titian's painting of Bacchus and Ariadne in a *camerino* of Alfonso d'Este had been completed shortly after the publication of the second edition of the *Furioso* in 1521.[23]

[19]The hunting metaphor is common in amorous contexts in Renaissance poetry; in a paradigm of this image, Ovid at *Metamorphoses* 1.532–8 compares erotic passion to the predatory chase of a hunting dog for its prey in Apollo's pursuit of Daphne.

[20]See Baldesar Castiglione, *The Book of the Courtier*, tr. George Bull (Baltimore: Penguin, 1967), pp. 323–29, on the question of the difference in quality between older and younger men as lovers, especially the tendency of youthful men to experience satiety and reject what they once craved.

[21]On love poetry as a popular diversion at the court of Ferrara, especially for women, see Werner L. Gundersheimer, *Ferrara: The Style of a Renaissance Despotism* (Princeton: Princeton University Press, 1973), pp. 252–53, who comments on the *giardino*, where love songs were often sung under the stars.

[22]A good study of the reception of Ovid in Renaissance France and Italy is Ann Moss, *Ovid in Renaissance France: A Survey of the Latin Editions of Ovid and Commentaries Printed in France before 1600* (London: Warburg Institute, 1982); she shows not only the scope of translations and commentaries on the *Heroides* but also the changing trends in scholarly interests, from the psychology of passion to rhetorical theory and textual criticism (pp. 8–16). See also Ettore Paratore, *Bibliografia ovidiana* (Sulmona: Comitato per le celebrazioni del bimillenario, 1958) for a list of editions published in the sixteenth century.

[23]Cecil Gould, *The Studio of Alfonso d'Este and Titian's Bacchus and Ariadne* (London: National Gallery, 1970), p. 3, notes that after receiving the commission from

Although scholars have long been aware of the numerous echoes of *Heroides* 10 in this episode, they have in general paid little attention to the subtle ways by which the poet changed his model.[24] An exception is Franco Pool, who recently argued that Ariosto was primarily interested in rivaling and surpassing Ovid's version rhetorically.[25] Given Olimpia's penchant for a highly literary discourse, the imitation is especially appropriate since it suggests that she has in fact read Ovid. An examination of the specific adaptations that Ariosto made will illustrate that his imitation of Ovid reflects a conflict between the pathos of Olimpia's abandonment by a callous man and the less admirable side of the woman herself, who responds without self-awareness and with little moral depth.

The poet begins Olimpia's story with a clever transformation of Ovid's text that should alert his careful reader. After addressing Theseus directly, Ariadne describes the setting in which she discovered her plight:[26]

It was the time when the earth is first sprinkled with clear frost and the birds sing plaintively, couched in foliage. (7–8)

Ariosto echoes Ovid's couplet with a similar description of setting:

Dawn of the golden rays scattered the ground with hoar frost, and the halcyons could be heard over the water lamenting their age-old sorrows. (10.20.3–6)

Like his model, the poet specifically mentions the frost on the ground and the mournful sound of the birds. But he mythologizes

---

Alfonso d'Este, Titian started the work in 1522 and sent it to Ferrara the following year.

[24]The major investigation of Ariosto's debt to Ovid and other classical sources in the Olimpia episode is Pio Rajna, *Le fonti dell'"Orlando Furioso"* (Florence: Sansoni, 1876), pp. 175–85, who provides a listing of the particular passages that echo *Heroides* 10 but does not attempt to develop any overview about their function.

[25]Franco Pool, *Interpretazione dell'"Orlando Furioso"* (Florence: La Nuova Italia, 1968), pp. 58–63, stresses the greater dramatic immediacy of Ariosto's passage in arousing suspense and confirming the dreadful truth of abandonment.

[26]Ovid, *Heroides, With the Greek Translation of Planudes,* ed. Arthur Palmer (Oxford: Clarendon Press, 1898). My quotations from *Heroides* 10 are from this edition. The translations are my own.

Ovid's simple description of the natural setting: now the goddess Aurora sprinkles the frost and Alcyone laments her misfortune.

A second mythological example refers to an episode in the *Metamorphoses* that Ariosto's fictional audience of ladies would probably recall with considerable feeling, since it was one of the greatly admired love stories in Ovid's poem.[27] Although the allusion to Alcyone's lament may seem to reinforce the elegiac tone of Olimpia's own story, it actually functions more by antithesis. In book 11 Ovid tells the story of Ceyx, who had to search for his brother and leave his wife Alcyone behind. The poet emphasizes the deep mutual love between husband and wife: after Ceyx is shipwrecked and his body washed ashore, Alcyone's grief is so intense that the gods out of pity reunite them eternally by transforming them into shorebirds (11.410–72). By alluding to this example of the pathos of true love, Ariosto puts the reader into a frame of mind that anticipates a similar story of mutual reciprocation of feeling and a reunion in another sphere of life. Subsequent events in the narrative, of course, ironically dispel that illusion. Ariosto, by weaving in this Ovidian myth of metamorphosis, may imply his own transformation of the great Roman poet who radically altered the meaning of the literary myths that he imitated. In this way Ariosto not only caters to his fictional courtly audience interested in love poetry but also signals to his perceptive reader the ironic possibilities latent in his adaptation of the classical Ariadne.

The poet imitates *Heroides* 10 closely, especially at the beginnning of his narrative of Olimpia's discovery of abandonment. He frequently translates specific phrases literally. His description of Olimpia's sudden awakening, for example, "Caccia il sonno il timor" (10.21.5), echoes Ovid's "excussere metus somnum" (13). Furthermore, he often cleverly imitates the rhetorical structures of *Heroides* 10. Ovid, for instance, repeats a phrase to frame the couplet in which he shows Ariadne groping for Theseus as she awakes:

[27]Love stories from Ovid's *Metamorphoses* seem to have been frequently adapted and presented for the d'Este family. Ovid's story of Procris and Cephalus, for example, was made the subject of a play, *Cefalò*, by Niccolo da Correggio, written and performed at the court of Ferrara. The great poet Boiardo had translated at least some of the *Metamorphoses* at Ferrara by 1494; see Werner L. Gundersheimer, *Art and Life at the Court of Ercole I d'Este: The 'De triumphis religionis' of Giovanni Sabadino degli Arienti* (Geneva: Droz, 1972), p. 21.

> Nullus erat: referoque manus iterumque retempto,
> Perque torum moveo bracchia: nullus erat. (11–12)

There was nobody; I return my hands and try again and move my arms over the bed; there was nobody.

Ariosto loosely translates this couplet but maintains the framing construction by which the circular action of the woman's hands is mirrored in the verse:

> Nessuno truova: a sé la man ritira:
> di nuovo tenta, e pur nessuno truova. (10.21.1–2)

She found nobody. She withdrew her hand. Again she tried: still nothing.

In another passage, which we discussed in the context of Ariadne's need for consolation by a beneficent nature, Ovid has Ariadne recollect her attempts to call out to Theseus by creating a pathetic fallacy and by infusing the verses with an alliterative *t* sound suggestive of his name:

> Reddebant nomen concava saxa tuum,
> Et quotiens ego te, totiens locus ipse vocabat:
> Ipse locus miserae ferre volebat opem. (22–24)

The hollow rocks returned your name, and as often as I called you, the place itself responded and wished to help me in my misery.

Ariosto's rendition is very similar:

> Bireno chiama: e al nome di Bireno
> rispondean gli Antri che pietà n'avieno. (10.22.7–8)

She called "Bireno," and at his name the sympathetic caves echoed "Bireno."

He borrows the motif of the resounding caves and even intensifies Ovid's effect. The heroine of *Heroides* 10 credited the cave with a desire to aid her; the poet here personifies the caves ("gli Antri") and endows them with pity ("pietà"). By repeating the name itself,

Ariosto literally creates a verbal echo in his verse that reflects the echo of the rocks.

Much as Ovid exploited the idea of vision in *Heroides* 10, Ariosto pays close attention to the heroine's ability to perceive clearly. As soon as she awakes from sleep, Olimpia's first act is to look: "She opened her eyes to look: no one to be seen." (10.21.5–6). Here Ariosto adds the element of vision to Ovid's passage, where Ariadne simply says "Frightened, I got up" (13). As Ariadne rushes off to catch sight of Theseus's ship, she uses three verbs of seeing:

> Luna fuit: specto, siquid nisi litora cernam;
> Quod videant, oculi nil nisi litus habent. (17–18)

There was a moon; I look to see if I can discern something except shore;
but as far as my eyes can see, they find nothing except shore.

Ariosto translates the passage closely and, by repeating the verb *vedere*, keeps the emphasis on the heroine's struggle to see. Olimpia

> va guardando (che splendea la luna)
> se veder cosa, fuor che 'l lito, puote;
> né, fuor che 'l lito, vede cosa alcuna. (10.22.4–6)

strained her eyes, the moon still being up, to see whether anything could
be made out beyond the shore—but she could see nothing, only the shore.

Ariadne claims that she thought she saw Theseus, then was doubtful: "I either saw him or it was as if I thought I saw him" (31); similarly, Olimpia "saw them in the distance, or thought she did" (10.24.1).

Ariosto exploits Ovid's emphasis on vision and shows the extent to which Olimpia relies on appearances, in contrast to the classical models. With another addition to Ovid's passage, Ariosto has his heroine, now sure of Bireno's departure, stare at the water ("da mirar l'acque," 10.26.7). Her next reference to vision, much more emphatic, suggests her desperate need to cling to the tangible and concrete. Unlike Ariadne, who uses the verb *video* once as she states her helplessness (69), Olimpia repeats the verb *vedere* three times in the corresponding passage:

"Uomo non veggio qui, non ci veggio opra
donde io possa stimar ch'uomo qui sia;
nave non veggio. . . ." (10.28.1–3)

"I see no man here, nor any sign to show that men live here. No ship do
I see. . . ."

As the episode progresses, Olimpia's vision becomes more problematic when compared to Ariadne's. We observed above that Ovid
goes beyond Catullus by having his heroine give vivid imaginative
form to her fears of attack:

Now, now I fear that wolves are about to come from here or there to
tear me apart with ravenous mouth; who knows whether this land nour-
ishes tawny lions? Perhaps Dia may also bear the savage tiger.
(83–86)

Olimpia utters similar fears:

"O what fear! I seem already to see bears and lions coming out of these
woods, and tigers and beasts armed by Nature with sharp fangs and claws
to rend me." (10.29.1–4)

Ariadne's remarks reflect her loss of bearings at the beginning of her
abandonment and are to some extent an understandable reaction to
dangers lurking in unfamiliar terrain. Olimpia's, however, are more
irrational. Unlike her model, she not only fears dreadful creatures
but actually claims to see the beasts coming after her. Her final
gesture in Canto 10 also alters the reference to vision in the *Heroides*.
She stares fixedly out to sea ("guarda il mare," 10.34.7), just as
Ariadne describes herself as "mare prospiciens" (49). The latter,
however, comments on her intense, motionless gaze out to sea in
the early part of her letter; the statement marks a turning point after
which she ceases to look for Theseus's ship in the distance. Instead,
she expresses her fears of isolation, exile, and ultimately death and
becomes detached from the traditional values that her predecessor
had espoused. Ariosto's heroine, by contrast, is totally fixed in her
predicament.

Besides focusing on vision, the poet further separates his heroine from her model in her consideration of the consequences of her situation. First, she views the anxiety that she now feels as a kind of death itself: "'But you—you are making me die a thousand deaths'" (10.29.8). Ovid's character utters a similar thought as she begins to express her fears about the probable sources of terror: "A thousand forms of death rush to my mind" (81). Whereas Ariadne simply reflects her terror, Olimpia concludes her account of dangers with this comment in order to place full responsibility on Bireno. She thus introduces the attitude that prevails throughout the rest of her speech, especially as she considers the possible sources of release from her desperate condition.

By reflecting on her situation, Olimpia resembles Catullus's heroine, who speaks strongly for social and moral principles. Yet ironically, in contrast to Ariadne, she reveals her lack of inner evaluation. She begins by considering the possibility of a rescue: "'But what if a ship put in right now to show mercy and take me away'" (10.30.1–2). She echoes Ariadne's first thoughts of escape: "Imagine that companions and winds and ship are granted to me" (63), in itself a reference to Catullus (64.178–79). Like Ariadne, Olimpia acknowledges that she cannot go back to her own country. But in pointing to her betrayal of father and country, Catullus's heroine sees her own responsibility for her situation. Ovid's Ariadne admits her betrayal of her father but then begins to sentimentalize her family and focus on her loss rather than on the moral issues. Olimpia emphasizes only Bireno's fault, that he took her homeland Holland away from her through fraud: "'Would I be taken back there to the land of my birth, seeing that you have falsely seized it from me?'" (10.30.6–7).

At this point, where Olimpia begins to consider what sources of refuge may remain open to her, the poet makes his predominant connection to the Catullan model but also suggests Vergil's Dido. Both of those characters undergo a similar process of self-questioning by which they investigate ways of extricating themselves from their difficult situations. In poem 64 Ariadne reflects a moral position strongly endorsed by the poet as she evokes the sacred nature of *fides*. In her more complex monologue in *Aeneid* 4, Dido considers the ethical implications of Aeneas's actions but also suggests her own failings. After the pathos of her cry "'en quid

ago?'" (4.534),[28] she rules out the possibilities: she cannot renew
relations with her former African suitors who are now hostile to
her, nor can she follow her lover to his destined kingdom in Italy,
since she has been scorned ("invisam," 541) and cannot uproot her
people a second time. While accusing Aeneas of being *perfidus* and
ingratus,[29] Dido recognizes her own failings, especially in breaking
her oath to remain faithful to her dead husband (552). This awareness is problematic, since the poet provides other perspectives on
the appropriateness of Dido's vow and alludes to her complex fusion of heroic ambitions and private passions. Her final act of suicide
reveals both the irrationality and the nobility of that character.

When viewed against this background, Olimpia's evaluation of
her situation can only seem shallow and unreflective. As she
ponders her second possibility, she finds Flanders also barred to her:
"'Shall I return to Flanders? But I have sold everything off which I
lived—little enough though this was—in order to aid you and deliv-
er you from prison.'" (10.31.5–7). Here again she finds Bireno
responsible for excluding another place of refuge: she cannot return
to Flanders because she has sold all her possessions there in order to
help her lover. Her first reproach, that Bireno has taken over as ruler
of Holland, is valid to some extent, though she fails to acknowledge
her own hasty act of transferring power to him and her inability to
see through his opportunistic nature. At this point, Olimpia does
not even consider that her decision to sell all her property in Flanders was rash and foolish, since she paid a vast sum for Bireno's
rescue to men who were all afraid of Cimosco's firearms and simply
took advantage of her lucrative offer (9.48–49).

Olimpia's inability to consider the full implications of her actions
is even more apparent as she poses her last possibility. She thus
contemplates a return to Frisia: "'Am I to go to Frisia, then, where I
might have been queen, but for your sake chose not to be? This was
the undoing of my father and my brothers, and spelled the end of all

---

[28]Vergil, *Opera*, ed. R. A. B. Mynors (Oxford: Clarendon Press, 1969). All
quotations from the *Aeneid* are from this edition, with *v* used for consonantal *u*. The
translations are my own.
[29]On the political obligations based on *fides* and *pietas* that Aeneas has contracted
with Dido, see Richard Monti, *The Dido Episode and the* Aeneid (Leiden: Brill, 1981),
esp. pp. 30–69.

my fortune'" (10.32.1–4). Here, she even blames Bireno for her refusal to serve as queen of Frisia. At this point she is blind to the truth, for in her earlier account to Orlando she herself implied that the young man was detained in Holland against his will by adverse winds. This unexpected circumstance gave her the opportunity to develop her interest in him and experience love for the first time.[30] Bireno's role in the whole affair seems at best a passive one. Most important, Olimpia herself bears the burden of her family's destruction, since she willfully kept her pledge of marriage a secret.

As she concludes this evaluation of her plight, Olimpia sums up her attitudes and expectations: "'I would not reproach you, thankless one, with all I have done for you, or use it against you—you know it as well as I do. A fine reward you give me for it!'" (10.32.5–8). It is certainly true that Bireno owes his fortune to her. He is at fault more so than Aeneas with Dido or Catullus's Theseus with Ariadne, since he has not only accepted her favors and sacrifices but has also married her. While having legitimate grounds for anger and hostility, Olimpia is ungraciously and unreflectively emphatic about the sacrifices that she has made for Bireno.

Unlike her classical models, she indicates no failure of her own in the entire affair. When she calls the man "ingrato," there is no sense of the complex nexus of associations at work in the Roman poems. Acting impulsively and rather mechanically, Olimpia is totally dependent upon rewards and gratitude in response to her efforts. She made herself the object of an unrealistic devotion through the workings of her imagination. According to Olimpia's literary code, Bireno was supposed to be a Lancelot rather than a Theseus. When placed in the unhappy condition of Ariadne and Dido, she knows the language of those two heroines but lacks their psychological and moral depth. The Catullan and Vergilian characters legitimately vilify the violation of *fides* and *gratia*; Olimpia by contrast seems unaware that the gratitude she expects has a shaky foundation, for

---

[30]Alfredo Bonadeo, "Olimpia," *Italica* 45 (1968), 48–57, discusses the subjective nature of Olimpia's passion; he ultimately connects this problem to the poet's own situation, his love for the selfish Alessandra Benucci, which may have prompted further reflection on the follies of human passion. In particular, Ariosto may have read Leone Ebreo's *Dialoghi*, a Neoplatonic work analyzing the relation of desire to love.

she has acted all along under her own delusions.[31] She seems, more-over, oblivious to her own insistence upon recompense; but her accusations in the preceding three stanzas belie her view that she is not primarily concerned about Bireno's indebtedness.

The poet places Olimpia's final words of lament in an ironic context. She concludes by expressing fears for her future and, like Ovid's Ariadne, hopes that she will not be captured and enslaved. Unlike her model, however, she states that she would rather have the wolves, lions, tigers, bears, and "'any fierce beast'" (10.33.4) consume her. At first glance, Olimpia seems to express anxieties reasonable for an individual in such a vulnerable situation. Although at this point neither the heroine nor the reader knows what will happen, the poet reveals that her statement is an ironic foreshadow-ing of events in canto 11: there, Olimpia is captured by pirates and is in fact left prey to the orc, a sea monster that feeds on young women who are offered as victims to its predatory assaults. Olimpia's per-ception is thus ironically prophetic.

To conclude the story of her abandonment, Ariosto compares her to two examples of Ovidian metamorphoses: "As though like Hecuba she had gone beserk at the sight of her last son Polydorus' corpse. Now she stood on a rock and stared at the sea; and she herself, no less than the rock, seemed to have turned to stone" (10.34.5–8). The first analogy, which refers to Hecuba's transfor-mation, recalls *Metamorphoses* 13, where Ovid describes the Trojan queen's madness after she sees the body of her dead son Polydorus and exacts revenge by gouging out his murderer's eyes; her fury rises to such a pitch that she finally loses her power of speech and is reduced to barking like a dog (538–75). A more immediate source for Ariosto, however, is the following passage from Dante's *Inferno*: "Hecuba sad, forlorn and captive, when she saw Polyxena dead and

[31]On a similar problem of gratitude in relation to the major character Orlando, who goes mad when his tributes are rejected by the ungrateful Angelica, see Andrea di Tommaso, "Boiardo/Ariosto: Textual Relations and Poetic Integrity," *Stanford Italian Review* 4 (1984), 87–88. D. S. Carne-Ross, "The One and the Many: A Reading of *Orlando Furioso*, Cantos 1 and 8," *Arion* 5 (1966), esp. 226–32, subtly discusses Orlando's "single vision in a universe where only multiple vision will serve." On the character of Olimpia, Mario Santoro, *L'anello di Angelica: Nuovi saggi ariosteschi* (Naples: Federico and Ardia, 1983), pp. 97–104, stresses the rational na-ture of her decisions throughout.

recognized with anguish her Polydorus on the beach, being out of her wits barked like a dog, so distraught was her mind with grief" (30.16–21).[32]

The particular context in which the allusion occurs continues the ironic literary characterization, for Dante refers to Hecuba in a long analogy introducing the canto of the falsifiers. He claims that the acts of madness by Athamas in Thebes or Hecuba in Troy were nothing in comparison to the punishments inflicted upon the sinners of this circle. Dante's description shows Hecuba, whose mind was completely overturned, in a pathetic, if horrifying, state. She is only a partial analogue for the falsifiers who are condemned to hell, since their violence reflects a willful discarding of their personality for unscrupulous purposes. Olimpia resembles Hecuba, who in her madness totally loses control of herself. Yet by the latter's proximity to the actual falsifiers in Dante's text, Ariosto further suggests that Olimpia has assumed a character that is not genuine. By situating his heroine in this Dantesque context, the poet thus reinforces the impression that she has adopted a literary persona in place of a real humanity.

This suggestion of impersonation is strengthened by the second metamorphosis, which echoes the following couplet in Ariadne's story: "Or looking at the sea, I sat rigidly on a rock, and was as much a stone as the seat itself" (49–50). An important difference between the two heroines is that Ariadne makes this comparison in the early part of her narrative in order to describe her reaction at losing sight of Theseus's ship. As the epistle progresses, she conceives of herself with images of motion and flexibility rather than of stasis, which show her pathetic distance from reality as the consequence of her fears of exile and death. Durling suggests that, by fixing Olimpia in a physical bind, Ariosto creates a useful transitional device that suspends her story and allows the poet to resume his account of Ruggiero's activities.[33] This image also serves a thematic function relevant to the episode at hand: limited by her literary

[32]Dante, *The Divine Comedy of Dante Alighieri*, tr. with commentary John D. Sinclair (1939; rpt. New York: Oxford University Press, 1961).

[33]Robert M. Durling, *The Figure of the Poet in Renaissance Epic* (Cambridge, Mass.: Harvard University Press, 1965), p. 119, draws many analogies between Ariosto's poem and Renaissance notions of the cosmos.

preconceptions and thus static in nature, Olimpia is calcified here in the text.

Ariosto concludes his ironic portrayal of Olimpia and his revision of the myth of Ariadne in canto 11. In canto 9 Olimpia lightly dismissed her legitimate social functions of daughter, sister, and then ruler through an obstinate constancy toward her object of desire. She then moved easily from lover to bride and in canto 10, with no reflection on her previous roles, is transformed into a despairing and angry *abbandonata*. In this context Olimpia seems too self-consciously derivative of the classical Ariadne. Again transformed in canto 11, she becomes a new Andromeda when she is chained to a rock and exposed to a sea monster, then rescued by a new Perseus, the hero Orlando.[34] Finally, she is married to Oberto and becomes queen of Ireland.

In this canto the poet brings her story and character to a logical conclusion. He implies that her attractiveness is only physical by a simile comparing her to a statue of Diana (11.58) and by a long passage describing the ideal proportions of her body (11.65–72). In the latter, Ariosto suggests the conventional idealized nature of his heroine as he enumerates the details of her anatomy in a series of literary clichés derived from the love poet's stock depiction of his mistress' charms.[35] He also relates her change of status "from countess to mighty queen" (11.80.2) in an ironic manner. Olimpia finally secures a place in her life (and in Ariosto's art) for what she is. When Oberto decides to marry her, he is motivated by lust aroused by viewing her beautiful naked body. His quickly kindled passion seems all too similar to Bireno's for the daughter of Cimosco. At the end of his description of Olimpia's charms, the poet mentions the king's response to her: "There was no concealing the blaze in his heart" (11.72.5–6). When Oberto tries to find appropriate clothing for Olimpia, his physical desire for her seems the sum of his interest as he keeps recalling her "splendid limbs" (11.75.6).

[34]On this mythological paradigm, see Robert W. Hanning, "Ariosto, Ovid, and the Painters: Mythological Paragone in *Orlando Furioso* X and XI," in *Ariosto 1974 in America*, ed. Aldo Scaglione (Ravenna: Longo, 1976), pp. 111–12; also Brand (above, note 5), p. 70.

[35]For a discussion of the conventional characteristics of female beauty in courtly love poetry, see Valency (above, note 8), pp. 173–74.

Ariosto assumes his audience's awareness of the conclusion to Ariadne's story in classical myth, especially in Catullus 64 and in Ovid's *Metamorphoses*: she is taken up by the god Bacchus and honored by a constellation in the sky.[36] With Oberto in the role of the classical god, Olimpia attains a similar status: she is also transported to a lofty, if not quite celestial, position. In effect, she fulfills the significance of her name: she too is now "Olympian." She thus ironically achieves the idealistic version of love as a transported state in the romance tradition.[37] If Ariosto can be said to challenge contemporary artists in this episode,[38] he may at this point be casting a final glance at Titian. That painter's rendition of the rescue of Ariadne by Bacchus manifestly suggests the virile young god's lust for the beautiful abandoned young woman.[39] In contrast to the woman who has had ridiculously unrealistic standards of love, Oberto sees the reality that is left when her coverings—literal and figurative—have been stripped away and desires the best that Olimpia has to offer.

It is probably true, as critics have observed, that in his final additions to the *Furioso* Ariosto reveals a greater complexity about human experience, which caused him to reject the pessimism and cynicism of the *Cinque Canti* as too limited. The episode of Olimpia reflects this deeper level of awareness. The poet is certainly not merely critical of this character. It is clear that Bireno took advantage of her and cynically deserted her. Yet he is not so different from numerous characters in this poem who are driven by irrational desires and shift from one object to another. Desire in the *Furioso* is fluid and unstable. The punishment that he receives, furthermore, is extreme, for he is killed at the hands of Oberto, who seems incensed

[36]On the fate of Ariadne after her abandonment by Theseus, see Catullus 64.251–64; Ovid, *Ars Amatoria* 1.525–64; *Metamorphoses* 8.174–82; and *Fasti* 3.459–516.

[37]On the exalted state of the lover in romance, see John Stevens, *Medieval Romance: Themes and Approaches* (London: Hutchinson, 1973), pp. 34–5.

[38]See Hanning (above, note 34), esp. pp. 110–16, on the poet's conscious efforts in books 10 and 11 to rival the skill and achievements of contemporary painters. He has some very good remarks about the end of the Olimpia episode, where the poet alludes to Renaissance artistic canons in the adoption of Zeuxis as the ideal model.

[39]See Erwin Panofsky, *Problems in Titian, Mostly Iconographic* (New York: New York University Press, 1969), pp. 143–44, on the literary sources for the actions and attitude of Bacchus.

beyond reason at Olimpia's fate. It is inadequate to say that Olimpia is an antithesis of the wicked and unfaithful women in some of the early and later cantos or that she is simply a tragic figure of suffering. Although to some extent burdens are unjustly inflicted upon her, the poet shows that the quality of her response and her own way of affecting events are equally important.

There is a tension between the Machiavellian political overtones, which scholars have tended to emphasize, and the naive erotic idealism of the woman herself. We thus find a character who is all too fallible and yields to the temptation of assimilating conventions and characters derived from fiction instead of building an identity through the trials of experience. She is poorly equipped to realize her ideals in a delicate situation that calls for tact and diplomacy; violence and death are the unfortunate result. If Olimpia is the victim of Bireno's callous behavior, Ariosto also reveals her blindness by exposing her literary pretensions through an adroit adaptation of Ovid's version of Ariadne. The poet's technique in this episode helps the reader to be on guard against making superficial, automatic identifications that do not hold up on deeper inspection. His adaptations of Ovid's Ariadne, along with allusions to Catullus and Vergil, cast doubt on Olimpia's unity of character and help to hold the narrative suspended between pathos and satire. While the narrator addresses the fictional audience of ladies on the naive level of total empathy with Olimpia, the poet leads his reader aware of the classical texts to a more detached point of view.

In the Olimpia episode, Ariosto has taken a kind of Ovidian approach as he explores through figurative use of metamorphosis another of the many characters who deceive themselves and lose a measure of their rational nature and human dignity. Yet he goes beyond the Roman poet by portraying a problem related to a later, more sophisticated age when printing made books readily available and when women had many more opportunities to become consumers of literature (and even, as in Ferrara, patrons of it).[40] An

---

[40]Women were a major audience of the romantic novel even in antiquity; see Tomas Hägg, *The Novel in Antiquity* (Berkeley: University of California Press, 1983), esp. pp. 90–108, on the increased literacy in the second century B.C. that allowed for a greater reading public, including people outside of the large urban areas and women generally.

untrained, susceptible mind can easily read itself into imaginative fiction, as Dante had much earlier recognized in his Francesca canto;[41] the results can sometimes be humorous and sometimes disastrous.

The Story of Cloridano and Medoro

In his episode of Cloridano and Medoro, Ariosto explores the implications of piety and fidelity from a different perspective. Unlike Olimpia, the two men do not act out of their own personal interests, but altruistically attempt to recover the bodies of their leader Dardinello. The poet based this episode on the night raid of Nisus and Euryalus in the *Aeneid* and on the mission of Hopleus and Dymas to recover their leaders' bodies in the *Thebaid*. The two Roman versions are essentially very different. Vergil eroticized the Nisus and Euryalus episode by subtly revealing the consequences of the love between these two young warriors, especially the narcissistic desire for glory, the self-destructive lust for material possessions, and the uncontrollable bloodlust of their attack on the enemy's camp. He thereby questions the piety and glory that underlie their quest. Statius, however, does not impute ambiguous motives to his two warriors. They reveal a true *pietas* for their leaders, even though Tydeus and to some extent Parthenopaeus are guilty of excesses in war. In Statius's world, few men indeed are exempted from the chaos and madness that causes all traditional values and forms of behavior to disintegrate. Hopleus and Dymas therefore seem all the more noble as their *amor* is truly selfless.

In combining the two Roman models, Ariosto imitates Statius primarily in the warriors' noble effort to retrieve the corpse of their fallen captain and Vergil in the warriors' attack upon sleeping enemy troops before they themselves are captured. He bases his characterization of Cloridano on the more experienced and erotically motivated Nisus and of Medoro on the pious Dymas, who is deter-

[41]On the influence of literature on Francesca's language, see Renato Poggioli, "Paolo and Francesca," in *Dante: A Collection of Critical Essays*, ed. John Freccero (Englewood Cliffs, N.J.: Prentice-Hall, 1965), pp. 61–77.

mined to provide a burial for his fallen leader. Ariosto also attributes great beauty to the younger man as Vergil does in his episode, but he makes him the object of a more extensive erotic interest. Significantly, he shifts Statius's focus on the social duty of his characters in a more sentimental direction. The remainder of this chapter will consider how *pietà* and *fede* lose their social grounding by observing the ways in which the poet adapts his sources.

My approach analyzes Ariosto's conflation of his two models and supplements the criticism that has tended to emphasize the influence of one classical model over the other. Thomas Greene concisely summarizes Ariosto's debt to Vergil by indicating the narrative elements that they have in common: two soldiers of unequal age, the slaughter of sleeping troops, the arrival of enemy cavalry, the flight into the woods, and the violent ending.[42] He also shows Ariosto's independence from his model, especially through his greater modulations of tone and his pragmatic characterization of Cloridano in comparison to Vergil's Nisus.[43] In an important study, Eduardo Saccone concentrates on the poet's relation to Statius. Noting the importance of *fede* in Ariosto's value system, he discusses Medoro's great fidelity to his leader and shows that the poet bestows fame and glory on the pair as the appropriate reward for their noble efforts.[44]

By modeling Cloridano on Nisus, Ariosto recalls the erotic basis of the relationship in the earlier episode. Vergil's character represents complex levels of eros. Contemplating the expedition, Nisus alludes to one aspect of his *cupido*, his love of glory. On the other hand, he would transfer to his friend the valuable war prizes that he expects to obtain. Eros includes the lust for reputation and for possessions as well as sexual drive. His intense passion for the younger Euryalus results in his own demise when he could have saved himself and continued the mission to Aeneas. Here, Cloridano feels an emotional, erotic attachment to the handsome young Medoro but

---

[42]Thomas M. Greene, *The Descent from Heaven: A Study in Epic Continuity* (New Haven: Yale University Press, 1963), pp. 125–29. Walter Moretti, "La storia di Cloridano e Medoro: Un esempio della umanizzazione ariostesca delle idealità eroiche e cavalleresche," *Convivium* 37 (1969), 543–51, also focuses on Vergil as Ariosto's model in this episode, which he interprets in highly idealistic terms.

[43]Ibid., esp. pp. 127–29.

[44]Eduardo Saccone, "Cloridano e Medoro, con alcuni argomenti per una lettura del primo *Furioso*," *MLN* 83 (1968), 67–99.

does not respond with the intense passion of his Vergilian counterpart. Furthermore, he does not embody the other levels of *cupido* that destroy Vergil's characters. Unlike Nisus, who hopes to obtain both fame and possessions, he does not initiate the mission to pass through enemy lines but merely agrees to his younger friend's proposal, even though he implies that it is foolish and cannot in all likelihood succeed. He does hope that the glory won from this exploit will be the payment for a noble death: "'anch'io famosa morte amo e disio'" (18.171.4). Yet the desire for fame is secondary; he does not seek a glory that will elevate him in the present but hopes to be remembered for his deed after his death. His primary motivation is an erotic feeling that accommodates him to the wishes of his friend, however foolhardy. The following statement conveys this important distinction: "'What joy am I to find in anything if I am left without you, Medor? Far better to die with you under arms than to die later of sorrow, should you be taken from me'" (18.171.5–8).

Cloridano's response upon discovering the sleeping troops removes the focus from the quest for glory in Vergil's account. As he catches sight of the sleeping camp, he expresses a pragmatic view: "'I'm not one to let an occasion slip by'" (18.173.2). By contrast, Nisus speaks with cold determination: "'Let the hand be bold: circumstances now call for action'" (9.320). The Moor simply conceives the idea of slaughtering the enemy as he sees them in a vulnerable position; he has not intended to seek an opportunity for demonstrating his prowess. As Greene observes, Cloridano's statement reflects the grim humor of a seasoned veteran.[45] The emphasis on chance ("l'occasioni") points to the cold, realistic attitude of grasping what comes your way. But it contradicts rather than reinforces the *cupido* in Vergil's passage, where the character seeks an opportunity for a potential source of the glory he craves.

Ariosto deletes another aspect of *cupido* in the *Aeneid*, the characters' bloodlust. First, he exaggerates the condition of the enemy in Vergil's text to such an extent that moral criticism of his two warriors' actions would be far less credible. In the *Aeneid*, when Nisus finds the Rutulians, the poet indicates why they are such easy vic-

[45]Greene (above, note 42), pp. 126–27.

tims: they are soundly asleep after an evening in which they celebrated the day's victory with wine (9.189). Here the Christians are not only relaxed with wine, they are "steeped to the eyes" in it (18.172.8). In addition, the poet de-emphasizes Cloridano's responsibility for the killing. Ariosto has eliminated an important suggestion of moral criticism in the *Aeneid*, where Vergil implies the impiety latent in Nisus's attack by noting that his first victim, Rhamnes, was a priest. This act sets the tone for the brutality that follows.[46] Cloridano's murder of the prophet is merely a fact of war.

The emphasis on the state of mind of the victims, moreover, lessens the responsibility of the two warriors for their actions. Cloridano first kills the augur Alfeo, who is described as "medico e mago e pien d'astrologia" (18.174.4). While Vergil comments that Rhamnes' gift of prophecy was of no use to him then (328), Ariosto adds that his character actually prophesied a long life for himself: "he had forecast his own death at a great age on his wife's bosom" (18.174.7–8). The poet here ironically points to the failure of the victim's expectations and the limitations of foreknowledge, for in this case prophecy turns out to be wrong.[47] As he reduces the status of prophecy, he implies that ultimately a man has no control over events.

Ariosto's imitation of the death of Rhoetus further reduces the implication of *cupido* as bloodlust. As we observed in the Vergil chapter, that passage is riveted with tensions in the language and even in the syntax. Although Rhoetus has tried to hide, Euryalus discovers him and eagerly buries his sword to the hilt in his victim's body. Vergil contrasts the life that he had celebrated shortly before with the death that he now suffers:

> He vomited up his red life-spirit and, dying, poured out wine mixed with blood. (349–50)

[46]See Vergil, *Aeneid VII-XII* (London: Macmillan, 1973), ed. with commentary R. D. Williams, ad loc.; since Rhamnes was presumably a *rex sacrificiorum*, his death begins the carnage with "irony and pathos."

[47]Caretti (above, note 7), ad loc., notes that Ariosto may allude to two well-known contemporary intellectuals versed in astrology, one of whom was a friend of Ippolito d'Este.

Ariosto imitates that scene here in the description of Grillo's last moments:

> Blood and wine gurgled out together through the same spigot, for his body held many a hogshead. (18.176.6–7)

The poet reduces Vergil's tragic sense of life cut short by exaggerating the enemy's state of drunkenness. Greene notes that this passage reflects a grim humor, as the poet describes the man's intoxication with an ironic remark: "He was dreaming of drink till Cloridan came to sort him out" (18.176.8).[48] While retaining the narrative details of dark blood and wine spurting out together, Ariosto minimizes Cloridano's responsibility and shifts the focus to Grillo's own state of mind. He again focuses on the ironic distance between a man's expectations and actual events, for he makes a point of stating that the victim had hoped for a sound and peaceful sleep (18.176.3–4). By thus distancing himself from the victim, Ariosto lessens the criticism of his own hero's actions. Finally, the poet's change of agent from Euryalus to the Nisus-figure Cloridano removes an important problem in Vergil's criticism of *cupido* as bloodlust: the younger man absorbs the ferocity from his more experienced friend and then exceeds his brutality. Ariosto has thus reduced the complexity between eros and heroic values implicit in his source.

The poet further reduces moral criticism by implying a higher power in control of events. Much like his model, he describes two victims who had stayed up late at a game (18.177.3–4). Vergil speculates on the fate of the men if they had not fallen asleep:

> Happy, if they had straightway extended that game into the night and had continued it to dawn. (337–38)

Ariosto closely follows his model:

> Happy would they have been had they known how to stay awake at their board until the sun rose across the Indus. (18.177.5–6)

Yet he goes on to add a comment about fate's dominance over human affairs:

[48]Greene (above, note 42), p. 127.

but Fate would be powerless over men if everyone could foretell the future. (18.177.7–8)

By further removing the moral responsibility from Cloridano, Ariosto implicitly challenges the possibility of a truly heroic view of the world through the individual's reliance on public values such as *virtù*.

Ariosto's adaptation of Vergil's powerful lion simile further lessens his warriors' bloodlust. The earlier poet concludes his account of Nisus's assault upon the sleeping enemy with this description:

> Just as an unfed lion ranging through the crowded sheepfolds (for mad hunger urges him on) both gouges and drags the tender flock mute with fear; he rages with bloody mouth. (339–41)

Here, the Moor is similarly compared to a lion:

> Just as a starving lion, lean and wizened from long fasting, in a crowded sheepfold; he kills, devours, and savages the feeble flock abandoned to his power. (18.178.1–4)

Although he begins with an exact translation,[49] Ariosto alters Vergil's analogy by toning down the excessive fury of the agent. He changes the operative word "vesana" ("mad") to the temporal adjective "lunga," by which he reasonably explains the lion's hunger. He does not include the phrase "fremit ore cruento," which graphically depicts the animal's raging madness in the *Aeneid*. Vergil's lion image adds to the surrealistic quality of an episode in which *virtus* and *pietas* have gone awry and so functions as a moral comment. Here the more neutral narrator implies neither pathos for the victims nor criticism of the aggressor. He further adapts his model by eliminating an important ambiguity. The simile in the *Aeneid* includes both Nisus and Euryalus as its referents. In the *Furioso* it

[49]Here I slightly alter Waldman's translation by rendering *come* as "just as" instead of "imagine" so as to keep the phrase a simile. For another discussion of this simile, see Kristin O. Murtaugh, *Ariosto and the Classical Simile, Harvard Studies in Romance Languages*, 36 (Cambridge, Mass.: Harvard University Press, 1980), pp. 96–99, who concentrates on the similarities to the original and sees more of an emphasis on movement in Ariosto's simile.

applies only to Cloridano and does not affect the characterization of Medoro.

Although Medoro corresponds to Euryalus, Ariosto does not implicate the younger man as much as Vergil does. By asserting that "he scorned to slay the common herd" (18.178.8), he reverses Vergil's description of Euryalus killing "many ordinary men without name in his midst" (343). Whereas Euryalus is indiscriminate in his slaughter, Medoro is restrained and selective. When the latter kills a man and his mistress lying in a tight embrace, the poet actually applauds the event and suggests that the two have deserved their fate and will be permanently united in the afterlife (18.179.6–8). In the case of Medoro's second pair of victims, the focus is on their frustrated expectations. Medoro is simply the agent who keeps the two brothers, newly knighted by Charlemagne, from receiving the extensive lands that they had been promised: "He had promised them lands in Frisia, too, and would have given them—but Medor prevented him" (18.180.7–8). Again Ariosto suggests the futility of heroic activity, since even the great Christian leader is foiled in his intentions to reward loyal service.

Materialism, another major facet of the *cupido* in Vergil's episode, loses its significance here. When Nisus decides to quit the bloody scene, Vergil suggests that the man is aware that he has gone too far in his lust for slaughter:

> (For he perceived that he was carried away by too much slaughter and greed). (354)

For Ariosto, Cloridano's motivation for leaving is strictly practical:

> They turned aside, fearing that they were bound to come upon one man still awake in so vast a host. (18.181.7–8)

The poet also eliminates Euryalus's foolish act of plunder in the *Aeneid* by which Vergil suggests a major tension between the values of *virtus* and *pietas*: the lust for slaughter has a counterpart in the desire for possessions that will add to one's glory. When the youth eagerly seizes a brightly crested helmet, his presence is revealed to the enemy (373–74) and ultimately leads to his death. Although Ariosto follows Vergil's account by noting that his two warriors could easily have plundered their victims, he explicitly states that neither was at all concerned with acquiring lucrative spoils: "And though they could have departed laden with booty, they deemed it gain enough if they could make good their escape" (18.182.1–2).

In his account of Cloridano's death, Ariosto also reveals the difference between Cloridano's feeling for Medoro and Nisus's for Euryalus. He eliminates the passion that characterizes even the last dying act of Vergil's hero. When he realizes that his efforts to save his friend from death at the hands of the enemy have failed, Nisus rushes savagely at the murderer and stabs him in the face. As others strike him down, he falls on the body of the younger man in a final burst of passion:

> Then, pierced through, he thrust himself over the lifeless body of his friend and at last found peace in the quiet of death. (444–45)

Cloridano also attempts to save Medoro by killing some of his captors but fails. Unlike his counterpart, however, he intends simply to die rather than to seek vengeance (19.15.1–4). And in contrast to Nisus's particularly violent death, his last moments are dispassionate and uninvolved, as he merely shows curiosity over the loss of his own lifeblood:

> He saw the sand turn red with his own blood, amid so many swords, and his end approaching. Now feeling his last strength gone, he dropped to the ground beside his friend. (19.15.5–8)

Although Ariosto has modeled Cloridano's and Medoro's attack on the sleeping camp on the night raid in the *Aeneid*, he has significantly distanced his two characters from Vergil's pair. They perform the same actions, but their motivations lack the complexity of the earlier characters'. Ariosto preserves the martial ambience but to a large extent eliminates the bases of the earlier heroic world. Although representing Vergil's older warrior, Cloridano does not exhibit complex associations with the ambivalent aspects of *cupido*: passion for glory, bloodlust, and greed. Only his erotic attraction to the handsome younger warrior is similar. Yet even there the difference is crucial: Cloridano may seem like a Nisus with Euryalus or a Heracles with Hylas, but Medoro does not play the role of the younger partner in a physical relationship. Each man seems driven by his own desires, Cloridano for the engagingly attractive Medoro, Medoro for his dead leader whom he adored, and, in the aftermath of the night raid, for the most elusive object of desire in the entire poem. Diverse and fluid, erotic drives here are not integrated into a nexus that makes social values so problematic in Vergil's text. When Ariosto refers to the "empia strage" (18.181.5) inflicted by the two warriors, he ironically reflects the difference between his perspective and Vergil's in the sphere of social criticism. The *empietà* of Cloridano and Medoro is their lack of pity, not a questionable or inadequate devotion to country, gods, or family.[50]

In imitating Statius's episode of Hopleus and Dymas, Ariosto makes the virtue of *pietà* more personal and sentimental. While Cloridano is the major protagonist representing the *Aeneid*, Medoro figures more prominently in the imitation of the *Thebaid*. The younger warrior resembles Statius's two characters in his devotion to his leader Dardinello. The heroes of the Roman epic have a high regard for their respective leaders that is appropriate for subordinates. The *dux*, or superior officer, represents the *patria*; absolute loyalty is owed to him in that capacity. Statius thus implies a complex of social and religious motivations when Hopleus conjures up a vision of the leader's mother reproaching Dymas for not returning her son's body (10.354–55).[51] Medoro, however, is motivated by private feelings. He indicates his reasons for seeking Dardinello's burial: "'When I think how good he always was to me, I feel that even if I gave my life to serve his fame I could not repay him or discharge

[50]For the semantic range of *pietà* and the related words *pio* and *pietade*, see Nicolo Tommaseo and Bernardo Bellini, eds., *Nuovo dizionario della lingua italiana* (Turin: Unione Tipografico-editrice, 1861–79).

[51]For a definition of *pietas* in Statius, see David Vessey, *Statius and the* Thebaid (Cambridge: Cambridge University Press, 1973), p. 80: "It involves love, duty and morality in a man's relationship with his family, his rulers, his fatherland and the gods." Vessey stresses that *pietas* is a vital concept for the poet, who even allegorizes it in the confrontation with Tisiphone, the personification of evil, in book 11; he emphasizes the piety of Hopleus and Dymas in wanting to fulfill the sacred duty of a man to bury the dead (pp. 116–17). A. J. Gossage, "Virgil and the Flavian Epic," in *Virgil*, ed. D. R. Dudley (London: Routledge and Kegan Paul, 1969), p. 73, points to Statius's emphasis on "close ties of duty and affection among members of a family." Thus, the Latin poet perceives a union between compassion and the obligations inherent in this primary social concept.

my immense debt to him'" (18.168.5–8). The young man views the fealty that a warrior owes to his lord in intensely personal, subjective terms. Because his leader has been kind ("umano") to him, he feels that he owes him an enormous debt ("oblighi immensi"). This perception of the relationship between lord and vassal is unconventional and does not square with traditional views on that formal social bond.[52]

Medoro is even eroticized as he searches for his leader's corpse. He utters a prayer to Diana on behalf of Dardinello that closely echoes Dymas's appeal to the same deity in the *Thebaid* (10.365–70). Yet in the latter Diana responds because the dead Parthenopaeus had venerated her (10.368–69); he is referred to as her "insignis alumnus" and as "tuus puer."[53] His *pietas* is thus the basis upon which the goddess acts on his behalf. Here it is not clear why the moon breaks through the clouds and illuminates the field for the warrior: "The Moon breached the clouds at his prayer (whether by chance or in answer to such faith)" (18.185.1–2). Unlike Statius, Ariosto places her appearance in a mythical context, Diana is "beautiful as the night when she gave herself naked into the arms of Endymion" (18.185.3–4). With this analogy between Medoro and Endymion, the poet suggests that his young hero has the power to seduce even the austere moon goddess, who in classical literature yielded only to the exceptionally beautiful Endymion. Ariosto adds an extra romantic element, for now the moon shines even more brightly on the spot where the dead leader lies (18.186.1–2).

Medoro's reaction to Dardinello's body reflects the increased sentimentality underlying the imitation of the *Thebaid*. Both Hopleus and Dymas are careful not to weep aloud because they do not wish to attract the enemy's attention:

They dared neither to speak nor to weep for a long while. (10.380–81)

Medoro, however, does not restrain his tears or sobbing:

[52]For the traditional view of this social and political relationship, see Marc Bloch, *Feudal Society*, tr. L. A. Manyon (Chicago: University of Chicago Press, 1961), esp. pp. 211–20.

[53]Statius, *Thebais et Achilleis*, ed. H. W. Garrod (Oxford: Clarendon Press, 1906). My quotations from Statius are from this edition, except for the minor alteration of *sed* for *sui* in line 417. The translations are my own.

> His whole face was bathed in bitter tears (there was a stream under each eyelid). He lamented with such sweetness, he could have made the winds stop to listen. (18.186.5–8)

In contrast to Statius's depiction of Dymas's self-control in his determination to provide a burial for his leader, Medoro manifests an effusively emotional state, a mark of his personal feelings for his leader.

Military fidelity becomes an expression of private desire for Medoro. Although showing some caution by lowering his voice, the young man is completely unconcerned with his own life: "Not that he was anxious for his own life if he were overheard—he hated his life and would gladly have quit it" (18.187.2–4). In the *Thebaid*, Statius claims simply that the two men regarded their leaders so highly that they valued their own lives less (349–50). Hopleus and Dymas do in fact wish to survive their bold deed. Medoro, however, emphatically claims to despise his own life so completely that he desires only death now that Dardinello is gone. He repeats this sentiment when he confronts Zerbino with a plea for his leader's burial: "'Further pity than this I do not crave nor would I have you think that I long to live. I care for my life only so far as it will enable me to bury my lord, no further'" (19.11.5–8).

The poet also reflects upon the significance of Medoro's piety by incorporating an extended epic simile from the *Thebaid*. The model compares Dymas hovering about Parthenopaeus to a lion protecting her cubs:

> As a lioness, whom Numidian hunters crowd upon in her rough den after she has given birth, stands erect over her newborn but with a doubtful mind, roaring wildly and wretchedly. She could chase off the crowd and break their weapons with her mouth. But love of her offspring conquers her cruel heart, and in the midst of her wrath she looks around at her cubs. (10.414–19)

Ariosto imitates this simile in a very close translation:

> Like a mother-bear attacked by a huntsman in her craggy mountain lair. She stands by her cubs, perplexed, and quivers with pity and rage at once: rage and her natural fierceness urge her to bare her claws and bloody her

chops, but mother-love softens her and draws her back, in the midst of her wrath, to take care of her young ones. (19.7.1–8)

Statius's simile sustains an epic tone: the lion is depicted as a warrior in a "savage" lair, able to throw the troops into confusion, but finally subject to an emotion that "conquers" her "cruel" heart. Ariosto sentimentalizes his description. The bear's young are "sons" rather than "offspring" or "cubs." While love "conquers" the lion's hard heart, it "softens" the bear's: the military connotation of "vincit" yields to the erotic suggestiveness of "intenerisce." By substituting the word "pietà" for Statius's description of sound, "miserabile" ("wretchedly"), the poet depicts the animal's tenderness, the emotional aspect of piety rather than familial obligation in a strict social sense. The *pietà* that Medoro exhibits for his leader thus comes from affection, not duty; its basis is private and subjective rather than public and social.

Ariosto further connects desire to *pietà* in his account of the enemy's reaction to the appealing young man. Although borrowing the scene from Statius, he changes the quality of the leader's response to the hero. In the *Thebaid*, Amphion's practical orders not to use violence on the captive are immediately disregarded:

> But now, although Amphion forbade them to use force, the man's left hand was cut off. (10.420–21)

In Ariosto's work, the captain Zerbino himself begins to handle Medoro roughly but then changes his tactics:

> He reached out and grasped his golden curls and tugged him forward petulantly—but when he laid eyes on the youth's handsome face he took pity on him and did not slay him. (19.10.5–8)

The *pietade* that Zerbino feels is a response to Medoro's beauty. Even for the young man's enemy, then, *pietade* has an erotic, sentimental underpinning that completely contrasts with the primary social significance of *pietas*, especially in a military context where duty to one's country and its cause comes first. In the Roman epic, the tenderness that Hopleus and Dymas feel for their leaders cannot outweigh the martial interests of their enemy; their piety is in conflict with the *virtus* that Amphion's men wish to display in their own fulfillment of duty.

Ariosto completely deviates from his classical models by eroticizing Medoro more overtly at the conclusion of the episode when he is rescued by Angelica. He brings in Cupid, the god of erotic poetry, as the agent of Angelica's change of heart toward men. Shot by his arrow, the beautiful princess who has been the object of desire for so many heroes in the poem now loses her haughtiness and actively pursues Medoro as her lover. Without knowing how great her response to the injured young soldier will be, Angelica begins to tend to his wounds and simultaneously feels a strange sensation overtaking her: "An unaccustomed sense of pity stole into her breast by some unused door, softening her hard heart" (19.20.5–7). She may be ignorant, but the reader has been prepared by the poet's description of Cupid waiting in the wings with his arrows and thus knows the nature of the woman's *pietade*. The rescue of the hero from death is thus transferred to the erotic domain, where sentimentality yields to lust. The poet describes this process as Angelica's *pietade* compels her to stay with Medoro until he is fully recovered: "So much did he mean to her—for such was the tenderness which pity had evoked in her when she had first set eyes on the prostrate youth" (19.26.2–4).

The formerly proud young woman burns with passion (19.26.5–7) and wastes away with longing; she is finally reduced to begging the humble soldier for "mercy" ("merce"). Medoro now becomes an agent of a different kind of *pietà*, the gratification that the beloved gives to the lover in erotic poetry.[54] The young man who had felt the "immense obligations" to his leader now expresses the same sentiments for his erotic mistress as he invokes the landscape where the two made love with a poetic statement of his "debt."[55] His transformation from the pious soldier tenderly wishing to bury his

[54] See Robert Ball, "Theological Semantics: Virgil's *Pietas* and Dante's *Pietà*," *Stanford Italian Review* 2 (1981), 72–74, for a discussion of the use of *pietà* in the erotic poetry of Dante and his predecessors. For an erotic use of *pietà* in the *Furioso*, see the poet's description of Angelica's lack of response to Sacripante's love lament (1.49).

[55] A. Bartlett Giamatti, "Headlong Horses, Headless Horsemen: An Essay on the Chivalric Epics of Pulci, Boiardo, and Ariosto," in *Italian Literature, Roots and Branches: Essays in Honor of Thomas Goddard Bergin*, eds. Giose Rimanelli and Ken-

leader to the pious lover offering his sexual "payment" is now complete: as with so many other characters in this poem, desire is easily transferred from one object to another.

Although he makes this episode appear similar to his classical models, Ariosto significantly differentiates his two protagonists from their predecessors. For Vergil, *pietas* is a complex social value, indispensible to Roman views of social cohesiveness. It is potentially destructive to the individual not only as the various areas of activity under its domain come into conflict but also as the very essence of these values is eroded by desire. Ariosto consistently veers away from Vergil's criticism as well as from Statius's more idealistic position. First, he performs a kind of *reductio ad absurdum* on Vergil's episode by exaggerating the drunken state of the enemy, by focusing on the irony of the victims' own thoughts and desires, by emphasizing the role of chance over the heroes' own actions, and by shifting Cloridano's motivation from the desire for glory to love for his friend (which Vergil's Nisus himself reveals at the end when he kills Volcens and in a paroxysm of grief falls on his dead friend's body). Conversely, Ariosto emphasizes the sentimentality in Statius's night raid, where *pietas* does in fact include the quality of tenderness but within the compass of performing duties to family, gods, and state. Medoro may be admirable in his own right, but Ariosto reduces his *pietà* to such a subjective level that it cannot function as a social value in a meaningful way, especially in a military context where a warrior's loyalty to his leader is a social obligation promoting the welfare of the society as a whole. Medoro survives his valiant but foolhardy effort that took the life of the capable warrior Cloridano. Yet he lives not to achieve great deeds in the military sphere but to become the object of Angelica's love. For Ariosto, then, piety and fidelity are essentially like so many other private drives in his poetic universe.

In the *Orlando Furioso*, the erotic is not only an impediment to heroic, social action, but it also reveals the extent to which the major

---

neth J. Atchity (New Haven: Yale University Press, 1976), p. 299, refers to the mercantile language by which Medoro can "pay" Angelica; he notes the ironic contrast with Petrarchan language of love in the same passage.

social values are themselves infused with private desires. Ariosto's revision of the abandoned female portrays the heroine acting by precepts derived from the private world of courtly literature and implementing those values in the larger social and political world. The poet goes well beyond Ovid, who made his heroine embody the precariousness of social values through the experience of abandonment. By reducing the sublime figure of his own predecessor Catullus, Ovid emphasized certain elegiac devices: the slow awakening from sleep with the vivid depiction of the woman's hands moving across the bed; the pathetic fallacy of the rocks echoing the woman's cries; the image of the ship receding in the distance; and the heroine's frozen posture on the beach. Ovid portrays the effect of abandonment on the psyche of his heroine, but Ariosto manipulates those very elements for a different kind of insight. He introduces Vergil's Dido as well as Catullus's Ariadne into his Ovidian imitation at a crucial point of evaluation of her situation and heightens the distance of his character from those models by her lack of real self-reflection.

In this case, Ariosto represents a kind of individual that the cultural conditions of his world seem to have fostered. By using the themes and motifs of romance to criticize that form, he implies how easily erotic literature can mislead the naive reader. Erotic fidelity becomes especially ironic here, as the woman takes it to such an extreme that she is completely oblivious to the moral consequences of her actions on behalf of her lover. Olimpia's fidelity to her family and country is subsumed by her obsession for Bireno. Unlike his classical predecessors Apollonius and Vergil, Ariosto does not use the eroticized female as a symbol of the weaknesses latent in the prevailing male-dominated social values. Nor, like Ovid, does he probe the state of mind of an individual under the circumstances of isolation. Desire does not seem to be transformed by the fear of exile or death but merely gets transferred to the next available object, in this case Oberto.

Olimpia willfully acts out a private notion of *fede* to the detriment of family and country, while Cloridano and Medoro transform *fede* and *pietà* on the political and social level into private values. The one, however noble, exhibits a fidelity to his leader based on personal affection, and the other is governed by an emotional bond to his young friend. In this episode, Ariosto consistently deletes the complex levels of significance that *cupido* bears in the *Aeneid*, including erotic passion, bloodlust, and greed. Conversely, he adds sentimental and erotic elements that emphasize the private over the social to his second model in Statius. Medoro's emotionally grounded *fede* to his leader differs from Dymas's loyalty, which is an exemplar of the social virtue that is so pervasively violated in the world of Statius's poem. Cloridano's motivation for the expedition is less *fede* or *pietà* than love for his young friend: he knows that Medoro's desire to retrieve Dardinello's body is folly, but he is unable to act upon his awareness under his friend's sway. The poet places almost every allusion to his two Roman models in an ironic light that prepares for the final stroke, the rescue of Medoro for the benefit of Angelica, the elusive object of desire for nearly all the heroes in the poem.

Ariosto's interplay with the classics throughout the *Orlando Furioso* offers a valuable approach to this complex work. In an important article on Astolfo's trip to the moon, David Quint has recently shown that Ariosto very cleverly adds a major allusion to Seneca's *Apocolocyntosis* in his parody of Dante's *Commedia*: he exposes the flattery of patrons by poets and suggests that immortality depends upon how much the subject of a literary work is willing to pay.[56] The poet consistently implies the problematic, potentially ironic, nature of his relation to traditional value systems. In the amusing episode of Astolfo transformed into a myrtle tree by Alcina, for instance, Ariosto cleverly combines a Vergilian with an Italian epic source in a context that is grounded in the erotic rather than in the heroic. There, he places Ruggiero's *pietà* in an ironic light; furthermore, he hints at the problem of poetic authority by adding allusions to Aeneas's discovery of the murdered Polydorus to his imitation of Dante's canto of Pier delle Vigne.[57] He often

[56]David Quint, "Astolfo's Voyage to the Moon," *Yale Italian Studies* 1 (1977), 398–408, reveals the intratextual system of signs created in that episode that play against Dante's sense of allegory as validated by authoritative texts.

[57]William J. Kennedy, "Ariosto's Ironic Allegory," *MLN* 88 (1973), 44–67, in his general discussion of allegory in the Alcina episode, draws some analogies between Ariosto's characters and their classical sources, especially Ruggiero with Aeneas and Melissa with Mercury. For an illuminating discussion of the problem of literary authority as an issue in the Pier delle Vigne episode, which is the model for the interchange between Ruggiero and Astolfo, see Giuseppe Mazzotta, *Dante, Poet of the Desert* (Princeton: Princeton University Press, 1979), pp. 188–90.

cleverly debunks the heroic in its entanglement with the erotic by imitating Ovid's *Metamorphoses*, which portrays love in all of its complexities and delusions. One of Ariosto's wittiest tales, Ruggiero's rescue of Angelica, derives much of its humor about erotic passion from the myth of Perseus and Andromeda in *Metamorphoses* 4.[58]

Even in the dramatic account of Ruggiero's struggle with Rodomonte at the end of the poem, Ariosto uses allusions to classical epic in ways that imply the frailty of traditional assumptions about the heroic. Aeneas and Turnus in the *Aeneid* are rivals in a dynastic struggle for Lavinia, but Rodomonte here is not a contender for Bradamante but rather an interrupter of Ruggiero's marriage feast for personal revenge. The narrative also shifts back to the erotic and personal as the poet explores Bradamante's doubts about Ruggiero's success against Rodomonte. The final simile of the poem, which describes the contest between the two heroes, echoes Vergil's comparison of Aeneas pursuing Turnus to a dog closing in on a stag. In his adaptation, Ariosto shifts the point of view to the Turnus-figure Rodomonte and significantly reduces the reader's empathy with Ruggiero at this crucial moment.[59] The final scene consistently recalls the end of the *Aeneid*, yet in revealing the private bases for human action, takes issue with Vergil's epic vision. Especially in his use of the erotic, Ariosto proves himself to be a worthy Renaissance successor to the Augustan Ovid.

[58]See Daniel Javitch, "Rescuing Ovid from the Allegorizers: The Liberation of Angelica, *Furioso* X," in *Ariosto 1974 in America*, ed. Aldo Scaglione (Ravenna: Longo, 1976), pp. 85–98, for a discussion of this episode as Ariosto's attempt to re-create the playfulness of Ovid's own narrative in reaction to the medieval moralizing tradition.

[59]Albert R. Ascoli, in a review of Daniela Delcorno–Branca's *L'Orlando Furioso e il romanzo cavalleresco medievale*, *Italica* 60 (1983), 278–81, comments on the questionable nature of Ruggiero's *virtus* in light of Rodomonte's lack of the invincible armor of Nimrod that he had earlier lost.

CHAPTER 5

Milton's Criticism of
Classical Epic in *Paradise Lost* 9

ALTHOUGH HE revived the genre in a monumental form, Milton's hostility to classical epic is in fact evident from the very opening of *Paradise Lost*, where the poet inverts elements of the conventional invocation to the Muse in Homer and Vergil.[1] Throughout books 1 and 2, as John Steadman has so well demonstrated, the poet consigns the values of classical epic to hell and makes Satan epitomize the weaknesses of the classical hero.[2] Perhaps nowhere is Milton more overtly critical than in the prologue of book 9:[3]

> Sad task, yet argument
> Not less but more Heroic than the wrath

[1]Davis P. Harding, *The Club of Hercules: Studies in the Classical Background of Paradise Lost*, *Illinois Studies in Language and Literature*, 50 (Urbana: University of Illinois Press, 1962) pp. 34–36, shows that Milton patterns the opening of *Paradise Lost* on its counterpart in the *Aeneid*, which implies Vergil's superiority to Homer; R. W. Condee, "The Formalized Openings of Milton's Epic Poems," *Journal of English and Germanic Philology* 50 (1951), 502–8, states that Milton evokes his two major predecessors in the genre in order to create a deliberate counterpoint.

[2]John M. Steadman, *Milton and the Renaissance Hero* (Oxford: Clarendon Press, 1967), discusses the signal characteristics of the classical epic hero that Milton assigns to Satan, including courage, wisdom, and leadership, but also acknowledges that the poet sometimes uses allusions to specific classical heroes in a positive way.

[3]John Milton, *Complete Poems and Major Prose*, ed. Merritt Y. Hughes (New York: Odyssey Press, 1957). My quotations from *Paradise Lost* are from this edition.

Of stern Achilles on his Foe pursu'd
Thrice Fugitive about Troy Wall; or rage
Of Turnus for Lavinia disespous'd,
Of Neptune's ire, or Juno's, that so long
Perplex'd the Greek, and Cytherea's Son. (13–19)

The erotic underlies much of the poet's criticism of these heroic characters. The reference to Turnus alludes to his fury over the interference with his marriage to Lavinia: the Rutulian leader is motivated to resist Aeneas out of personal desire for the young woman as well as for dynastic reasons. The comment on Juno recalls that she sustained her hostility to the Trojans in part because Paris chose Venus as the most beautiful, desirable goddess (*Aeneid* 1.26–27). Even the hero whom Vergil refers to with the adjective *pius* or by the patronymic *Anchisiades* is here called "Cytherea's Son." The matronymic itself is certainly unusual for heroes in ancient patriarchal societies, but all the more unflattering here as it calls attention to the sexual origins of Aeneas's mother, born off the island of Cythera from the castrated genitals of Uranus.

Milton indicates that his own concerns far transcend the egoistic personal interests and political ambitions depicted in classical epic, yet scholars have not adequately shown how the strong criticism voiced by the poet specifically affects the narrative of book 9, in love as well as in the traditional heroic virtues. To what extent is the nature of the traditional hero at question in this book? By examining the relationship of Adam and Eve, we consider Milton's representation of this pair in connection with the paradigm of the female abandoned by the callous hero. Eve, of course, is not actually abandoned by Adam. But the poet allusively summons the model of Aeneas's affair with Dido and his abandonment of her in Vergil's epic. Milton adapts this story by shifting some key elements of Vergil's account from the male to the female protagonist and thus makes his characterization far more complex. In addition, another "hero" enters this episode in the form of Satan, who lures the woman with erotic language and then leaves her to a dreadful fate. In that context, Milton alludes not only to the *Aeneid* but also to the *Odyssey* and an important Renaissance epic deeply influenced by Vergil, the *Gerusalemme Liberata*: his echoes imply a critical judgment on the classical epic tradition. By his subtle incorporation of the abandoned female model, then, this poet continues the debate about the nature of heroic values but moves in a radically different direction from his major predecessors in epic poetry.

Within the biblical subject of man's disobedience and the consequent loss of Eden, *Paradise Lost* 9 narrates the Fall in the context of Adam's and Eve's marital relations. Milton certainly had important precedents for his emphasis on love, not only in sixteenth-century theory of the genre, particularly the *Discorsi* of Torquato Tasso, but also, of course, in the major Renaissance romantic epics.[4] We have already observed that, after many amorous digressions, the *Orlando Furioso* ends with a dynastic marriage. Tasso's *Gerusalemme Liberata* and Spenser's *Faerie Queene* also link the welfare of the city with love and marriage.[5] Yet Milton goes far beyond those earlier works by integrating marriage itself into the narrative rather than simply making it the goal toward which the action proceeds. Several critics have recently observed that *Paradise Lost* reflects upon the reciprocity and balance of obligations between Adam and Eve as a paradigm of male and female relations in marriage.[6] In this poem, marriage is the major image of both the flawed reality and the ideal

[4]See Torquato Tasso, *Discourses on the Heroic Poem*, ed. Mariella Cavalchini and Irene Samuel (Oxford: Clarendon Press, 1973), pp. 44–49, for a defense of the appropriateness of love in epic; comparing the heroic themes of love and wrath, Tasso stresses that because the former is a "noble habit of the will" as well as a passion connected with the sensitive appetites, it generates actions that are more noble and worthy of a hero.

[5]For the influence of Spenser's attitude toward love in the *Faerie Queene* on *Paradise Lost*, see William Haller, "'Hail Wedded Love,'" *ELH* 13 (1946), 79–97; and Paul N. Siegel, "Milton and the Humanist Attitude toward Women," *Journal of the History of Ideas* 11 (1950), 42–53.

[6]The pioneering work on this subject was done in the late sixties and early seventies. On the need for growth and change in Milton's paradise, see Irene Samuel, "*Paradise Lost*," in *Critical Approaches to Six Major English Works*, ed. R. M. Lumiansky and Herschel Baker (Philadelphia: University of Pennsylvania Press, 1968), pp. 237–43; and Barbara K. Lewalski, "Innocence and Experience in Milton's Eden," in *New Essays on* Paradise Lost, ed. Thomas Kranidas (Berkeley: University of California Press, 1969), pp. 86–117. On the appropriateness of Eve's decision to work alone, see Diane K. McColley, "Free Will and Obedience in the Separation Scene of *Paradise Lost*," *Studies in English Literature* 12 (1972), 103–20, who emphasizes Eve's serious interest in her work; and Stella P. Revard, "Eve and the Doctrine of Responsibility in *Paradise Lost*," *PMLA* 88 (1973), 69–78. More recent studies are cited in specific contexts.

vision; by the unique nature of this union Milton gives marriage the status of a new heroic value.[7]

His representation of marriage in the case of Adam and Eve may be viewed as a poetic enactment of the ideals contained in his various prose writings. Milton expressed his views on this major seventeenth-century issue in several prose tracts, including the seminal *Areopagitica*.[8] Like other Protestant thinkers of his day, he viewed marriage as a fellowship and partnership in which the rational powers of both members were necessary.[9] As the work of Stella Revard, Joan Webber, and Diane McColley has revealed, Eve's role in this relationship is more important and more complex than has been generally acknowledged. Traditionally, scholars have tended to reduce Eve in various ways. She has often been regarded as a "second thought" of God's creation and inherently limited, inferior to Adam in nature as well as in degree. Her significance in the poem, especially in book 9, has sometimes been reduced to an allegorical representation of *ratio* (or *anima*) in contrast to the *intellectus* (or *mens*) represented by Adam.[10] In exploring Milton's social vision in *Paradise Lost* through the poet's revision of Spenser, Maureen Quilligan perceives Eve as Milton's model for his contemporary female, will

---

[7]See Diane K. McColley, *Milton's Eve* (Urbana: University of Illinois Press, 1983), esp. pp. 32–57; and Joan M. Webber, "The Politics of Poetry: Feminism and *Paradise Lost*," *Milton Studies* 14 (1980), 3–24, who responds to Sandra Gilbert's view that Milton created Eve as a "divine afterthought" by showing that Eve's subjectivity and Adam's intellectualism, while positive in themselves, need to be mutually tempered.

[8]Purvis E. Boyette, "Milton's Divorce Tracts and the Law of Marriage," *Tulane Studies in English* 17 (1969), 73–92, discusses Milton's concept of "companionability" in the divorce pamphlets and provides a balanced view of the differences between the poet and his contemporaries. David Aers and Bob Hodge, "'Rational Burning': Milton on Sex and Marriage," *Milton Studies* 13 (1979), 3–33, discuss the progress of Milton's thinking on marriage in his political writings, such as the *Doctrine and Discipline of Divorce* and *Tetrachordon*, as well as in *Paradise Lost* and find his position problematic; they suggest that he allowed for more independence for the female in his great epic than in his male-oriented political pamphlets, in which real power ultimately resides in the hands of the husband.

[9]Marilyn R. Farwell, "Eve, the Separation Scene, and the Renaissance Idea of Androgyny," *Milton Studies* 16 (1982), 3–20, notes that the Puritan belief in fellowship in marriage relies on Renaissance humanistic views on women as rational creatures who can be educated.

[10]On the background of the allegorical, reductive interpretation of Eve, see McColley (above, note 7), pp. 9–17.

ingly accepting a "mediated" position in relation to the male.[11] The full implications of the poet's representation of Eve must, of course, remain open to debate. Yet it is certainly possible that Milton creates an ideal vision in *Paradise Lost* that is intended to influence his society on a subtle level of attitude and behavior rather than to define gender roles in a more rigid way.

Throughout *Paradise Lost* Milton stresses the complementary nature of male and female. If Eve is less rational and intellectual than Adam, she is also more intuitive and creative.[12] Barbara Lewalski has shown that in book 4 Eve, in contrast to her inferiority in the absolute hierarchy, is not only a partner engaging in the georgic tasks in the Garden but also reveals an astonishing imaginative faculty by creating, as it were, the love sonnet.[13] Her involvement with Adam extends to the sphere of religious piety, and she shares with him the creation of the eloquent morning hymn in book 5 (160–208). She also learns to recognize and overcome her potential for narcissism by the love that she learns to show the world through her husband's help.[14] In his conversation with Raphael in book 8, Adam certainly reveals his stronger interest in intellectual matters; Eve's primary access to that sphere is through his assistance. During the same interchange with Raphael, the hero shows his tendency toward irresponsible, irrational passion for Eve, which he must learn to control. Each gains from the other and tempers natural deficiencies. In that way, Eve is a cooperative partner in a union whose primary bond is responsible love. While Milton reveals the harmony of this relationship in books 4 through 8, in book 9 he relates not only the failure of Adam's and Eve's love but also their dynamic attempts at developing their interdependence.

Critics have discussed the long conversation between Adam and

[11]Maureen Quilligan, *Milton's Spenser: The Politics of Reading* (Ithaca: Cornell University Press, 1983), esp. pp. 226–42.

[12]On Eve's association with imaginative faculties, see Joan M. Webber, *Milton and His Epic Tradition* (Seattle: University of Washington Press, 1979), pp. 147–48.

[13]See Barbara K. Lewalski, Paradise Lost *and the Rhetoric of Literary Forms* (Princeton: Princeton University Press, 1985), p. 189, in the context of Milton's use of generic expectations in his account of Eden.

[14]Leslie Brisman, *Milton's Poetry of Choice and Its Romantic Heirs* (Ithaca: Cornell University Press, 1973), pp. 160–61, observes that Eve is saved from self-love by a voice that introduces time to her, as it simultaneously brings Adam into her existence.

Eve early in book 9 (205–84) as an illustration of the learning process that the two undergo concerning their mutual responsibilities rather than merely as a display of willfulness on Eve's part. Their exchange focuses on the advisability of Eve's desire to go off and work by herself for a while and is central to an understanding of Milton's position on the balance between male and female responsibility. Revard has perceived a basic issue underlying this dialogue: "Happiness cannot exist without liberty, and liberty can function only if man and woman are permitted independently to affirm 'Faith, Love, Virtue' by trial."[15] McColley has further explained that at the point where Adam fears "'lest harm / Befall thee sever'd from me'" (251–52), the conversation weighs ideas of Christian liberty and responsibility that long occupied Milton's thought.[16] Eve is not ignorant of the potential danger to their security, since she acknowledges that she listened to Adam's discussion with Raphael on the subject of Satan's intrusion into Eden (274–78). Her responses to Adam's objections reveal an independence of mind that closely approximates Miltonic thought, especially in the *Areopagitica*.[17] Eve makes several points in common with Milton's own expressed views: baseness recoils on itself rather than on its object; to live in confinement for fear of an enemy constrains virtue as well as sin; harmony is important for all things relating to union with God, while variety is appropriate in all else; freedom is essential for those in God's image because a "narrow circuit" is a presumption against the Spirit; it is necessary for an individual to stand on one's own faith; and it is impossible to be happy when one is compelled by external policing rather than led by a virtuous education. It has been argued that Eve distorts Milton's views and puts them into an inappropriate context.[18] Yet her positions are at least partially relevant to Eden, since the fundamental question of liberty

---

[15]Revard (above, note 6), 73.

[16]McColley (above, note 7), pp. 170–81.

[17]Ibid., pp. 172–77, on whom I base my summary of the connections between the separation scene and *Areopagitica*.

[18]John S. Diekhoff, "Eve, the Devil, and the *Areopagitica*," *MLQ* 5 (1944), 429–34, argues that Adam does not reject Eve's contention that temptation itself is not debasing and that for Milton trial is necessary only in man's fallen state. On the first point, Adam in his conversation with Eve seems to emphasize her weakness and thereby implies that temptation is too dangerous for her; on the second, Milton in

and restraint in the private relationship of marriage applies as much to the archetype as to seventeenth-century examples. If Eve thus presents the case for Christian liberty, Adam ends his arguments with a strong plea for responsibility in the context of freedom by reminding her that virtue can be harmed if it does not adhere rigorously to God's word.

Eve's initial broaching of the subject to Adam illustrates the delicate balance and complexity of their relationship. Milton begins the dialogue by having Eve specifically suggest the ways by which they may work independently:

> "Let us divide our labors, thou where choice
> Leads thee, or where most needs, whether to wind
> The Woodbine round this Arbor, or direct
> The clasping Ivy where to climb, while I
> In yonder Spring of Roses intermixt
> With Myrtle, find what to redress till Noon." (214–19)

The plants and flowers mentioned here have a long tradition of allegorical interpretation involving specific associations with love: ivy and woodbine stand for fidelity in marriage and for friendship, roses and myrtle for divine and conjugal love.[19] Fowler notes that the ivy is a symbol of conjugal union and also of the integration of *mens* and *anima*.[20] But, as McColley has observed, the plants in this passage not only have a variety of positive symbolic connections with love; each also traditionally has a negative connotation suggesting *cupiditas* as well as *caritas*.[21] It is certainly possible, then, that Milton suggests Eve's concern for her relationship with her husband, her fear that Adam's tendency toward excessive passion may

---

the scene in *Paradise Lost* itself does not seem to suggest that trial is in any way wrong, even for Eve. If she is too eager for such temptation, Adam too precipitously encourages her. On the problems with the positions of both characters in this dialogue, see Lewalski (above, note 13), pp. 233–37.

[19]Erwin Panofsky, *Studies in Iconology: Humanistic Themes in the Art of the Renaissance* (1939; rpt. New York: Harper and Row, 1962), illustrates the various kinds of connections between Venus and the plants traditionally associated with her in the Renaissance.

[20]Milton, *The Poems of John Milton*, ed. John Carey and Alastair Fowler (London: Longman, 1968), ad loc.

[21]McColley (above, note 7), p. 147.

endanger their life together as it seems to hinder their work. Rather than allegorize Eve as a defective *anima*, Milton presents her as seriously tending not only her garden but also her loving union with Adam. He may well imply that Eve is excessively diligent about her work and that she overestimates the need for increased efficiency.[22] But it is important that both Adam and Eve misemphasize certain points as they earnestly exchange their different points of view. It is unsatisfactory to say that Eve is merely willful and Adam negligent in his leadership over his wife.[23]

At the end of their conversation, Milton alludes to an important moment in the representation of the vulnerable female in epic by describing Eve's departure with an extended simile:

> and like a Wood-Nymph light,
> Oread or Dryad, or of Delia's Train,
> Betook her to the Groves, but Delia's self
> In gait surpass'd and Goddess-like deport,
> Though not as shee with Bow and Quiver arm'd,
> But with such Gard'ning Tools as Art yet rude,
> Guiltless of fire had form'd, or Angels brought. (386–92)

Scholars have approached this simile from various points of view. Alastair Fowler emphasizes a negative characterization of Eve in the detail of the quiver, which she lacks, as an emblem of counsel in the allegorical tradition and in an ambiguity in the word "light," which may mean not only "nimble" but also "unsteady, fickle."[24] Others have concentrated on the visual function of this simile as an engaging depiction of Eve's beauty. Isabel MacCaffrey, for example, observes that Milton stresses the uniqueness of his character here: "No son or daughter can be quite as wonderful as these originals."[25] This view emphasizes Milton's sense of the priority of his biblical material over pagan and earlier Renaissance literary subjects; Fowler's stresses an allegorical interpretation that underestimates the com-

---

[22]See Lewalski (above, note 13), p. 233.

[23]See, for example, Dennis H. Burden, *The Logical Epic: A Study of the Argument of Paradise Lost* (Cambridge, Mass.: Harvard University Press, 1967), pp. 89–92, on Adam's failure to maintain proper leadership over his wife.

[24]Fowler (above, note 20), ad loc.

[25]Isabel G. MacCaffrey, Paradise Lost *as "Myth"* (Cambridge, Mass.: Harvard University Press, 1959), p. 122.

plexity of human interaction. As we observed in our discussions of Apollonius and Vergil, this elegant simile has a long history from Homer onward in the context of the love of a female character for the hero.[26]

The archetype of the Diana simile in the *Odyssey* (6.102–8) conveys an impression of the chaste beauty of the young Phaeacian princess just before she meets the hero and becomes interested in him. As we noted, Nausikaa's awakening sexual desires and expectation of marriage contrast her with the virgin goddess Artemis. Although Nausikaa tries to encourage Odysseus as a suitor, the hero responds with flattery but avoids any commitment and leaves the Phaeacian kingdom with considerable riches. In the *Argonautica*, Apollonius gives the Homeric simile sinister overtones through his depiction of Medea going off to her assignation with Jason: her physical separation from her companions and the association with Hecate suggest the young woman's lack of social integration. Medea then casts off all scruples in joining with Jason, and Apollonius makes his simile a bridge that illustrates the irreversible change from innocent chastity to destructive passion.

Vergil develops the transitional function of the Diana simile even more fully by applying it to Dido just before she sees Aeneas for the first time. Here he depicts Dido as she surveys the new city Carthage: "Just as on the banks of the Eurotas or along the ridges of Mount Cynthus Diana leads her troops; a thousand Oreads in attendance cluster around her. She bears a quiver on her shoulder and as she walks towers above all the goddesses. (Latona's heart silently feels pleasure.)" (1.498–502).[27] This complex simile presents Dido as a more mature woman of experience, a political leader who bears the responsibility of building a new city. It also conveys a psychological complexity in Dido's problematic sexuality: her repression of her sexuality after vowing never to marry again upon her husband's death but also her resemblance to Venus, who shortly before

---

[26]In general, commentators have oddly failed to notice this allusion; an exception is Harding (above, note 1), pp. 87–88, who finds that the Vergilian source reinforces the sense of Eve's "headstrong desires."

[27]Vergil, *Opera*, ed. R. A. B. Mynors (Oxford: Clarendon Press, 1969). My quotations from the *Aeneid* are from this edition, with the substitution of *v* for consonantal *u*. The translations are my own.

appeared to Aeneas disguised as a huntress like Diana. Although sympathetic to the psychological struggle of his compelling character, the poet is distanced from the deep problems that ultimately make her incompatible with the social vision projected by his epic. Her own interest in heroic activity and in the glory that attends it influences her desire for Aeneas. At the same time, she cannot balance passion and political responsibility. Her unfortunate suicide, furthermore, is induced to a large extent by her guilt over betraying her husband and by the loss of her reputation for fidelity.

Milton specifically recalls Vergil's Diana simile by mentioning elements not in Homer's or Apollonius's versions: the Oreads as a particular group of nymphs and the quiver that the goddess carries. He echoes the phrase "gradiensque deas supereminet omnes" from the *Aeneid*, but also uses language that challenges the superiority of his predecessor: "but Delia's self / In gait surpassed and goddess-like deport" (388–89). By referring to Eve's greater stature, Milton implies that he wishes to differentiate his character from her model. First, he sets his simile in the context of a marital union. Far from having repressed her sexuality as did Dido, Eve has a close, loving relationship with Adam. The poet points to her gentle, tender nature as he introduces the simile: "Thus saying, from her Husband's hand her hand / Soft she withdrew" (385–86). This simile suggests another ironic discrepancy with the *Aeneid*: at the point of expressing her independence, Eve is leaving Adam. Her gesture, however, represents a desire for a temporary separation, motivated to some extent by the hero's own excessive fondness for her, in contrast to the lack of strong emotional attachment in the male classical counterparts.

Like many of Milton's allusions to the classics, this comparison suggests a complex similarity with its model. Eve as well as Dido is engaged in labor, though Eve's consists of pruning and cutting. The poet refers to the specific nature of this activity: "But with such Gard'ning tools as Art yet rude, / Guiltless of fire had form'd, or Angels brought" (391–92). Another simile immediately follows and reinforces this point: Eve is compared to Pales, Pomona, and Ceres (393–96). Fowler notes that the analogue with Pomona is morally unfavorable, since Milton "specifically refers to her seduction by the disguised Vertumnus."[28] Yet that simile may not only proleptically suggest Eve's "seduction" by Satan but may also imply her immediate situation and intention. As the model for this analogy, Ovid's passage in *Metamorphoses* 14 makes the sexual union of Pomona and Vertumnus a representation of agricultural productivity: the fruit trees take on the seasonal activity (implied by the etymology of Vertumnus in the word *verto*, "to turn") of germination, growth, maturation, and decay.[29] In Milton's Diana simile, Eve is delicately poised between Adam and the garden, between union and independence. Both Eve and Dido have important responsibilities, but Dido is successful and productive only before her love for Aeneas develops. Eve, on the contrary, relies on Adam's affection and his support for her continuing attempts to develop her relation to the larger world.

After Eve's departure, Milton also alludes to the archetype of the abandoned female in Homer's *Odyssey*. Having entered into the Garden and seeing Eve alone, Satan passes through the plots of flowers and plants, which the poet thus describes:

> Spot more delicious than those Gardens feign'd
> Or of reviv'd Adonis, or renown'd
> Alcinous, host of old Laertes' Son. (439–41)

In the second part of this analogy, Milton compares the intruder to the Homeric hero who enters the fabulous gardens of the Phaeacian king on his way to the palace after meeting the princess Nausikaa and encouraging her interest in him (7.112–32). While Odysseus's purpose is certainly not as sinister as the archfiend's, there are some disturbing similarities. Both have a flirtation with an inexperienced young woman and manipulate her to gain their own ends. For the Homeric hero, Nausikaa is a convenient means to a safe reception at the royal palace, where he can gradually reveal his character as a hero through his fascinating account of his travels after the Trojan War. He will also acquire rich gifts to compensate for the loss of his war booty and thus can restore his position as king of Ithaca more securely. In order to get revenge on God, Satan actually wishes to

[28]Fowler (above, note 20), ad loc.

[29]See David J. Littlefield, "Pomona and Vertumnus: A Fruition of History in Ovid's *Metamorphoses*," *Arion* 4 (1965), 465–73.

destroy Eve's blissful existence, but he is essentially similar to the classical hero in manipulatively using the female as an instrument for self-aggrandizement. Both, moreover, are primarily interested in their own *kleos*, or reputation: Scheria enables Odysseus to fully reestablish his heroic identity, and Eden provides Satan with the opportunity to restore his damaged reputation, as he openly acknowledges:

> "that destruction wide may range:
> To mee shall be the glory sole among
> Th'infernal Powers, in one day to have marr'd
> What he Almighty styl'd." (134–37)

In this context, Milton uses another epic paradigm of the vulnerable female that reinforces the implications of the Dido-Nausikaa model. Satan's awareness that Eve is working alone is first described by a charming pastoral simile (445–54). But the poet quickly dispels the blissful pastoral vision as he describes Eve's effect on Satan and the immediate return of his malice:

> Her graceful Innocence, her every Air
> Of gesture or least action overaw'd
> His Malice, and with rapine sweet bereav'd
> His fierceness of the fierce intent it brought:
> That space the Evil one abstracted stood
> From his own evil, and for the time remain'd
> Stupidly good, of enmity disarm'd,
>
> . . .
>
> then soon
> Fierce hate he recollects. (459–71)

This passage echoes the major Renaissance poem that attempted to re-create Vergilian epic. In book 2 of the *Gerusalemme Liberata*, Aladino, the king of Jerusalem, is outraged by the theft of a Christian statue that had been placed in the mosque and decides to persecute the Christians *en masse* for this violation. The beautiful virgin Sofronia then valiantly offers herself as victim for the act that she did not commit. As he sees her, Aladino's ferocity is thus momentarily quelled:[30]

[30]Torquato Tasso, *Gerusalemme Liberata*, ed. Lanfranco Caretti (Turin: Einaudi, 1971). My quotations from Tasso's epic are from this edition. The English is *Jerusalem Delivered*, tr. Edward Fairfax (New York: Capricorn Books, 1963).

A l'onesta baldanza, a l'improviso
folgorar di bellezze altere e sante,
quasi confuso il re, quasi conquiso,
frenò lo sdegno, e placò il fer sembiante. (2.20.1–4)

> Her modest boldness and that light'ning ray
> Which her sweet beauty streamed on his face
> Had strook the prince with wonder and dismay,
> Hanged his cheer and clear'd his moody grace.

Like Satan, he becomes momentarily overawed:

> It was amazement, wonder and delight,
> Although not love, that moved his cruel sense. (21.1–2)

Then he too recovers his hateful, malicious nature: "The wretch of new enraged at the same" (224.1).

Milton recalls Tasso's passage through both the similarity of content and specific verbal echoes: the first two lines describing Eve's beauty and innocence suggest Tasso's depiction of Sofronia; Satan's state of being "overaw'd" and "bereav'd" of his anger parallels Aladino's condition as "confuso" and "conquiso"; Satan is "stupidly good" much as for Aladino "fu stupor." The episode of Sofronia is one example of the ambivalent perspective on love that characterizes Tasso's poem. The two major characters, Rinaldo and Tancredi, exemplify the problem of warriors led astray and unable to perform their military duties properly because of their erotic obsessions. Love debilitates Rinaldo, who comes to his senses only after seeing his debased, effeminate self in the surface of a shield (16.28). When made aware of his useless inertia during his affair with Armida, he can finally abandon his subservient condition and fulfill his destiny as a warrior. Tancredi's idealized love for Clorinda is finally destroyed in book 12, after he has unwittingly killed her in combat and then receives her healing words of spiritual love in a dream. Judith Kates thus sums up the poet's position: "The distraction of love and its trance of inward concentration, isolating the spirit from the outside world, cannot exist for Tasso in the same nature that accomplishes great deeds and achieves its salvation."[31]

[31]Judith A. Kates, *Tasso and Milton: The Problem of Christian Epic* (Lewisburg: Bucknell University Press, 1983), p. 99.

Tasso's use of Sofronia in book 2 is another example of this perspective on the role of love in the committed Christian. Sofronia is a heroic character, a Christian militant who acts boldly for the faith when the ruler of Jerusalem decides to persecute the Christians for the theft of the statue of the Virgin Mary. Since the pagans themselves originally stole the statue from the Christians with the hope that it would bring them good fortune, their act recalls the theft by the Greeks of the Palladium, the token of Troy's safety. Through her efforts to take the blame and receive the punishment for recovery of the statue, Sofronia as a Christian hero in a sense reverses the act of pagan heroism by which Odysseus and Diomedes stole the image of Athena. But like Rinaldo and Tancredi after they have abandoned love, Sofronia is an active Christian who is single-minded in her religious zeal. Tasso emphasizes her absolute dedication by weaving her self-sacrifice into the story of Olindo's passionate love for her. The poet presents this young man's passion as one of the many cases of "love as an unknown, unreciprocated devotion or as frustrated physical desire."[32] When his attempt to rescue Sofronia from death by confessing to the crime fails, Olindo is bound to the stake with the young woman and gives vent to his feelings. His bold outburst ("'Yet happy were my death . . . If this I could obtain, that breast to breast / Thy bosom might receive my yielded sprite,'" 2.35.1–4) reflects the depth of his frustration and torment. Sofronia's failure to respond to human sexuality is the indirect cause of his foolish act of daring and his continued agony at the stake. Only the fortuitous arrival of the female warrior Clorinda saves the pair. In what appears to be an uneasy gesture, Sofronia then accepts Olindo's love and agrees to marry him. Although far distant in time from Apollonius or Vergil, Tasso reflects a similar skepticism toward love that makes Milton's allusion to his epic highly appropriate.

If Satan in *Paradise Lost* 9 is like Aladino, Eve is a more complex analogue of Sofronia. Like Tasso's heroine, she is bold in her willingness to confront danger.[33] Yet the differences between the two

[32]C. P. Brand, *Torquato Tasso: A Study of the Poet and of His Contribution to English Literature* (Cambridge: Cambridge University Press, 1965), p. 102.
[33]See Milton, *Paradise Lost: Books IX and X*, ed. with commentary J. Martin Evans (Cambridge: Cambridge University Press, 1973), pp. 27–28, for the view that Eve is like a romance heroine in her daring confrontation with Satan.

are marked. Tasso's character lacks the capacity for natural human love, but Milton's can be defined by her constantly developing spirit of love not only for her husband but for all of God's creation. At Satan's very first glimpse of Eve alone, Milton describes the loving care with which she is tending the garden:

> so thick the Roses bushing round
> About her glow'd, oft stooping to support
> Each Flow'r of slender stalk, whose head though gay
> Carnation, Purple, Azure, or speckt with Gold,
> Hung drooping unsustain'd, them she upstays
> Gently with Myrtle band. (426–31)

The poet not only shows her seriously engaged in her labor with nature but again joins the roses with myrtle, plants whose allegorical significance was noted in Eve's conversation with Adam. He seems to imply that she is in fact concerned with the *caritas* that she implied might falter in a situation where amorous tendencies are not controlled. Eve, however, will lapse in her love of God because she allows Satan to challenge God's goodness and she temporarily abandons her love of Him. In contrast, Sofronia, having sublimated her sexuality, is totally motivated by her religious zeal and unwavering love of God. Finally, Milton emphasizes the importance of human responsibility to an extent that Tasso does not. Choice is available to Eve in the crucial moment as much as it is later to Adam.[34] Unlike Sofronia, Eve does not find a fortuitous rescuer but must fully accept the consequences of her actions.

Satan shows his Odysseus-like verbal powers, and Milton further develops his criticism of love in his predecessors' poems and intimates his own distance from those works. He alludes to Homer's hero as the archfiend approaches Eve by noting that he is "more duteous at her call, / Than at Circean call the Herd disguis'd" (521–

[34]On this point, see especially Elaine B. Safer, "'Sufficient to Have Stood': Eve's Responsibility in Book IX," *Milton Quarterly* 6 (1972), 10–14, who shows that although Eve has a lower position in the cosmos, Milton shows her competence to accept her own responsibility. J. M. Evans, "Mortals' Chiefest Enemy," *Milton Studies* 20 (1984), 111–26, discusses Eve's fall in connection with the negligence that Adam had warned her about through the multiple connotations of the word "secure" in the conversation scene.

22). Yet he reverses the significance: Satan as Odysseus is the tempter, Eve as Circe is not. The poet heightens the speciousness of Satan's first address to Eve through its literary nature, for it is in essence a courtly love poem that elevates a beautiful woman to the status of a divinity and makes her an object of idolatry.[35] With insidious rhetoric Satan is master of a literary form for which Milton had only contempt.[36] He first addresses Eve by suggesting her supremacy and by playing upon connotations of the word *wonder*: " 'Wonder not, sovran Mistress, if perhaps / Thou canst, who are sole Wonder.' " (532–33).[37] He continues punning, especially with the word *fair*, and openly raises Eve to the level of supreme deity:

> "Fairest resemblance of the thy Maker fair,
> Thee all things living gaze on, all things thine
> By gift, and thy Celestial Beauty adore
>
> . . .
>
> In this enclosure wild, these Beasts among,
> Beholders rude, and shallow to discern
> Half what in thee is fair, one man except,
> Who sees thee? (and what is one?) who shouldst be seen
> A Goddess among Gods, ador'd and serv'd." (538–47)

While he does not corrupt Eve with this courtly flattery, Satan has more success as he insidiously explains the origin of the miracle that has supposedly provided the serpent with a voice. His prologue to this important speech begins in what appears to continue his ingratiating manner:

[35]D. S. Berkeley, " 'Precieuse' Gallantry and the Seduction of Eve," *Notes and Queries* 196 (1951), 337–39. Anne D. Ferry, *Milton's Epic Voice: The Narrator in Paradise Lost* (Cambridge, Mass.: Harvard University Press, 1963), pp. 141–45, also has a good analysis of Satan as a courtly love poet. Francis C. Blessington, *Paradise Lost and the Classical Epic* (London: Routledge and Kegan Paul, 1979), p. 59, observes that in the reference to Eve as a goddess (540) Satan is like Odysseus when he asks Nausikaa if she is a mortal or a goddess (*Od*. 6.149).

[36]David Parker, "The Love Poems of *Paradise Lost* and the Petrarchan Tradition," *Ariel* 3 (1972), 34–43, discusses Milton's ironic uses of the Petrarchan and courtly tradition in some of his love poems.

[37]Burden (above, note 23), pp. 141–42, discusses Satan's use of a characteristic quality of epic in his references to "wonder."

"Empress of this fair World, resplendent Eve,
Easy to mee it is to tell thee all
What thou command'st and right thou should'st be obey'd." (568–70)

These lines echo a subtly erotic passage in the *Aeneid*, in which the wind god Aeolus speaks to Juno:

Aeolus spoke thus in response: "It is your labor to decide what you wish, oh queen; it is right for me to obey your orders." (1.76–77)

Satan's sycophantic tone also characterizes Aeolus's response to Juno, for in the classical epic the minor deity readily submits to the manipulative designs of the queen of the gods. This Olympian divinity reveals her essentially ruthless and malicious character by her efforts to destroy the Trojans; she resents her inability thus far to prevent the Trojan refugees from reaching their new homeland (1.37–45). She makes use of a highly seductive rhetoric in order to obtain Aeolus's help in stirring up trouble for the Trojans. In offering him the gift of her most beautiful nymph as his wife, the goddess heightens the rhetorical appeal of her offer. She states: "'quarum quae forma pulcherrima Deiopeia'" (1.72). The heavily spondaic first half of the line builds up to the climactic mention of the nymph's name. The word *Deiopeia*, which means something like "she of the awesome face," cleverly glosses the descriptive phrase, "pulcherrima forma" ("most beautiful appearance"). The wind god's ingratiating response (76–80) reveals the amoral nature of Vergil's divinities, in this case their susceptibility to lust.

Milton attributes the qualities of both Aeolus and Juno to Satan. Like the wind god, Satan uses erotic language that reflects the impact of Eve's attractiveness, though he must prevent thoughts of her beauty from impeding his vengeful purposes. Even more than the queen of the gods, he employs a seductive rhetoric specifically in order to accomplish destructive acts that are motivated by hatred and resentment at the loss of status in the cosmos. As a result of her bargain with Aeolus, Juno irrationally and unjustly inflicted pain and misery on the Trojans. Milton's view of this pagan goddess has already been suggested in the prologue of book 9, where she is described as one "who so long perplex'd the Greek and Cytherea's Son" (19).

Just before Satan begins his final speech to Eve, Milton points to his great rhetorical skills:

> As when of old some Orator renown'd
> In Athens or free Rome, where Eloquence
> Flourish'd, since mute, to some great cause addrest,
> Stood in himself collected, while each part,
> Motion, each act won audience ere the tongue,
> Sometimes in highth began, as no delay
> Of Preface brooking through his Zeal of Right. (670–76)

After reemphasizing the effect the fruit has had on himself, Satan suggests that God wishes to keep Adam and Eve from eating it in order to restrict their development and maintain His superiority over them. He concludes his long discourse with questions designed to make Eve herself doubt God's intentions and violate the command not to eat the fruit:

> "Or is it envy, and can envy dwell
> In heav'nly breasts? these, these and many more
> Causes import your need of this fair Fruit.
> Goddess humane, reach then, and freely taste." (729–32)

These final words thus culminate Satan's insidious attempt to corrupt Eve's love of God and faith in Him by insinuating His fear of man's potential and by elevating her own position in the cosmos. Significantly, the questions that the demon poses paraphrase a powerful passage at the beginning of the *Aeneid*, where the poet comments on Juno's persistent hostility to Aeneas and the Trojans: "tantaene animis caelestibus irae?" (1.11), "can there be such wrath in heavenly spirits?" Milton shows that Satan can exploit classical rhetoric for his own advantage, as he echoes Vergil's deeply felt expression of confusion at the dark powers in the universe. What Vergil reveals about Juno, who vents her anger by trying to hold the hero back from his destined course out of spite, Satan unjustly suggests about God in *Paradise Lost*. By embodying elements of the classical divinity, poet, and orator, Satan exhibits a formidable power in the temptation scene.[38] The archfiend has indeed reflected the rhetorical skills of the master tactician Odysseus with a young woman far less sophisticated than Nausikaa. Even so, Milton stresses that Eve should have resisted:

> He ended, and his words replete with guile
> Into her heart too easy entrance won:
> Fixt on the Fruit she gaz'd, which to behold
> Might tempt alone, and in her ears the sound
> Yet rung of his persuasive words, impregn'd
> With Reason, to her seeming, and with Truth. (733–38)

When Eve actually eats the forbidden fruit, the poet records the moment with an important allusion to *Aeneid* 4. Nature itself responds to Eve's transgression:

> Earth felt the wound, and Nature from her seat
> Sighing through all her Works gave signs of woe,
> That all was lost. (782–84)

Similarly, Vergil shows earth's reaction to the union of Dido and Aeneas after a storm has brought them together in a cave:

> lightning flashed and the heaven was witness to the union, and the nymphs shrieked from the mountain top. (4.167–68)

Critics have observed that Milton again shows the greater magnitude of his own theme by implying the permanent effects of the Fall on the earth itself as well as on the entire human race and that he makes a significant addition to his model by having nature respond a second time, when Adam completes the Fall.[39] The context of Vergil's description also shows a difference in the causes responsible for such devastating consequences. The Roman poet makes the protagonists to some extent victims of divine self-interest. But on the human side he places the burden of responsibility on Dido. By

---

[38]For Milton's views on the power of oratory, see Joseph A. Wittreich, Jr., "Milton's Idea of the Orator," *Milton Quarterly* 6 (1972), 38–40.

[39]On this echo of the *Aeneid*, see Willard Connely, "Imprints of the *Aeneid* on *Paradise Lost*," *CJ* 18 (1923), 466–76, who indicates that nature's response after Adam's sin most closely imitates the passage in *Aeneid* 4.

commenting that the woman gave her "fault" (*culpa*) the name of marriage, he implies that she feels guilty about breaking her vow to her husband and is covering up her actions with a veil of respectability. The anger and violence that erupt when Aeneas reveals his intentions thus in large measure result from Dido's problematic sexuality. While granting Eve her share of the responsibility for man's fall from grace, Milton corrects Vergil's emphasis on the female irrationality ultimately at the root of the historical chaos in the Roman world. For when Adam participates in Eve's error and completes the Fall, the cosmic effects are even more pronounced:

> Sky low'r'd, and muttering Thunder, some sad drops
> Wept at completing of the mortal Sin
> Original. (1002–4).

Milton differs sharply with his classical predecessors by connecting love with pious behavior. For him, love is a necessary aid to piety; the failure of that bond between Adam and Eve destroys their genuinely virtuous existence. In several passages portraying critical moments during the Fall, he compares Adam specifically to the hero of the *Aeneid*. Like the Diana simile earlier in book 9, these echoes recall the ill-fated relationship between the hero and the Carthaginian queen. And as Eve resembles but also differs from Dido, so Adam is a complex analogue of Aeneas. In response to Eve's transgression of God's command, Milton clearly recalls the Roman hero. After learning that the serpent persuaded her to taste the apple and that she has found the effects miraculous, Adam is stunned. The poet thus describes his physical reaction:

> amaz'd,
> Astonied stood and Blank, while horror chill
> Ran through his veins, and all his joints relax'd. (889–91)

Aeneas has a very similar response to traumatic situations, especially when he reacts to Mercury's warning in book 4 that he should leave Carthage and continue on his mission to Italy, for he is struck dumb and becomes speechless (4.279–80). He also reacts similarly to the storm sent by Aeolus in book 1, where his limbs go limp (1.92). A response to situations outside of the normal course of human events through this kind of physical incapacitation is a hallmark of the Roman hero. Adam's loss of bearings here in book 9 seems a direct reflection of his Vergilian forebear, especially in *Aeneid* 4, where Aeneas's anxiety and guilt for his laxity surface. But the significance of their responses is much different. Whereas Vergil's hero has stayed too long with Dido, Milton's has delayed and failed to seek Eve, even though he fears that Eve may have encountered danger.

In addition to the similar emotional reaction, the Christian hero verbally echoes his pagan model. Before eating the fruit himself, Adam responds to Eve's plight with two speeches. The first acknowledges the enormity of her transgression; the second suggests that God may relent and spare her. Yet in both he proclaims his willingness to die with her. Two specific phrases concisely summarize his purpose: "'for with thee / Certain my resolution is to Die'" (906–7) and "'Certain to undergo like doom'" (953).[40] The first expression reflects Aeneas's perception of Dido's irrational state and the second, the hero's own intention of leaving. While echoing each other, the two phrases in the *Aeneid* ironically reveal the polarized attitudes of the two characters and suggest the inherent incongruity of male and female in the Roman epic. In *Aeneid* 4, Dido is consumed with passion and is unable to endure what she considers a breach of faith by Aeneas. Guilty at having shirked his responsibilities, especially toward his son Ascanius, who is destined to rule over the future city of Alba Longa, and unwilling to face Dido's passionate reaction, Aeneas decides to leave ("iam certus eundi," 4.554). When in a dream vision the god Mercury describes this woman as "mutabile" unpredictable, and "certa mori" (4.564) at the prospect of his departure, the hero can act only by fleeing at once.

The Latin phrases point to Aeneas' commitment to piety in the Roman sense, while Milton shows Adam's failure of Christian piety. Aeneas perhaps responds too hastily by leaving, since he does

---

[40]These echoes of the *Aeneid* have long been recognized by scholars: Hughes (above, note 3), ad loc., notes the translation of *certus eundi*; more recently, Wolfgang E. H. Rudat, "Milton's Dido and Aeneas: The Fall in *Paradise Lost* and the Vergilian Tradition," *Classical and Modern Literature* 2 (1981), 33–46, discusses these two allusions to the *Aeneid* but interprets their significance differently from this essay. In particular, he sees Eve as a *femina ambigua*, "guilty of the guiles which Mercury had falsely imputed to Dido," and implies that Adam should have separated from Eve.

nothing to prevent or forestall Dido's self-destruction. For his part, Adam is clearly precipitous in his decision to die as soon as he has heard what Eve has done. He is at this point completely guiltless; it is Eve who has betrayed Milton's hero. Not only did she succumb to temptation that she should have resisted, at least by returning to seek Adam's help sooner,[41] but realizing that her husband may be given a new wife to replace her when she has died, she also determined to make him share her fate rather than marry "another Eve" (828–31). On the other hand, although Adam is thus far innocent, his echo of "certa mori" is only superficially noble. His first assertion that he will share Eve's fate is egocentric; he betrays a concern with how Eve's disobedience will affect himself.[42] As the following excerpt reveals, the hero says nothing about the woman's plight but speaks only of his own:

> "How can I live without thee, how forgo
> Thy sweet Converse and Love so dearly join'd,
> To live again in these wild Woods forlorn?
> Should God create another Eve, and I
> Another Rib afford, yet loss of thee
> Would never from my heart; no, no, I feel
> The Link of Nature draw me: Flesh of Flesh,
> Bone of my Bone thou art, and from thy State
> Mine never shall be parted, bliss or woe." (908–16)

Adam here exhibits the impulsiveness that Aeneas attributes to Dido in his dream vision where the apparition of Mercury tells him that she is "certa mori." Although Dido finally takes the extreme

[41]On the problem of Eve's failure to seek her husband's help when Satan begins to tempt her, see Revard (above, note 6), 77, who perceptively suggests that Milton's Satan would perhaps have been able to corrupt the two together or even Adam alone and that if Eve's faith and love for God had remained firm, she would not have fallen at all. On the other hand, Joan S. Bennett, "'Go': Milton's Antinomianism and the Separation Scene in *Paradise Lost*, Book 9," *PMLA* 98 (1983), 388–404, discusses the "voluntarist antinomianism" of Eve and the "humanistic antinomianism" of Adam in the separation scene. Milton thus places their decisions in a contemporary intellectual context that implicitly criticizes both characters.

[42]See Robert Crosman, *Reading* Paradise Lost (Bloomington: Indiana University Press, 1980), pp. 177–78.

course of suicide, she first tries to alleviate her suffering by urging the hero to delay his departure for a while, then considers the possibilities and determines to die after deciding that she has lost her much prized fame for loyalty to her dead husband and has left herself exposed to aggression from the hostile African tribes. Adam, however, does not even consider the long-range consequences of his actions but instead reacts to the immediate impact of life without his wife. He is like Dido in her weakest moment. Furthermore, he can only perceive the future perversely through his present state of mind. The woods without Eve would simply be "wild" and he "forlorn"; and his assertion that the "link of nature" would not allow him to be satisfied even with "another Eve" limits the significance of his relation to the being created from his rib to a physical bond.

The context of his second address, which alludes to Aeneas through the phrase " 'certain to undergo like doom,' " draws further similarities and contrasts with Vergil's hero. When Aeneas by being "certus eundi" forsakes his own personal pleasure so as to seek his destined kingdom in Italy, he reflects the full extent of his piety—to the gods who oversee the founding of Rome, to the Trojan people who are to be resettled, and to his son Ascanius who is destined one day to rule over Alba Longa, the mother-city of Rome. Adam, by contrast, violates all levels of the polysemantic word piety, especially the religious sphere that most interested Milton. As one of the poet's contemporaries defined it, piety is "a moral vertue which causes us to have an affection and esteem for God and Holy Things."[43]

In his long speech (921–59), Adam reveals his impiety toward God. He begins his address to Eve with a critical attitude toward her boldness but he at once adopts a fatalistic position: " 'But past who can recall, or done undo? / Not God Omnipotent, nor Fate' " (926–27). He further challenges God's authority and power by suggesting that since the serpent has already tried the fruit, they too may not commit so grave an offense by eating it (928–32), and since the serpent has already attained a higher state, they may ultimately

---

[43]Boyette (above, note 8), 87, cites Edward Phillips's definition in *The New World of Words; or, A Universal English Dictionary* (5th ed., 1696).

become "'Gods, or Angels Demi-gods'" by tasting the fruit (933–37). Moreover, he denies the unconditional nature of the divine command to them by indicating that God would be likely to change His mind rather than to destroy the two creatures "dignifi'd so high," lest He should waste His effort and expose Himself to the ridicule of Satan (938–51). By thus questioning God's omnipotence, Adam demonstrates his lack of piety, which induces affection for God. His determination to die with Eve further reflects impiety toward God because it contradicts His intention that the first couple procreate and propagate the human race. In this respect, Adam's moral failure also has a political significance related to his function as founder of a new race.

The hero's swift decision to die with his wife bears on the question of piety in another important way. To Milton, marriage is a "mutuall help to piety."[44] Adam here rejects the piety that his marriage should promote by failing to consider the possibility of interceding with God on Eve's behalf. By showing that the unfallen man does not try to redeem the fallen woman but instead rushes into a plan to die with her, Milton implies how far he is from genuine love and piety. Critics have noted that Adam's failure to seek God's pardon for Eve's transgression suggests a strong contrast with the Son's generous offer in book 3 to sacrifice Himself in payment for man's sin.[45] The poet in fact seems to call attention to this discrepancy when he has Eve exclaim: "'O glorious trial of exceeding Love, / Illustrious evidence, example high!'" (961–62). Her words ironically recall the angels' exclamation of admiration at the Son's magnificent gesture of charity: "'O unexampl'd love, / Love nowhere to be found less than Divine!'" (3.410–11).

By expressing his solidarity with Eve, Adam compares unfavorably with Aeneas in piety, yet Milton suggests a much greater level of complexity in his hero's motivation and decision. Although poorly applied, Adam's basic impulse to remain with Eve is in itself positive. Those critics who find the hero's error in his failure to divorce himself from his wife take an approach that seems to agree

---

[44]See *Tetrachordon* in *Complete Prose Works of Milton*, ed. Douglas Bush, John S. Diekhoff, et al. (New Haven: Yale University Press, 1959), p. 599.

[45]See John C. Ulreich, Jr., "'Sufficient to Have Stood': Adam's Responsibility in Book IX," *Milton Quarterly* 5 (1971), 41.

with Vergil's solution to Aeneas's situation but not with Milton's in *Paradise Lost*.[46] By failing to respond adequately to Eve's dilemma through some attempt at mediation with God, Adam remains with Eve only superficially and does nothing to prevent the deep breakdown of their union, which is manifest at the end of book 9 after he too has eaten the fruit.

Adam and Eve pervert their love for each other by violating their piety to God. After they have completed the Fall, Milton recalls classical epic as a means of emphasizing their loss of genuine affection. Filled with delusions about their superior new abilities, Adam and Eve assume for themselves the attributes of divinity. As the poet observes, they

> fancy that they feel
> Divinity within them breeding wings
> Wherewith to scorn the Earth. (1009–11)

At this point, they engage in a ridiculous parody of the Platonic myth of divine ascent that Milton earlier used in a positive context.[47] They also reenact two well-known erotic scenes from classical epic, as the poet describes their first interest in sex as mere play rather than the natural expression of their loving relationship. Adam states his desires in the language of love poetry:

> "For never did thy Beauty since the day
> I saw thee first and wedded thee, adorn'd
> With all perfections, so inflame my sense
> With ador to enjoy thee." (1029–32)

While conveying his lust for Eve, Adam also alludes to classical epic, specifically Paris's invitation to Helen in the *Iliad*.[48] For after

---

[46]Burden (above, note 23), p. 163, stresses that Adam's major error was in not divorcing himself from Eve. By contrast, Webber (above, note 11), pp. 147–48, comments on Eve's association with nature and Adam's with reason, an interdependence that would require Adam to remain with Eve in order to avoid the consequences of his potentially too rational nature.

[47]See Douglas Bush, "Ironic and Ambiguous Allusion in *Paradise Lost*," *Journal of English and Germanic Philology* 60 (1961), 639–40.

[48]Ibid., 640.

being rescued from battle by Aphrodite, the Trojan hero similarly attempts to persuade Helen to satisfy his amorous desires:[49]

> "Never before as now has passion enmeshed my senses,
> not when I took you the first time from Lakedaimon the lovely
> and caught you up and carried you away in seafaring vessels,
> and lay with you in the bed of love on the island of Kranae,
> not even then, as now, did I love you and sweet desire seize me."
>   (3.442–46)

Milton could hardly have found a more fitting model for Adam's seduction speech, since the classical character is the archetype of the self-indulgent, adulterous lover who flaunts accepted social values and disregards the opinion of his heroic peers as he seeks private satisfaction.[50] Although he reveals Paris's flaws, especially in this scene where Helen reproaches him after his unmanly conduct in the war at Troy, Homer perceives him to some extent as a victim of Aphrodite's gift of charm and good looks. He similarly shows Helen compelled by Aphrodite to submit even when she wishes to reject Paris's desires.

The passage here in *Paradise Lost* also echoes a second seduction speech in the *Iliad*, Zeus's to Hera (14.313–28). There the king of the gods himself falls victim to the wiles of his wife Hera, who wishes to keep him unaware of her machinations on behalf of the Greeks on the battlefield at Troy. After asserting that "'never before has love for any goddess or woman / so melted about the heart inside me,'" the philandering Zeus proceeds to compare his present feelings to his amorous desires for various women. This second model not only reflects lust but also reemphasizes the manipulative self-interest that induces Hera to shift the course of events on the battlefield in favor of the Greeks. In *Paradise Lost*, Adam's seduction of Eve is more serious because it introduces lust among humans. Milton here prefaces their carnality with an image of disease:

---

[49]Homer, *Iliad*, tr. Richmond Lattimore (Chicago: University of Chicago Press, 1951). My quotations from the *Iliad* are from Lattimore.

[50]See James M. Redfield, *Nature and Culture in the* Iliad: *The Tragedy of Hector* (Chicago: University of Chicago Press, 1975), pp. 113–15.

> So said he, and forbore not glance or toy
> Of amorous intent, well understood
> Of Eve, whose Eye darted contagious Fire. (1034–36)

The scene in which the two consummate their new passion also has an important underpinning in classical epic. The poet describes Adam leading Eve off to a bed of lush flowers:

> He led her nothing loath; Flow'rs were the Couch,
> Pansies, and Violets, and Asphodel,
> And Hyacinth, Earth's freshest softest lap. (1039–41)

As commentators have noted, this description alludes to the above-mentioned scene between Zeus and Hera in *Iliad* 14, where the goddess lures her husband away from the Trojan War in order to keep him ignorant of her plan to rouse the Greeks more fiercely against the Trojans.[51] To insure her success at forestalling the king of the Olympians, the Greek goddess takes great pains to guarantee her seductiveness, even by borrowing Aphrodite's infallible *zonē*. She is so enticing that Zeus, as we have observed, claims to be more aroused than ever before. The actual scene of their sexual encounter is a lush bed of flowers much like Adam's and Eve's after the Fall:

> underneath them the divine earth broke into young, fresh
> grass, and into dewy clover, crocus and hyacinth
> so thick and soft it held the hard ground deep away from them.
> (14.347–49)

Against that background of deceit and carnality, Adam's and Eve's bed loses all connotations of innocence. By recalling the *Iliad* passage, Milton makes their lovemaking a contrast to the genuine bliss of their prelapsarian sex. The allusion also serves as a commentary on the values underlying the Homeric epic. The scene in the *Iliad* is an ironic moment of marital harmony, for the king and queen of the gods have a loveless marriage characterized by constant

---

[51]Bush (above, note 47), 40. Blessington (above, note 35), pp. 62–63, notes that Milton corrects Homer's theological error by attributing such conduct to human rather than divine agents; he also notes the ironic change in detail from Homer's dewy cloud to the offensive vapors that here surround the lovers (1044–51).

infidelities on Zeus's part and incessant jealousy on Hera's.[52] Adam's and Eve's debased scene of passion thus dramatizes the fundamental incompatibility and antagonism between male and female in the classical epic tradition and reinforces the need for genuine affection in marital relations.

Adam's stature is further diminished by his assumption of the role of the abandoned female from classical epic, especially that of Dido and Ariadne. He begins by reproaching Eve: "'Is this the Love, is this the recompense / Of mine to thee, ingrateful Eve'" (1163–64). This opening rings familiar tones from the classical models: Dido refers to "noster amor" (4.307) in her initial reproach to Aeneas and emphasizes his lack of gratitude (4.373–74). When he claims "'Thus it shall befall / Him who to worth in Woman overtrusting'" (1182–83), Adam recalls the scathing words of Catullus's Ariadne: "'Now let no woman believe a man when he swears anything'" (64.143). In his pettiest response to Eve, then, the hero is no more than a pitiful, but also vengeful, heroine from Vergilian and Catullan epic.

In *Paradise Lost*, the restoration of Adam's and Eve's piety takes place through Eve's renewal of genuine married love. Whereas Dido impedes the hero's progress and is governed by values that ultimately make her self-destructive, Eve provides the impetus for regeneration. She begins this process when she offers to take the burden upon herself on the day of judgment (10.932–36); her love for her husband is also a genuine gesture of piety. Her words furthermore echo Christ's offer of self-sacrifice (2.236–37) in a positive way:

> "On me, sole cause to thee of all this woe,
> Mee mee only just object of his ire." (935–36)

Adam, by contrast, has at this point remained self-defensive and depressed. Obsessed with what he has lost for both himself and his future offspring, he is unable to motivate himself to show a spirit of genuine repentance. But after Eve makes the first overtures and considers some possible solutions to their dilemma, Adam once

[52]Renaissance poets frequently refer to Jupiter's philandering; see Douglas Bush, *Mythology and the Renaissance Tradition in English Poetry*, rev. ed. (New York: Norton, 1963), for example, pp. 66, 70, 104, 109, 126, and 151.

again participates in a dialogue that reveals their need for mutual encouragement and correction. To avoid inflicting the evils resulting from their sin on their descendants, she at first suggests that they refrain from the pleasures of sex but then immediately realizes the difficulty of such a deprivation (979–98). As a desperate final solution, she suggests that they actively seek death or, alternatively, commit suicide (999–1006). Although Eve hopes to spare future generations the misery resulting from the Fall, Adam has the intellectual power to realize that her solutions are futile. To her Dido-like, impulsive thought of ending their problems by suicide, he recalls God's prophecy that Eve's seed will achieve revenge on Satan (1030–40). He then takes hope from the charity they have already received from God since their sin and considers how they may lighten their burdens through His further grace.

As a *concordia discors*, a union of her greater intuitiveness and imagination and his superior intellect and reason, the marriage of Adam and Eve is necessary to restore the piety that each member separately violated. Neither can meaningfully exist alone. Eve needs Adam's generally sounder understanding of their world, but he benefits especially from her greater spontaneity and the balance of her views on issues that he too only partially comprehends. By renewing their mutual interdependence, Adam and Eve can regain the Eden that they have physically lost through a greater "paradise within." While indicating the essential solitariness of Vergil's hero in the two allusions to his piety, Milton emphasizes the importance of a true cooperation between male and female. Eve fosters the love that enables the two to return to God, especially by cementing the union that in itself promotes piety as a preeminent virtue in both partners. In this way, she both aids Adam in attaining a higher, truly heroic, status and herself has the same positive potential.

Milton's attitude toward classical literature, especially epic, is not so uniformly negative as his allusions in *Paradise Lost* 9 suggest. As Lewalski has recently shown, he incorporated traditional literary kinds in contexts that reflect their positive value. He assimilates the eclogue and the georgic in books 4 and 8, for example, as a means of illustrating the perfection of Eden before the Fall.[53] Conversely, not

[53]Lewalski (above, note 13), pp. 173–95.

all examples of classical genres placed in negative contexts in *Paradise Lost* imply criticism of the models. Milton certainly does not find anything fundamentally wrong with classical or Elizabethan tragedy when he has Satan posture as a tragic hero. Such allusions that distort the original are frequently a means to distinguish more sharply the genuine from the spurious. The poet also adapts many classical literary forms and employs them in ways that show their need for modification in a Christian context. The classical lyric form, the hymn, is reoriented toward a Christian ethos; the angels, for example, praise God for His effulgent glory and for His reflection in the Son who expressed unparalleled love in offering to die for mankind (3.372–415). In accommodating and adapting classical genres, Milton employed allusions variously, as he could assume the reader's general awareness about the meanings inherent in those forms.

Although he often takes advantage of the thematic potential of the various genres, Milton frequently alludes to specific works for more polemical purposes. He takes a very critical position on certain aspects of classical and Renaissance epic. The *Aeneid*, the most important structural and stylistic model for *Paradise Lost*, also forms the core of the poet's polemic in book 9. His recollection of the piety of the hero Aeneas indicates that it is totally inappropriate for Adam to emulate the Roman model of heroism, in which public responsibilities overwhelm the more basic human concerns of a religious and familial nature. By recalling the Greek hero Odysseus at the moment when Satan enters the Garden to corrupt Eve through his rhetoric, Milton suggests the classical emphasis on verbal skill as one means of demonstrating and reinforcing one's individual *kleos* and exposes the erotic, seductive underpinning to that skill. In *Paradise Lost*, by contrast, true glory is ultimately theocentric, emanating from God and returning to Him, and cannot accommodate the egocentric quality of the classical heroes.[54] If Satan takes the classical position on this value, the poet reaffirms its genuine nature, as all things "send up silent praise / To the Creator" (9.195–96) and Adam and Eve lose their natural physical splendor at the end of the book ("O how unlike / To that first naked glory," 1114–15). Per-

[54]See John P. Rumrich, "Milton and the Meaning of Glory," *Milton Studies* 20 (1984), 75–86, on the influence of the Hebrew *kabod* and Greek *doxa* on Milton's concept of glory in *Paradise Lost*.

haps most important, Milton employs allusions to erotic contexts in classical epic ironically so as to validate the love that promotes a true piety and glory in Adam and Eve. The failure of the earlier works in this respect underscores the limitations of their larger value system.

As he undermines his predecessors' ethical structures, the poet adapts the literary traditions that give form to epic values in significantly different ways. By incorporating multiple allusions that tend to achieve a similar effect or point in the same direction, Milton does not readily allow for the kind of ambivalence that permits either a positive or a skeptical interpretation, as Vergil does in the Nisus and Euryalus episode with his uneasy fusion of Homer and Euripides. A moral point of view is thus more firmly impressed upon the reader. As Adam, for example, reenacts the dalliance of Paris with Helen and of Zeus with Hera in the *Iliad*, the poet strengthens the debasement of the hero's first expression of lust. More complexly, the multiple allusions to the *Aeneid* reject the disunity between Vergil's Dido and Aeneas by showing Adam's and Eve's need for mutual reinforcement.

In *Paradise Lost* as in all the other works that we have discussed, the simile is a major vehicle for expressing the tensions and values of the epic. James Whaler long ago observed that Milton's similes are highly articulated, complex units characterized by "logical patterns," a density of detail used "homologously," and sometimes a proleptic function that foreshadows significant events in the poem.[55] Like the other poets, moreover, Milton relies heavily on literary allusions to inform his similes with subtle levels of significance. His famous bee simile, for instance, which describes the assemblage of fallen angels after the building of Pandaemonium (1.768–75), alludes to two classical uses of the same analogy: *Iliad* 2.87–90, where the Greek troops come together in response to Agamemnon's call, and *Aeneid* 1.430–36, where the Carthaginians are busily engaged in building their new city. The allusion to the Roman epic especially makes the heroism of Satan and the fallen angels ironic, for Vergil clearly suggests the future destruction of Carthage by the Romans in the final scene of book 4. There, he compares Dido's death to the fall of Carthage itself (669–71), which he thus attributes to lust. Milton further heightens the irony of his

[55]James Whaler, "The Miltonic Simile," *PMLA* 46 (1931), 1034–74.

analogy by echoing Vergil's fourth *Georgic*, in which the bees are rather humorously depicted as glorious and heroic and are compared to Cyclopes working under Mt. Etna, a location that came to represent Hell in Medieval typology.[56]

While often exploiting the ironies within Vergil's own texts and using his models as a vehicle for moral judgment, the poet incorporates other classical similes for more polemical purposes. As McColley has shown, analogues between Eve and various mythical characters, such as Venus, Circe, and Proserpina, imply similarities balanced by significant differences; Milton thus wishes to reveal Eve's potentially positive qualities where she may seem to be as vulnerable or corrupt as the classical counterpart.[57] The erotic allusions in *Paradise Lost* often contain levels of meaning that reinforce rather than negate or qualify the potentially beneficial, and often rational, aspects of Eve as the poem's representative of the female. The Diana simile in book 9 is an important example of this complex cross-referencing. Eve's superiority to her model applies to more than physical appearance; it also extends to her relations with her husband, in contrast to the problematic sexuality of Vergil's character, which ultimately causes irredeemable chaos. By integrating his simile into a cluster of literary allusions concerned with women's relation to heroism, Milton has made the simile an important means of elevating the female and the erotic in epic and thus brought the genre to an ending point. Like the earlier poet Ariosto, he looks at the erotic female not merely in terms of male values. But Milton more idealistically projects a new vision of an ideal that may be attained with effort. The commitment that has traditionally been relegated to the public sphere now has an important private counterpart; piety, fidelity, and glory can only be fully implemented through the cooperation of male and female.

[56]See Davis P. Harding, "Milton's Bee-Simile," *Journal of English and Germanic Philology* 60 (1961), 664–69, on the Homeric and Vergilian epic antecedents and the additional influence of the *Georgics* passage; Geoffrey Hartman, "Milton's Counterplot," *ELH* 25 (1958), 1–12; rpt. in *Critical Essays on Milton from* ELH (Baltimore: Johns Hopkins Press, 1969), pp. 151–62, includes a discussion of Milton's transformation of the *Aeneid* simile in the context of his "counterplot" revealing the nature of order in God's universe.

[57]Diane McColley, "Shapes of Things Divine: Eve and Myth in *Paradise Lost*," *Sixteenth Century Journal* 9 (1978), 47–55.

Selected Bibliography

T HIS LIST cites works related to the main themes of my study of the epic. It includes books and articles that helped to shape my thinking on the erotic and social values within the heroic tradition and the imitative techniques employed by poets. Other works more peripheral to the main subject may be found in the notes. Editions of primary sources do not appear here.

Aers, David, and Hodge, Bob. "'Rational Burning': Milton on Sex and Marriage." *Milton Studies* 13 (1979): 3–33.
Anderson, William S. "The *Heroides*." In *Ovid*, edited by J. W. Binns, 49–83. London: Routledge and Kegan Paul, 1973.
———. "*Pastor Aeneas*: On Pastoral Themes in the *Aeneid*." *Transactions of the American Philological Association* 99 (1968): 1–17.
Ascoli, Albert R. *Ariosto's Bitter Harmony: Crisis and Evasion in the Italian Renaissance*. Princeton: Princeton University Press, 1987.
Barkhuizen, J. H. "The Psychological Characterization of Medea in Apollonius of Rhodes, *Argonautica* 3,744–824." *Acta Classica* 22 (1979): 33–48.
Beye, Charles R. *Epic and Romance in the* Argonautica *of Apollonius*. Carbondale: Southern Illinois University Press, 1982.
———. "Jason as Love-hero in Apollonios' *Argonautika*. *Greek, Roman and Byzantine Studies* 10 (1969): 31–55.
Blessington, Francis C. Paradise Lost *and the Classical Epic*. London: Routledge and Kegan Paul, 1979.
Bonadeo, Alfredo. "Olimpia." *Italica* 45 (1968): 47–58.

Selected Bibliography

Bono, Barbara J. *Literary Transvaluation: From Vergilian Epic to Shakespearian Tragicomedy*. Berkeley: University of California Press, 1984.

Boyette, Purvis E. "Milton's Divorce Tracts and the Law of Marriage." *Tulane Studies in English* 17 (1969): 73–92.

Brand, C. P. *Ludovico Ariosto: A Preface to the "Orlando Furioso."* Edinburgh: Edinburgh University Press, 1974.

Burden, Dennis H. *The Logical Epic: A Study of the Argument of* Paradise Lost Cambridge, Mass.: Harvard University Press, 1967.

Burgess, J. F. "*Pietas* in Virgil and Statius." *Proceedings of the Virgil Society* 11 (1971–72): 48–61.

Bush, Douglas. "Ironic and Ambiguous Allusion in *Paradise Lost*." *Journal of English and Germanic Philology* 60 (1961): 631–40.

Campbell, Malcolm. *Echoes and Imitations of Early Epic in Apollonius Rhodius*. Leiden: Brill, 1981.

——. *Studies in the Third Book of Apollonius Rhodius'* Argonautica. Hildesheim: Georg Olms, 1983.

Carson, Anne. *Eros the Bittersweet: An Essay*. Princeton: Princeton University Press, 1986.

Carspecken, John F. "Apollonius Rhodius and the Homeric Epic." *Yale Classical Studies* 13 (1956): 35–143.

Clack, Jerry. "The Medea Similes of Apollonius Rhodius." *Classical Journal* 68 (1973): 310–15.

Colie, Rosalie. *The Resources of Kind: Genre-Theory in the Renaissance*. Berkeley: University of California Press, 1973.

Collins, John F. "Studies in Book One of the *Argonautica* of Apollonius Rhodius." Ph.D. dissertation, Columbia University, 1967.

Connely, Willard. "Imprints of the *Aeneid* on *Paradise Lost*." *Classical Journal* 18 (1923): 466–76.

Couat, Auguste. *Alexandrian Poetry under the First Three Ptolemies, 324–222 B.C.* Translated by James Loeb. London: Heinemann, 1931.

Curran, Leo C. "Catullus 64 and the Heroic Age." *Yale Classical Studies* 21 (1969): 171–92.

Diekhoff, John S. "Eve, the Devil, and the *Areopagitica*." *Modern Language Quarterly* 5 (1944): 429–34.

Duckworth, George E. "The Significance of Nisus and Euryalus for *Aeneid* IX–XII." *American Journal of Philology* 88 (1967): 129–50.

Durling, Robert M. *The Figure of the Poet in Renaissance Epic*. Cambridge, Mass.: Harvard University Press, 1965.

Earl, Donald. *The Moral and Political Tradition of Rome*. Ithaca: Cornell University Press, 1967.

Evans, J. M. "Mortals' Chiefest Enemy." *Milton Studies* 20 (1984): 111–26.

Selected Bibliography

Farwell, Marilyn R. "Eve, the Separation Scene, and the Renaissance Idea of Androgyny." *Milton Studies* 16 (1982): 3–20.

Fenik, Bernard. "The Influence of Euripides on Vergil's *Aeneid*." Ph.D. diss., Princeton University, 1960.

Ferry, Anne D. *Milton's Epic Voice: The Narrator in* Paradise Lost. Cambridge, Mass.: Harvard University Press: 1963.

Fitzgerald, G. J. "Nisus and Euryalus: A Paradigm of Futile Behaviour and the Tragedy of Youth." In *Cicero and Virgil: Studies in Honour of Harold Hunt*, edited by John R. C. Martyn, 114–37. Amsterdam: Hakkert, 1972.

Foley, Helene P. "'Reverse Similes' and Sex Roles in the *Odyssey*." *Arethusa* 11 (1978): 7–26.

Forsyth, Phyllis Y. "Catullus: The Mythic Persona." *Latomus* 35 (1976): 555–66.

Foucault, Michel. *The History of Sexuality*. Translated by Robert Hurley. New York: Pantheon Books, 1978.

Fränkel, Hermann. "Apollonius Rhodius as a Narrator in *Argonautica* a. 1 140." *Transactions of the American Philological Association* 83 (1952): 144–55.

———. "Ein Don Quijote unter den Argonauten des Apollonios." *Museum Helveticum* 17 (1960): 1–20.

———. *Noten zu den* Argonautika *des Apollonios*. Munich: Beck, 1968.

———. *Ovid: A Poet between Two Worlds*. Berkeley: University of California Press, 1945.

———. "Problems of Text and Interpretation in Apollonius' *Argonautica*." *American Journal of Philology* 71 (1950): 113–33.

Garson, R. W. "Homeric Echoes in Apollonius Rhodius' *Argonautica*." *Classical Philology* 67 (1972): 1–9.

George, Edward V. "Poet and Characters in Apollonius Rhodius' Lemnian Episode." *Hermes* 100 (1972): 47–63

Giamatti, A. Bartlett. *The Earthly Paradise and the Renaissance Epic*. Princeton: Princeton University Press, 1966.

———. "Headlong Horses, Headless Horsemen: An Essay on the Chivalric Epics of Pulci, Boiardo, and Ariosto." In *Italian Literature, Roots and Branches: Essays in Honor of Thomas Goddard Bergin*, edited by Giose Rimanelli and Kenneth J. Atchity, 265–307. New Haven: Yale University Press, 1976.

Gillis, Daniel. *Eros and Death in the* Aeneid. Rome: L'Erma di Bretschneider, 1983.

Gransden, K. W. *Virgil's* Iliad: *An Essay on Epic Narrative*. Cambridge: Cambridge University Press, 1984.

Greene, Thomas M. *The Descent from Heaven: A Study in Epic Continuity*. New Haven: Yale University Press, 1963.

———. *The Light In Troy: Imitation and Discovery in Renaissance Poetry.* New Haven: Yale University Press, 1982.

Griffiths, Frederick T. "Home before Lunch: The Emancipated Woman in Theocritus." In *Reflections of Women in Antiquity*, edited by Helene P. Foley, 247–73. New York: Gordon and Breach, 1981.

Händel, Paul. *Beobachtungen zur Epischen Technik des Apollonios Rhodios.* Zetemata 7. Munich: Beck, 1954.

Hanning, Robert W. "Ariosto, Ovid, and the Painters: Mythical Paragone in *Orlando Furioso* X and XI." In *Ariosto 1974 in America: Atti del congresso ariostesche, dicembre 1974*, edited by Aldo Scaglione, 99–116. Ravenna: Longo, 1976.

Harding, Davis P. *The Club of Heracles: Studies in the Classical Background of Paradise Lost. Illinois Studies in Language and Literature*, 50. Urbana: University of Illinois Press, 1962.

Heiserman, Arthur. *The Novel before the Novel: Essays and Discussions about the Beginnings of Prose Fiction in the West.* Chicago: University of Chicago Press, 1977.

Jacobson, Howard. *Ovid's* Heroides. Princeton: Princeton University Press, 1974.

Javitch, Daniel. "Rescuing Ovid from the Allegorizers: The Liberation of Angelica, *Furioso* X." In *Ariosto 1974 in America: Atti del congresso ariostesche, dicembre 1974*, edited by Aldo Scaglione, 85–98. Ravenna: Longo, 1976.

Jenkyns, Richard. *Three Classical Poets: Sappho, Catullus, and Juvenal.* Cambridge, Mass.: Harvard University Press, 1982.

Johnson, W. R. *Darkness Visible: A Study of Vergil's Aeneid.* Berkeley: University of California Press, 1976.

———. "Aeneas and the Ironies of *Pietas*." *Classical Journal* 60 (1965): 360–64.

Kates, Judith. *Tasso and Milton: The Problem of Christian Epic.* Lewisburg: Bucknell University Press, 1983.

Kennedy, William J. "Ariosto's Ironic Allegory." *Modern Language Notes* 88 (1973): 44–67.

Klein, Theodore M. "Apollonius Rhodius, *Vates Ludens*: Eros' Golden Ball (*Arg.* 3.115–150)." *Classical World* 34 (1980–81): 223—25.

Knight, W. F. Jackson. *Roman Vergil*, 2d ed. London: Faber and Faber, 1945.

Konstan, David. *Catullus' Indictment of Rome: The Meaning of Catullus 64.* Amsterdam: Hakkert, 1977.

Lawall, Gilbert. "Apollonius' *Argonautica*: Jason as Anti-Hero." *Yale Classical Studies* 19 (1966): 119–69.

———. *Theocritus' Coan Pastorals: A Poetry Book.* Washington, D.C.: Center for Hellenic Studies, 1967.

Lee, M. O. *Fathers and Sons in Virgil's Aeneid.* Albany: State University of New York Press, 1979.

Lennox, P. G. "Apollonius, *Argonautica* 3,1.ff. and Homer." *Hermes* 108 (1980): 45–73.

———. "Virgil's Night-Episode Re-examined (*Aeneid* IX, 176–449)." *Hermes* 105 (1977): 331–42.

Levin, Donald N. *Apollonius' Argonautica Re-examined, I: The Neglected First and Second Books*. Leiden: Brill, 1971.

———. "*Diplax Porphureē.*" *Rivista di Filologia e di Istruzione Classica* 98 (1970): 17–36.

Lewalski, Barbara K. "Innocence and Experience in Milton's Eden." In *New Essays on* Paradise Lost, edited by Thomas Kranidas, 86–117. Berkeley: University of California Press, 1969.

———. Paradise Lost *and the Rhetoric of Literary Forms*. Princeton: Princeton University Press, 1985.

Livrea, Enrico. "Una 'tecnica allusiva' apolloniana alla luce dell'esegesi omerica alesandrina." *Studi Italiani di Filologica Classica* 44 (1972): 231–43.

Lyne, R. O. A. M. *The Latin Love Poets: From Catullus to Horace*. Oxford: Clarendon Press, 1980.

MacCaffrey, Isabel G. Paradise Lost *as Myth*. Cambridge, Mass.: Harvard University Press, 1959.

McColley, Diane K. "Free Will and Obedience in the Separation Scene of *Paradise Lost.*" *Studies in English Literature* 12 (1972): 103–20.

———. *Milton's Eve*. Urbana: University of Illinois Press, 1983.

———. "Shapes of Things Divine: Eve and Myth in *Paradise Lost.*" *Sixteenth Century Journal* 9 (1978): 47–55.

McGushin, P. "Catullus' Sanctae Foedus Amicitiae." *Classical Philology* 62 (1967): 85–93.

Mazzotta, Giuseppe. *The World at Play in Boccaccio's* Decameron. Princeton: Princeton University Press, 1986.

Monti, Richard. *The Dido Episode and the* Aeneid: *Roman Social and Political Values in the Epic*. Leiden: Brill, 1981.

Moretti, Walter. "La storia di Cloridano e Medoro: Un esempio della umanizzazione ariostesca delle idealità eroiche e cavalleresche." *Convivium* 37 (1969): 543–51.

Murtaugh, Kristin O. *Ariosto and the Classical Simile. Harvard Studies in Romance Languages*, 36. Cambridge, Mass.: Harvard University Press, 1980.

Otis, Brooks. *Ovid as an Epic Poet*, 2d ed. Cambridge: Cambridge University Press, 1970.

———. *Virgil: A Study in Civilized Poetry*. Oxford: Clarendon Press, 1963.

Paduano, Guido. "L'episodio di Talos: Osservazioni sull' esperienza magica nelle *Argonautiche* di Apollonio Rodio." *Studi Classici e Orientali* 19 (1970): 46–67.

Palombi, Maria Grazia. "Eracle e Ila nelle *Argonautiche* di Apollonio Rodio." *Studi Classici e Orientali* 35 (1985): 71–92.

Parker, Patricia A. *Inescapable Romance: Studies in the Poetics of a Mode.* Princeton: Princeton University Press, 1979.

Perkell, Christine G. "On Creusa, Dido, and the Quality of Victory in Virgil's *Aeneid.*" In *Reflections of Women in Antiquity*, edited by Helene P. Foley, 355–77. New York: Gordon and Breach, 1981.

Perotta, Gennaro. "Il carme 64 di Catullo e i suoi pretesi originali ellenistici." *Athenaeum* 9 (1931), 177–222 and 370–409.

Phinney, Edward, Jr. "Narrative Unity in the *Argonautica*, the Medea-Jason Romance." *Transactions of the American Philological Association* 98 (1967): 327–41.

———. "Hellenistic Painting and the Poetic Style of Apollonius." *Classical Journal* 62 (1967): 145–49.

Pool, Franco. *Interpretazione dell' "Orlando Furioso."* Florence: La Nuova Italia, 1968.

Pöschl, Viktor. *The Art of Vergil: Image and Symbol in the* Aeneid. Translated by Gerda Seligson. 1962; rpt. Ann Arbor: University of Michigan Press, 1970.

———. "Virgile et la tragédie." In *Présence de Virgile: Actes du Colloque des 9, 11, et 12 Décembre 1976*, edited by Raymond Chevallier, 73–79. Paris: Les Belles Lettres, 1978.

Pucci, Pietro. *Odysseus Polutropos: Intertextual Readings in the* Odyssey *and the* Iliad. Ithaca: Cornell University Press, 1987.

Putnam, Michael C. J. "The Art of Catullus 64." *Harvard Studies in Classical Philology* 65 (1961): 165–205.

———. "*Pius* Aeneas and the Metamorphosis of Lausus." *Arethusa* 14 (1981): 139–56.

Quilligan, Maureen. *Milton's Spenser: The Politics of Reading.* Ithaca: Cornell University Press, 1983.

Quint, David. "Astolfo's Voyage to the Moon." *Yale Italian Studies* 1 (1977): 398–408.

———. *Origin and Originality in Renaissance Literature: Versions of the Source.* New Haven: Yale University Press, 1983.

Rajna, Pio. *Le fonti dell'"Orlando Furioso."* Florence: Sansoni, 1876.

Redfield, James M. *Nature and Culture in the* Iliad: *The Tragedy of Hector.* Chicago: University of Chicago Press, 1975.

Revard, Stella P. "Eve and the Doctrine of Responsibility in *Paradise Lost.*" *PMLA* 88 (1973): 69–78.

Rhorer, Catherine C. "Red and White in Ovid's *Metamorphoses*: The Mulberry Tree in the Tale of Pyramus and Thisbe." *Ramus* 9 (1980): 79–88.

Rose, Amy. "Clothing Imagery in Apollonius's *Argonautika*." *Quaderni Urbinati di Cultura Classica* 50 (1985): 29–44.

Rosivach, Vincent J. "Hector in the *Rhesus*." *Hermes* 106 (1978): 54–73.

Rudat, Wolfgang E. H. "Milton's Dido and Aeneas: The Fall in *Paradise Lost* and the Vergilian Tradition." *Classical and Modern Literature* 2 (1981): 33–46.

Rumrich, John P. "Milton and the Meaning of Glory." *Milton Studies* 20 (1984): 75–86.

Saccone, Eduardo. "Cloridano e Medoro, con alcuni argomenti per una lettura del primo *Furioso*." *Modern Language Notes* 83 (1968): 67–99.

Safer, Elaine B. "'Sufficient to Have Stood': Eve's Responsibility in Book IX." *Milton Quarterly* 6 (1972): 10–14.

Santoro, Mario. *L'anello di Angelica: Nuovi saggi ariostesche*. Naples: Federico and Ardia, 1983.

Schmidt, E. A. "Ariadne bei Catull und Ovid." *Gymnasium* 74 (1967): 489–501.

Segal, Charles. "The Song of Iopas in the *Aeneid*." *Hermes* 99 (1971): 336–49.

Segre, Cesare. *Esperienze ariostesche*. Pisa: Nistri-Lischi, 1966.

Shapiro, H. A. "Jason's Cloak." *Transactions of the American Philological Association* 110 (1980): 263–86.

Siegel, Paul N. "Milton and the Humanist Attitude toward Women." *Journal of the History of Ideas* 11 (1950): 42–53.

Steadman, John M. *Milton and the Renaissance Hero*. Oxford: Clarendon Press, 1967.

Tatum, James. "Allusion and Interpretation in *Aen*. 6.440–76." *American Journal of Philology* 105 (1984): 434–52.

_____. "Apollonius of Rhodes and the Resourceless Hero of *Paradise Regained*." *Milton Studies* 22 (1986): 255–70.

Thompson, Douglas S. F. "Aspects of Unity in Catullus 64." *Classical Journal* 57 (1961): 49–57.

Thornton, M. K. "The Adaptation of Homer's Artemis-Nausikaa Simile in the *Aeneid*." *Latomus* 44 (1985): 615–22.

West, Grace S. "Cacneus and Dido." *Transactions of the American Philological Association* 110 (1980): 315–24.

Wiseman, T. P. *Catullus and His World: A Reappraisal*. Cambridge: Cambridge University Press, 1985.

Vance, Eugene. "Sylvia's Pet Stag: Wildness and Domesticity in Virgil's *Aeneid*." *Arethusa* 14 (1981): 127–38.

_____. "Warfare and the Structure of Thought in Virgil's *Aeneid*." *Quaderni Urbinati di Cultura Classica* 15 (1973): 111–62.

Verducci, Florence. *Ovid's Toyshop of the Heart: Epistulae Heroidum*. Princeton: Princeton University Press, 1985.

Vessey, David. *Status and the* Thebaid. Cambridge: Cambridge University Press, 1973.

Webber, Joan M. *Milton and His Epic Tradition*. Seattle: University of Washington Press, 1979.

Whaler, James. "The Miltonic Simile." *PMLA* 46 (1931): 1034–74.

Williams, Gordon. *Tradition and Originality in Roman Poetry*. Oxford: Clarendon Press, 1968.

Zanker, Graham. "The Love Theme in Apollonius Rhodius' *Argonautica*." *Wiener Studien* n.s. 13 (1979): 52–75.

Zeitlin, Froma. "Playing the Other: Theater, Theatricality, and the Feminine in Greek Drama." *Representations* 11 (1985): 63–94.

Index

Index

Cupido (*cont.*)
    connected to bloodlust, 97–102, 172–
    76; to greed, 70, 76–77, 95–97,
    176–77; to *pietas*, 104–5

Dante, 152, 165–66, 170
Diana, 72–74, 103–4, 167, 179, 194–97
    See also Artemis
Dido, 72–85
    influenced by Ariadne, 80–84; by
      Medea, 74–75, 78; by Nausikaa,
      72–74
    influence on Adam, 208–9, 214; on
      Eve, 195–97, 205–6, 215; on Olim-
      pia, 162–65
Diomedes, 88–92, 98–99, 103–4
Dolon, 89–92
Domus, 125–27, 138–40
    See also Familial love
Duckworth, George E., 88, 93n
Durling, Robert M., 166

Earl, Donald, 79n, 95n, 139n
Ereuthos, 29–31, 33–34, 48–49
    and *aidōs,* 57
Eros, 43–44, 119–20
    See also Cupid/ Love
Eukleia, 53, 79
Euripides:
    Hippolytus, 10, 78
    Medea, 10–11, 51–55, 61, 68, 74–75,
      80–81, 118–23, 144–45
    Rhesus, 89–92, 99–100, 107–8
Eusebeia, 26–27, 50, 103
Eve, 192–215
    influenced by Dido, 195–97, 205–6,
      214–15; by Sofronia, 198–201

Fama. See Gloria/ fama
Familial love, 105–8, 125–27, 138–40
Fede. See Fides
Fenik, Bernard, 89, 95n, 98, 99n
Fides, 79–82, 127–28, 138–39
    and *fede,* 150, 155, 162–64, 172, 180
    and fidelity, 214, 218
Fitzgerald, G. J., 88
Foucault, Michel, 15–16
Fowler, Alastair, 193–94, 196–97
Fränkel, Hermann, 6n, 21, 33n, 55, 59,
    130–31, 143n

George, Edward V., 27, 33n
Giamatti, A. Bartlett, 1, 182–83n
Gillis, Daniel, 70, 76n, 86n, 102n

Gloria/ fama, 79–85, 92–95, 111–12,
    121, 171–72
    contrasted with Christian glory, 216
    See also Kleos
Golden Fleece, 30–31, 53
Greene, Thomas M., 2–3, 171–72, 174

Hanning, Robert W., 167n, 168n
Harding, Davis P., 187n, 195n
Helen of Troy, 5–8, 28–29, 211–12
Hera, 26–27, 40–41, 63, 213
    See also Juno
Heracles, 15, 50, 64–65
Homer:
    archetype for abandoned female in
      epic, 8–10; for night raid, 13–15
    influence on Apollonius, 24–25, 48–
      50, 52–54, 58–61, 67; on Milton,
      197–98, 200–202, 211–14, 217; on
      Vergil, 72–74, 89–92, 98–101,
      103–4
    views on love, 6–8
Homoerotic love, 15–16, 64, 87–88,
    177–78
Hypsipyle, 45–51

Influence, literary
    concept of, 2–4
    See also Apollonius, Catullus, Homer,
      Milton, Ovid, Statius, Vergil;
      Ariadne, Cloridano and Medoro,
      Dido, Medea, Nausikaa, Odysseus,
      Satan

Jacobson, Howard, 129n, 130, 143n
Jason, 24–27, 30–31, 43–44, 49–51, 61–
    67
    influenced by Odysseus, 25–26, 61–63
Jason's cloak, 24–39
Johnson, W. R., 68n, 86, 102, 107n
Juno, 80, 187–88, 203–4
    See also Hera

Kates, Judith A., 18n, 199
Kennedy, William J., 185n
Klein, Theodore M., 19n, 43
Kleos, 11, 15–16, 55, 61–62, 79, 90–92,
    198
    See also Gloria/ fama
Konstan, David, 80n, 105n, 116–17n,
    199n, 126n

Lawall, Gilbert, 21–22, 25
Lee, M. O., 87–88, 104n
Lemnian women, 45–51

Index

Vance, Eugene, 74n, 83n
Venus, 73, 75, 119–20, 187–88
  See also Aphrodite
Verducci, Florence, 130, 133, 135n, 142n
Vergil:
  Dido in, 72–85
  influenced by Apollonius, 74–75, 80–
    81; by Catullus, 80, 102; by Eu-
    ripides, 74–75, 80–81, 89–92, 99–
    100, 107–8; by Homer, 72–74, 89–
    92, 98–101, 103–4
  influence on Ariosto, 162–63, 172–77,
    185–86; on Milton, 188, 195–96,
    203–9, 217

Nisus and Euryalus in, 87–108
  references to the *Georgics,* 69–70, 76,
    94–95, 217–18
Vessey, David, 16n, 178n
Virtus, 25, 70, 74, 97–100, 109–10
  See also Aretē
Visual arts:
  influence on epic, 29–30, 34–39, 58–
    59, 122, 168

Webber, Joan M., 190, 191n, 211n
West, Grace S., 71n
Williams, Gordon, 76, 78n, 116n
Wiseman, T. P., 125n

Library of Congress Cataloging-in-Publication Data

Pavlock, Barbara.
    Eros, imitation, and the epic tradition / Barbara Pavlock.
        p.   cm.
    Includes bibliographical references.
    ISBN 0–8014–2321–X (alk. paper)
        1. Epic poetry, Classical—History and criticism.   2. Epic poetry—Classical
influences.   3. Imitation (in literature)   4. Homer—Influence.   5. Virgil.
Aeneis.   6. Ariosto, Lodovico. 1474–1533. Orlando furioso.   7. Milton, John. 1608–
1674. Paradise lost.   I. Title.
PA3022.E6P38   1990
873'.01'09—dc20   89–36639